Nikon® D5600

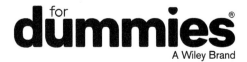

for dummies®
A Wiley Brand

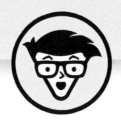

Nikon®
D5600™

by Julie Adair King

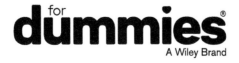
A Wiley Brand

Nikon® D5600™ For Dummies®

Published by: **John Wiley & Sons, Inc.,** 111 River Street, Hoboken, NJ 07030-5774, www.wiley.com

Copyright © 2017 by John Wiley & Sons, Inc., Hoboken, New Jersey

Published simultaneously in Canada

Contents at a Glance

Introduction 1

Part 1: Fast Track to Super Snaps 5

CHAPTER 1: First Steps, First Shots 7

CHAPTER 2: Reviewing Five Essential Picture-Taking Options 45

Part 2: Taking Creative Control 85

CHAPTER 3: Taking Charge of Exposure 87

CHAPTER 4: Controlling Focus and Depth of Field 129

CHAPTER 5: Mastering Color Controls 157

CHAPTER 6: Putting It All Together 177

CHAPTER 7: Shooting, Viewing, and Trimming Movies 197

Part 3: After the Shot 221

CHAPTER 8: Playback Mode: Viewing Your Photos 223

CHAPTER 9: Working with Picture and Movie Files 247

Part 4: The Part of Tens 275

CHAPTER 10: Ten More Ways to Customize Your Camera 277

CHAPTER 11: Ten Fun (And Practical) Features to Explore on a Rainy Day 291

Appendix: Intro to Nikon SnapBridge 309

Index 319

Table of Contents

INTRODUCTION 1
    About This Book. 1
    How This Book Is Organized 2
    Icons and Other Stuff to Note 3
    Where to Go from Here 3

PART 1: FAST TRACK TO SUPER SNAPS 5

CHAPTER 1: **First Steps, First Shots** 7
    Preparing the Camera for Initial Use 7
    Checking Out External Controls 11
        Topside controls 11
        Back-of-the-body controls 13
        Front-left features 16
        Hidden connections 17
    Enabling and Using the Touchscreen 18
    Navigating Menus 21
    Viewing Critical Picture Settings 24
    Adjusting Settings via the Control Strip 27
    Familiarizing Yourself with the Lens 28
    Working with Memory Cards 32
    Taking a Few Final Setup Steps 34
        Cruising the Setup menu 34
        Custom Setting options 36
        Restoring default settings 37
    Shooting Pictures in Auto Mode 38
        Viewfinder photography in Auto mode 38
        Live View photography in Auto mode 40

CHAPTER 2: **Reviewing Five Essential Picture-Taking
Options** 45
    Choosing an Exposure Mode. 46
        Beginner exposure modes. 46
        Advanced exposure modes: P, S, A, and M 49
    Setting the Release Mode. 49
        Single Frame and Quiet Shutter modes. 51
        Continuous (burst mode) shooting. 52
        Self-timer shooting 54
        Investigating other shutter-release options 55

Checking Image Size and Image Quality 61
 Considering the Image Size setting (resolution) 61
 Understanding Image Quality options (JPEG or Raw). 65
 Setting Image Size and Image Quality 69
Adding Flash. 72
 Enabling and disabling flash 72
 Choosing a Flash mode. 73
 Adjusting flash output. 79
 Controlling flash output manually 82

PART 2: TAKING CREATIVE CONTROL 85

CHAPTER 3: **Taking Charge of Exposure**. 87
Introducing the Exposure Trio: Aperture,
Shutter Speed, and ISO. 88
 Aperture affects depth of field 90
 Shutter speed affects motion blur 91
 ISO affects image noise 93
 Doing the exposure balancing act 94
Stepping Up to Advanced Exposure Modes (P, S, A, and M) 96
Checking the Exposure Meter 98
Choosing an Exposure Metering Mode 101
Setting Aperture, Shutter Speed, and ISO 103
 Adjusting aperture and shutter speed. 103
 Controlling ISO. 107
Solving Exposure Problems 110
 Applying Exposure Compensation 111
 Expanding tonal range 115
 Eliminating vignetting 121
 Using autoexposure lock 123
Bracketing Exposures 124

CHAPTER 4: **Controlling Focus and Depth of Field** 129
Choosing Automatic or Manual Focusing 130
Exploring Standard Focusing Options
(Viewfinder Photography) 131
 Mastering the D5600 focus system 132
 Focusing manually. 143
Focusing in Live View Mode 145
 Using Live View autofocus 146
 Manual focusing in Live View mode 151
 Zooming in to check focus 152
Manipulating Depth of Field 152

CHAPTER 5: **Mastering Color Controls** 157
Adjusting the White Balance Setting 157
Changing the White Balance setting 159
Fine-tuning White Balance settings 162
Creating white balance presets 163
Bracketing white balance 166
Taking a Quick Look at Picture Controls 170

CHAPTER 6: **Putting It All Together** 177
Recapping Basic Picture Settings 178
Shooting Still Portraits 179
Capturing Action 185
Capturing Scenic Vistas 188
Capturing Dynamic Close-Ups 191
Coping with Special Situations 193

CHAPTER 7: **Shooting, Viewing, and Trimming Movies** 197
Shooting Movies Using Default Settings 198
Adjusting Video Settings 202
Controlling Audio 206
Setting microphone sensitivity 207
Reducing wind noise 209
Exploring Other Recording Options 210
Manipulating Movie Exposure 212
Screening Your Movies 214
Trimming Movies 216
Saving a Movie Frame As a Still Image 218

PART 3: AFTER THE SHOT 221

CHAPTER 8: **Playback Mode: Viewing Your Photos** 223
Picture Playback 101 224
Choosing Which Images to View 225
Adjusting Playback Timing 226
Enabling Automatic Picture Rotation 227
Shifting to Thumbnails Display 229
Displaying Photos in Calendar View 230
Zooming in for a closer view 232
Viewing Picture Data 234
File Information mode 235
Highlights (blinkies) mode 237
RGB Histogram mode 238
Shooting Data display mode 241
Overview mode 242
Viewing Your Photos on a Television 244

CHAPTER 9: **Working with Picture and Movie Files** 247

Rating Photos and Movies 248
Protecting Files. 251
Deleting Files 252
Deleting files one at a time 252
Deleting all files 253
Deleting a batch of selected files 253
Taking a Look at Nikon's Photo Software. 255
Downloading Pictures to the Computer. 258
Connecting via USB 260
Starting the file-transfer process. 260
Downloading using Nikon ViewNX-i 261
Processing Raw (NEF) Files. 265
Processing Raw images in the camera. 266
Processing Raw files in Capture NX-D .268
Preparing Pictures for Online Sharing 271
Prepping online photos using ViewNX-i. 271
Resizing pictures in the camera. 273

PART 4: THE PART OF TENS. 275

CHAPTER 10: **Ten More Ways to Customize Your Camera** 277

Adding Comments and Copyright Notices. .277
Adding an image comment 278
Adding a copyright notice. 279
Creating a Custom Storage Folder 280
Customizing Filenames. 281
Changing the Information Display Style. 282
Keeping the Information Display Hidden. 283
Creating Your Own Menu. 284
Adjusting Automatic Shutdown Timing 286
Customizing a Few Buttons 287
Assigning a Touch Function Role. 289
Reversing the Command Dial Orientation. 290

CHAPTER 11: **Ten Fun (And Practical) Features to Explore
on a Rainy Day** 291

Applying the Retouch Menu Filters. 292
Removing Red-Eye. 295
Fixing Tilting and Distorted Images 295
Manipulating Exposure and Color 297
Cropping Your Photo 298
Adding Special Effects to Existing Photos 300
Shooting in Effects Mode 302

Creating a Dust Reference File 306
Printing Directly from the Camera 307
Presenting a Slide Show 307

APPENDIX: INTRO TO NIKON SNAPBRIDGE 309

What Can I Do with SnapBridge? 310
Setting Up the Camera for SnapBridge 311
Connecting to Your Smart Device 312
Taking a Look at SnapBridge Functions 314
Connect tab 315
Gallery tab 315
Camera tab 315
Other tab 317

INDEX 319

Introduction

Nikon. The name has been associated with top-flight photography equipment for generations, and the D5600 only enriches that reputation, offering terrific features for capturing both still photos and high-definition digital movies. But the fun doesn't stop after the shoot: On top of everything else, the D5600 enables you to transfer photos wirelessly to certain smartphones and tablets so that you can instantly share images online. You can even use your smart device as a wireless remote control.

In fact, the D5600 offers so many features that sorting them all out can be more than a little confusing. And therein lies the point of *Nikon D5600 For Dummies:* With the help of this book, you can take full advantage of everything the camera has to offer, even if you're brand new to photography.

About This Book

Unlike many photography books, this one doesn't require any previous knowledge of photography or digital imaging to make sense of things. In classic *For Dummies* style, everything is explained in easy-to-understand language, with lots of illustrations to help clear up any confusion.

However, even if you have some photography experience — or quite a bit of experience, for that matter — this book has plenty to offer. I provide detailed information about all the camera's advanced exposure, focus, and color controls, explaining not just what each feature does but why and how to put it to best use.

In short, what you have in your hands is the paperback version of an in-depth photography workshop tailored specifically to your Nikon picture-taking powerhouse.

How This Book Is Organized

This book is organized into four parts, each devoted to a different aspect of using your camera. Although chapters flow in a sequence that's designed to take you from absolute beginner to experienced user, I've also made each chapter as self-standing as possible so that you can explore the topics that interest you in any order you please.

Here's a brief preview of what you can find in each part of the book:

» **Part 1: Fast Track to Super Snaps:** Part 1 contains two chapters to help you get up and running. Chapter 1 guides you through initial camera setup, shows you how to view and adjust camera settings, and walks you through the steps of taking your first pictures using the Auto exposure mode. Chapter 2 introduces you to other exposure modes and explains basic picture options such as Release mode, Image Size (resolution), and Image Quality (JPEG or Raw). The end of Chapter 2 provides information on using flash.

» **Part 2: Taking Creative Control:** Chapters in this part help you unleash the full power of your camera by detailing the advanced shooting modes (P, S, A, and M). Chapter 3 covers the critical topic of exposure; Chapter 4 explains how to manipulate focus; and Chapter 5 discusses color controls. Chapter 6 summarizes techniques explained in earlier chapters, providing a quick-reference guide to the camera settings and shooting strategies that produce the best results for portraits, action shots, landscape scenes, and close-ups. Chapter 7 shifts gears, moving from still photography to HD movie recording.

» **Part 3: After the Shot:** Chapter 8 explains picture playback features and how to connect your camera to a TV for large-screen playback. Chapter 9 topics include rating, deleting, and protecting photos, downloading images to your computer, processing Raw files, and resizing pictures for online sharing.

» **Part 4: The Part of Tens:** In famous *For Dummies* tradition, this book concludes with two top-ten lists containing additional bits of information and advice. Chapter 10 details options for customizing your camera. Chapter 11 covers the tools found on the camera's Retouch menu, shows you how to use the Effects exposure mode, and explains a few other features that may come in handy on occasion, such as creating a slide show featuring your best work.

» **Appendix: Intro to Nikon SnapBridge:** Nikon SnapBridge is an app you can install on certain Android and Apple iOS smartphones and tablets. It's this app that enables you to use the camera's wireless functions to connect your D5600 to your smart device. After making the connection, you can transfer photos to the device for viewing or easy uploading to social media sites or online photo-storage sites. You also can use the smart device as a wireless remote control. Check out the appendix for an overview of these features.

>> **Cheat sheet:** When you have a minute or two, visit www.dummies.com and enter the name of this book in the search box. You'll find a link to a cheat sheet, which provides a handy reference to your camera's buttons, controls, and exposure modes.

Icons and Other Stuff to Note

If this isn't your first *For Dummies* book, you may be familiar with the large, round icons that decorate its margins. If not, here's your very own icon-decoder ring:

TIP

The Tip icon flags information that will save you time, effort, money, or some other valuable resource, including your sanity. Tips also point out techniques that help you get the best results from specific camera features.

WARNING

When you see this icon, look alive. It indicates a potential danger zone that can result in much wailing and teeth-gnashing if ignored. In other words, this is stuff that you really don't want to learn the hard way.

TECHNICAL
STUFF

Lots of information in this book is of a technical nature — digital photography is a technical animal, after all. But when I present a detail that is useful mainly for impressing your tech-geek friends, I mark it with this icon.

REMEMBER

I apply this icon either to introduce information that is especially worth storing in your brain's long-term memory or to remind you of a fact that may have been displaced from that memory by another pressing fact.

Additionally, replicas of some of your camera's buttons and onscreen graphics appear in the margins and in some tables. I include these images to provide quick reminders of the appearance of the button or option being discussed.

Where to Go from Here

To wrap up this preamble, I want to stress that if you initially think that digital photography is too confusing or too technical for you, you're in very good company. *Everyone* finds this stuff mind-boggling at first. So take it slowly, experimenting with just one or two new camera settings or techniques at first. Then every time you go on a photo outing, make it a point to add one or two more shooting skills to your repertoire.

I know it's hard to believe when you're just starting out, but it really won't be long before everything starts to come together. With some time, patience, and practice, you'll soon wield your camera like a pro, dialing in the necessary settings to capture your creative vision almost instinctively.

So without further ado, I invite you to grab your camera, a cup of whatever it is you prefer to sip while you read, and start exploring the rest of this book. Your D5600 is the perfect partner for your photographic journey, and I'm grateful for the opportunity to act as your tour guide.

1

Fast Track to Super Snaps

Familiarize yourself with the basics of using your camera, from attaching lenses to navigating menus.

Get step-by-step help with shooting your first pictures in Auto mode.

Find out how to select the exposure mode, Release mode, Image Size (resolution), and Image Quality (JPEG or Raw file type).

Discover options available for flash photography.

IN THIS CHAPTER

» **Preparing the camera for its first outing**

» **Getting acquainted with the touchscreen and other camera features**

» **Viewing and adjusting camera settings**

» **Setting a few basic preferences**

» **Taking a picture in Auto mode**

Chapter **1**

First Steps, First Shots

S hooting for the first time with a camera as sophisticated as the Nikon D5600 can produce a blend of excitement and anxiety. On one hand, you can't wait to start using your new equipment, but on the other, you're a little intimidated by all its buttons, dials, and menu options.

Well, fear not: This chapter provides the information you need to start getting comfortable with your D5600. The first section walks you through initial camera setup; following that, you can discover how to view and adjust picture settings and get my take on additional setup options. At the end of the chapter, I explain how to take pictures using Auto mode, which offers point-and-shoot simplicity until you're ready for more advanced options.

Preparing the Camera for Initial Use

After unpacking your camera, you have to assemble a few parts. In addition to the camera body and the supplied battery (be sure to charge it before the first use), you need a lens and a memory card. Later sections in this chapter provide details about working with lenses and memory cards, but here's what you need to know up front:

>> **Lens:** You can mount a wide range of lenses on your D5600, but some aren't compatible with all camera features. For example, to enjoy autofocusing, you need an AF-P or AF-S lens. (The 18–55mm lens featured in this book and sold in a kit with the D5600 body is an AF-P lens.) The camera's instruction manual offers details about lens compatibility. (The full manual is available online at the Nikon Download Center.)

TECHNICAL
STUFF

The *AF* in AF-S and AF-P stands for *autofocus*. The *S* in AF-S stands for a *silent wave* focusing motor; the *P* refers to an autofocusing technology known as a "stepping motor." Both are designed to deliver faster and quieter autofocusing. How you implement autofocusing differs between the two types, however. Read more about this issue later in this chapter, in the section "Familiarizing Yourself with the Lens."

>> **SD (Secure Digital) memory card:** Your camera accepts only this type of card. Most SD cards carry the designation SDHC (for *High Capacity*) or SDXC (for *eXtended Capacity*), depending on how many gigabytes (GB) of data they hold. SDHC cards hold from 4GB to 32GB of data; the SDXC moniker is assigned to cards with capacities greater than 32GB.

With camera, lens, battery, and card within reach, take these steps:

1. **Turn the camera off.**

2. **Install the battery into the compartment on the bottom of the camera.**

3. **Attach a lens.**

   First, remove the caps that cover the front of the camera and the back of the lens. Then align the *mounting index* (white dot) on the lens with the one on the camera body, as shown in Figure 1-1. After placing the lens on the camera mount, rotate the lens toward the shutter-button side of the camera. You should feel a solid click as the lens locks into place.

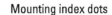

Mounting index dots

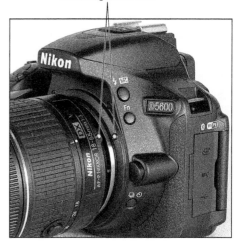

FIGURE 1-1:
Align the white dot on the lens with the one on the camera body.

4. **Insert a memory card.**

   Open the card-slot cover on the right side of the camera and orient the card as shown in Figure 1-2 (the label faces the back of the camera). Push the card gently into the slot and close the cover. The memory-card access light, labeled in the figure, illuminates briefly to let you know that the camera recognizes the card.

5. **Rotate the monitor to the desired viewing position.**

   When you first take the camera out of its box, the monitor is positioned with the screen facing inward, protecting it from scratches and smudges. Gently lift the right side of the monitor up and away from the camera back. You can then rotate the monitor to move it into the traditional position on the camera back, as shown on the left in Figure 1-3, or swing the monitor out to get a different viewing angle, as shown on the right.

Memory-card access light

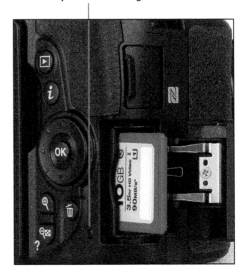

FIGURE 1-2:
Insert the memory card with the label facing the back of the camera.

Multi Selector/OK button

FIGURE 1-3:
Here are just two possible monitor positions.

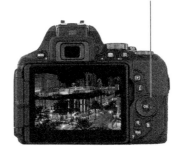
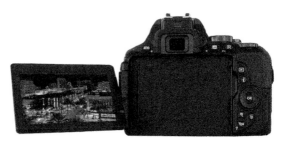

6. **Turn on the camera.**

7. **Set the language, time zone, and date.**

   When you power up the camera for the first time, you can't do anything until you take this step.

The easiest way to adjust the settings is to use the touchscreen, which is enabled by default. To select an option or display a menu of settings, just tap it on the screen, just as you do with any touchscreen device. If you see an OK symbol in the lower-right corner of the screen, tap it to finalize your selection and return to the previous screen. To exit a screen without making changes, tap the exit arrow shown in the upper-right corner of the screen.

If you prefer, you also can use the Multi Selector and OK button, labeled in Figure 1-3, to navigate menus. You can find more details about using the touchscreen and other ways to adjust settings later in this chapter.

8. **Adjust the viewfinder to your eyesight.**

This step is critical; if you don't set the viewfinder to your eyesight, subjects that appear out of focus in the viewfinder might actually be in focus, and vice versa. If you wear glasses while shooting, adjust the viewfinder with your glasses on.

You set viewfinder focus by rotating the adjustment dial labeled in Figure 1-4. After taking off the lens cap and making sure that the camera is turned on, look through the viewfinder and press the shutter button halfway. In dim lighting, the flash may pop up. Ignore it for now and concentrate on the row of data that appears at the bottom of the viewfinder screen. Rotate the dial until that data appears sharpest. The markings in the center of the viewfinder, which relate to autofocusing, also become more or less sharp. Ignore the scene you see through the lens; that won't change because you're not actually focusing the camera. When you finish, press down on the flash unit to close it if necessary.

Viewfinder adjustment dial

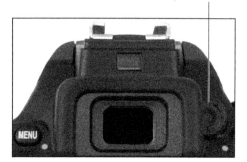

FIGURE 1-4:
Rotate this dial to set the viewfinder focus for your eyesight.

9. **If using a retractable lens, unlock and extend the lens.**

The lens barrels of AF-P kit lenses, as well as some AF-S lenses, extend and retract. When you're not shooting, you can retract the lens so that it takes up less space in your camera bag. But before you can take a picture or even access most camera menu items, you must unlock and extend the lens. A message appears on the monitor to remind you of this step.

To extend the lens, press the lens lock button, highlighted in Figure 1-5, while rotating the lens barrel toward the shutter-button side of the camera. To retract the lens, press the button while rotating the lens in the other direction.

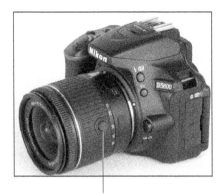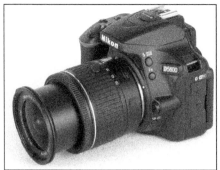

FIGURE 1-5:
If using a
retractable
lens, press
the lens lock
button while
rotating the
lens barrel to
extend and
retract the
lens.

Lens lock button

That's all there is to it — your camera is now ready to go. From here, my recommendation is that you keep reading this chapter to familiarize yourself with the main camera features and basic operation. But if you're anxious to take a picture right away, skip to the last section of the chapter, which guides you through the basic process. Just promise that at some point, you'll read the pages in between, because they do contain important information.

Checking Out External Controls

Scattered across your camera's exterior are numerous features that you use to change picture-taking settings, review your photos, and perform various other operations. In later chapters, I discuss all your camera's functions in detail and provide the exact steps to follow to access them. This section provides just a basic "what's this thing do?" guide to each control. (Don't worry about memorizing the button names; throughout the book, I show pictures of buttons in the page margins to help you know exactly which one to press.)

REMEMBER

Keep in mind, too, that you can adjust many settings by simply tapping the touchscreen, which is sometimes faster than fiddling with the camera buttons. I explain how to use the touchscreen later in this chapter.

Topside controls

Your virtual tour begins with the bird's-eye view shown in Figure 1-6. There are a number of features of note here:

>> **Shutter button/power switch:** Okay, I'm pretty sure you already figured out this combo button. But you may not be aware that you need to press the

shutter button in two stages: Press and hold the button halfway and wait for the camera to initiate exposure metering and, if you're using autofocusing, to set the focusing distance. Then press the button the rest of the way to take the picture.

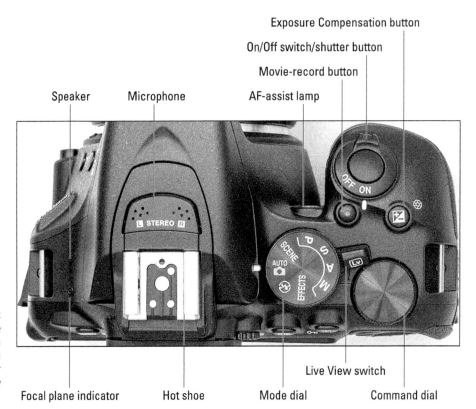

Exposure Compensation button

On/Off switch/shutter button

Movie-record button

Speaker   Microphone   AF-assist lamp

FIGURE 1-6:
Rotate the Live View switch to shift from viewfinder to Live View photography.

Focal plane indicator   Hot shoe   Mode dial   Command dial

Live View switch

>> **Mode dial:** With this dial, you choose the exposure mode, which determines which picture-taking settings you can control. You get a number of automatic, beginner modes as well as four advanced modes (P, S, A, and M). Effects mode enables you to apply special effects as an image or movie is captured; the Scene setting accesses automatic modes designed for specific types of shots (portraits, landscapes, and so on). Chapter 2 introduces you to each exposure mode.

>> **Command dial:** After you activate certain camera features, you rotate this dial, labeled in the figure, to select a setting. For example, to choose a shutter speed when shooting in shutter-priority (S) mode, you rotate the Command dial.

>> **Exposure Compensation button:** The main use of this button is to apply Exposure Compensation, which enables you to tweak autoexposure results when using some exposure modes. Hold the button down while rotating the Command dial to adjust the setting. Chapter 3 explains Exposure Compensation.

>> **Live View switch:** Rotate this switch to turn *Live View* on and off. In Live View mode, the scene in front of the lens appears on the monitor, and you can't see anything through the viewfinder. You then can compose a photo using the monitor. For movie recording, you must use Live View; you can't shoot a movie using the viewfinder. The last section of this chapter introduces you to Live View photography; see Chapter 7 for help with movie making.

>> **Record button:** After shifting to Live View mode, press this button to start recording a movie. Press it again to stop recording.

>> **AF-assist light:** In dim lighting, this light turns on briefly to help the camera locate your focusing target. The light also comes on when you use red-eye reduction flash and the Self-Timer shutter-release mode, both covered in Chapter 2.

>> **Flash hot shoe:** *Hot shoe* is photography-speak for a terminal that enables you to connect an external flash. On the D5600, the hot shoe also serves as a mount for the optional Nikon ME-1 and ME-W1 stereo microphones.

>> **Microphone:** If you don't attach an external microphone, movie audio is recorded using the camera's built-in microphone.

>> **Speaker:** When you play a movie, sound comes out of these holes.

TIP

>> **Focal plane indicator:** If you need to know the exact distance between your subject and the camera, as you might if you need to photograph objects for scientific or legal documentation, the focal plane indicator is key. The mark indicates the plane at which light coming through the lens is focused onto the camera's image sensor. Basing your measurement on this mark produces a more accurate camera-to-subject distance than using the end of the lens or another external point on the camera body as your reference point.

Back-of-the-body controls

On the back of the camera, shown in Figure 1–7, you find the following features:

>> **Menu button:** Press this button to access menus of camera options. See "Navigating Menus," later in this chapter, for details.

>> **Viewfinder adjustment dial:** Rotate this dial to adjust the viewfinder focus to your eyesight; see the first section of this chapter for details.

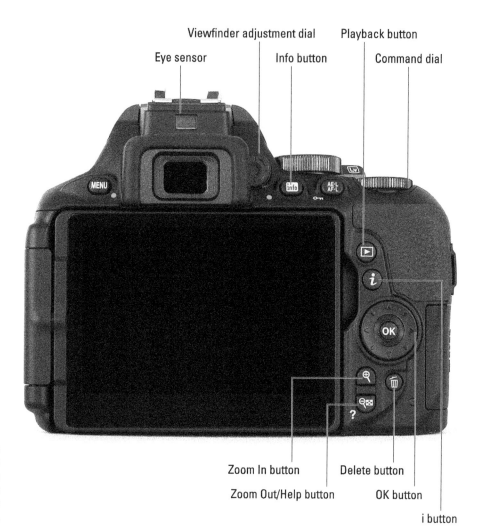

Viewfinder adjustment dial

Playback button

Eye sensor

Info button

Command dial

FIGURE 1-7:
For quick
access to
primary picture
settings, press
the *i* button.

Zoom In button

Delete button

Zoom Out/Help button

OK button

i button

>> **Eye sensor:** This window senses when you put your eye to the viewfinder and, in response, turns off the monitor to save battery power. Not working? Open the Setup menu and check the status of the item named Info Display Auto Off. The option should be set to On, as it is by default. If that's not the issue, you may simply need to press your eye closer to the viewfinder. Also, when you wear glasses, sometimes the sensor can't detect your eye. You do have the option of pressing the Info button, labeled in the figure, to turn the monitor on and off.

>> **Info button:** When using the viewfinder to compose photos, press this button to display the Information screen, which shows key camera settings and various bits of information, such as the battery status. To turn off the screen, press Info again.

You also can display the screen by pressing the shutter button halfway and releasing it.

In Live View mode, pressing the Info button changes the type and amount of data that appears on the preview.

>> **AE-L/AF-L button:** During shooting, pressing this button initiates autoexposure lock (AE-L) and autofocus lock (AF-L). Chapter 3 explains autoexposure lock; Chapter 4 talks about autofocus lock.

In playback mode, pressing the button locks the picture file — hence the little key symbol that appears near the button — so that it isn't erased if you use the picture-delete functions. See Chapter 9 for details. (The picture *is* erased if you format the memory card, however.)

>> **Playback button:** Press this button to switch the camera to picture-review mode. Chapter 8 details playback features.

>> *i* **button:** During shooting, pressing this button activates a control strip that enables quick access to certain picture settings. I provide details in the later section "Adjusting Settings via the Control Strip." Press *i* again to exit the control strip. In Playback mode, pressing the button brings up a small menu that enables you to rate photos, edit them using the Retouch menu features, and tag them for later wireless transmission to a smartphone or tablet. I refer to the Playback menu as the *i-button menu*.

>> **Multi Selector/OK button:** This dual-natured control plays a role in many camera functions. You press the outer edges of the Multi Selector left, right, up, or down to navigate camera menus and access certain other options. At the center of the control is the OK button, which you press to finalize a menu selection or another camera adjustment.

In this book, the instruction "Press the Multi Selector left" means to press the left edge of the control. "Press the Multi Selector right" means to press the right edge, and so on.

>> **Delete button:** Sporting a trash can icon, the universal symbol for delete, this button enables you to erase pictures from your memory card. Chapter 9 explains the steps.

>> **Zoom In and Zoom Out buttons:** These buttons have several purposes, depending on what camera function you're using:

- *Picture playback:* In still-photo playback mode, pressing the Zoom In button magnifies the image; pressing Zoom Out reduces the magnification. After you display a photo at its normal magnification, you can press Zoom Out repeatedly to shift to thumbnails view, which displays multiple image previews at a time, and then to Calendar view, which simplifies the job of tracking down all pictures taken on a certain date. Pressing Zoom In cycles the display in the other direction.

- *Movie playback:* Press Zoom In to increase audio volume; press Zoom Out to lower it.

- *Live View mode:* Pressing the Zoom In button magnifies the live preview so you can check focus more closely. Pressing Zoom Out reduces the magnification amount. (Chapter 4 details this feature.)

TIP

Additionally, if you see a question mark symbol on a menu screen or other display, pressing the Zoom Out button displays a Help screen that contains information about the feature you're using. (Note the question mark symbol beneath the button.)

Both buttons also come into play when you use certain other camera features, such as applying changes from the Retouch menu.

Front-left features

The front-left side of the camera, shown in Figure 1-8, sports these features:

» **Flash button:** In some exposure modes, pressing this button raises the built-in flash. In other modes, the camera controls whether flash is enabled.

By holding the Flash button down and rotating the Command dial, you can adjust the Flash mode (Fill Flash, Red-Eye Reduction, and so on). In some exposure modes, you also can adjust the flash power by pressing the button while simultaneously pressing the Exposure Compensation button and rotating the Command dial. The little +/– symbol that appears below the Flash button — the same symbol that's on the Exposure Compensation button — is a reminder of the button's role in flash-power adjustment.

Check out Chapter 2 for details on flash options.

Flash button

Fn (Function) button

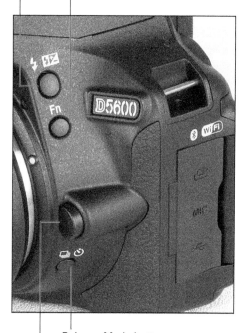

Release Mode button

Lens-release button

FIGURE 1-8:
Press the Flash button to use the built-in flash in P, S, A, or M mode.

>> **Function (Fn) button:** By default, this button gives you quick access to the ISO setting, which controls the camera's sensitivity to light. (Chapter 3 explains.) If you don't adjust that setting often, you can use the button to perform a variety of other operations. Chapter 10 shows you how to change the button's purpose. (**Note:** All instructions in this book assume that you haven't changed the function of this or any other button.)

>> **Lens-release button:** Press this button to disengage the lens from the camera's lens mount so you can remove the lens. (If you're using a retractable lens, collapse the lens first.)

>> **Release Mode button:** Press this button to display a screen where you can select the shutter-release mode. By default, the option is set to Single Frame, which results in one picture each time you press the shutter button. You can explore other options in Chapter 2.

Hidden connections

Open the covers on the left and right sides of the camera, to access the following connection ports, labeled in Figure 1-9:

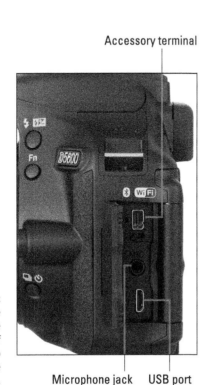
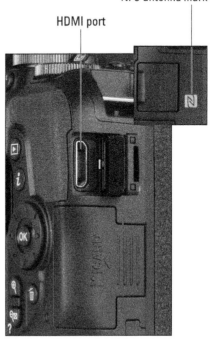

NFC antenna mark

Accessory terminal   HDMI port

FIGURE 1-9:
Open the covers on the sides of the camera to reveal these connections.

Microphone jack   USB port

- **Accessory terminal:** This terminal accepts the following accessories: Nikon MC-DC2 remote shutter-release cable; WR-1 and WR-R10 wireless remote controllers; and GP-1/GP-1A GPS units. I don't cover these accessories, but the manual that comes with each device can get you up and running.

- **Microphone jack:** If you're not happy with the audio quality provided by the internal microphone, you can plug in an external microphone, such as the Nikon ME-1 mic. The jack accepts a 3.5mm plug.

- **USB port:** Through this port, you can connect your camera to your computer via USB connection for picture downloading. However, Nikon doesn't supply the necessary USB cable (Nikon UC-E20). You can buy one for about $12, but before you go to that expense, check out Chapter 9 for details about downloading through a memory-card reader. For information about wireless file transfer to a smartphone, tablet, or other compatible device, head for this book's appendix.

- **HDMI port:** You use this port, found on the right side of the camera, to connect your camera to a high-definition TV, but you need to buy an HDMI cable to do so. Look for a cable that has a Type C connector on one end (this end goes into the camera) and a regular, Type A connector on the other end. Chapter 8 offers details on television playback.

Just below the HMDI port is a door that leads to the memory–card slot. (See the first section of this chapter for help installing a memory card.) If you turn the camera over, you find a tripod socket, which enables you to mount the camera on a tripod that uses a ¼-inch screw, plus the battery chamber.

TECHNICAL STUFF

In case you're wondering, the two symbols above the left port door are there simply to remind you of two of the camera's wireless connection technologies: Bluetooth and Wi-Fi. On the right side of the camera, the N symbol (shown in the outset on the right side of Figure 1-9) reminds you that the D5600 also offers Near Field Communication (NFC), a feature that enables you to link two NFC devices by placing them next to each other.

Enabling and Using the Touchscreen

When manufacturers first started putting touchscreens on dSLRs, I thought, "Meh, just a gimmick." But after discovering how much easier it is to adjust camera settings by using the touchscreen instead of pressing buttons and rotating dials — well, let's just say that I was wrong in my initial assessment. Yes, I said it: "I was wrong."

If you've used a smartphone, tablet, or other touchscreen device, working with the camera's touchscreen will feel familiar. Just as with those devices, you communicate with the camera via these *gestures*, which are specific ways to touch the screen:

>> **Tap:** Tap a finger lightly on the screen.

>> **Drag (or swipe):** Drag your finger up, down, right, or left across the screen.

>> **Flick:** Drag a finger quickly across the screen.

>> **Pinch in/pinch out:** *Pinching* enables you to quickly adjust the magnification of an image during picture playback. To magnify the image, pinch out. That is, place your thumb and your pointer finger in the center of the screen and then drag both fingers outward to the edges of the screen. To zoom out, pinch in, dragging your thumb and finger from the outer edge of the screen toward the center.

TIP

By default, the touchscreen is enabled for both shooting and playback. But you can disable it entirely or use it just for playback if you wish. The following steps walk you through the process of adjusting this option and give you some practice in using the touchscreen:

1. **Press the Menu button to display the camera menus.**

   Sadly, there's no touchscreen control that takes you to the menus.

2. **Tap the Setup menu icon (wrench symbol) to select that menu, as shown on the left in Figure 1-10.**

Setup menu icon   Scroll bar   Exit without making changes

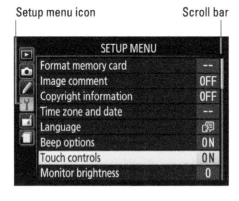
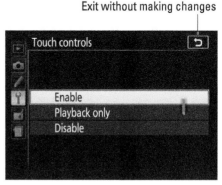

FIGURE 1-10:
Enable or disable the touchscreen via this Setup menu option.

3. **Tap the Touch Controls option, highlighted in the figure.**

   You see the screen shown on the right in Figure 1-10.

4. **To turn the touchscreen off for shooting functions but leave it enabled for playback, tap Playback Only. To disable the touchscreen altogether, tap Disable.**

REMEMBER

   On many screens, an exit arrow appears in the top-right corner of the screen (refer to Figure 1-10). Tap this arrow to exit the screen. On some screens, you must tap an OK symbol or take some other action to lock in your changes before exiting the screen. (Instructions throughout the book let you know when that's necessary.)

If you choose Playback Only or Disable, you can't use the touchscreen to revert to the original, Enable, setting. Instead, you must use the Multi Selector and OK button to do the job. (See the next section for help navigating menus using these controls.)

A couple final tips about the touchscreen:

>> **On the Information and Live View displays, a white border around a symbol indicates that you can tap that symbol to access the setting.** For example, the border around the *i* symbol in the lower-right corner of Figure 1-11 tells you that you can tap that area to perform the same action as pressing the *i* button.

TIP

>> **For viewfinder photography, you can tap your thumb anywhere on the right half of the screen to perform a specific function.** Nikon refers to this feature as the Touch Function. When the Touch Function feature is enabled, you see the FN symbol at the top of the Information display, labeled in Figure 1-11.

Touch Function enabled

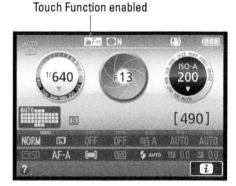

FIGURE 1-11:
This symbol tells you that the Touch Function feature is enabled.

By default, the Touch Function is set to display an alignment grid in the viewfinder. Try it: With your eye to the viewfinder, tap your right thumb on the right half of the screen. The grid should appear in the viewfinder. Tap again to hide the grid.

If you swing the monitor out to the left side of the camera, you can tap anywhere on the monitor to take advantage of the Touch Function. You still must have your eye to the viewfinder to make this feature work, however; it doesn't work for Live View photography or movie shooting.

Don't need a viewfinder grid? Use the Assign Touch Fn option on the Custom Setting menu to make the camera perform a different task when you tap. (Chapter 10 has details.) If you set the option to None, the Touch Function symbol disappears from the Information display.

>> **During Live View shooting, you can tap the screen to set focus and take a picture.** The last section of this chapter tells you more about this feature, known as the Touch Shutter. You also can tell the camera to set focus only when you tap.

WARNING

>> **Don't apply a screen protector.** Applying a screen protector can actually damage the monitor and make it less responsive to your touch.

One final bit of touchscreen advice: If you're wearing the camera on a neck strap and the touchscreen is enabled, it's possible to inadvertently "tap" a touchscreen symbol with your chest and not notice it. By default, the touchscreen emits a sound when you tap a symbol, but in a noisy environment, it's easy to miss that audio warning. The only solutions are to turn the camera off between shots, disable the touchscreen, or rotate the monitor to the closed (face in) position.

Navigating Menus

REMEMBER

Although you can change some settings by using the camera's external buttons or by tapping touchscreen symbols, other options are accessible only via the menus.

To access the menus, press the Menu button. You see a screen similar to the one shown in Figure 1-12. The icons along the left side of the screen represent the available menus. To the right of the icon strip are options associated with the current menu. Table 1-1 offers a quick guide to the menus.

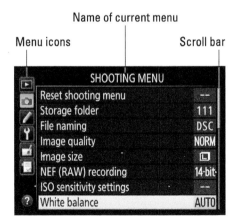

FIGURE 1-12:
The scroll bar indicates that the menu is a multi-page affair.

TABLE 1-1 **D5600 Menus**

Symbol	Open This Menu . . .	To Access These Functions
▶	Playback	Viewing, deleting, and protecting pictures
◉	Shooting	Basic photography settings
✎	Custom Setting	Advanced photography options and some basic camera operations
⚲	Setup	Additional basic camera operations
🖌	Retouch	Photo and movie editing options
▤ ▤	My Menu/Recent Settings	Your custom menu or a menu listing the 20 most recently used menu options

Here's what you need to know to work your way though menu screens:

>> **To select a different menu:** Tap the menu's icon or press the Multi Selector left to activate the icon strip, press up or down to select the menu you want to view, and then press right to access the menu's options.

>> **To select and adjust a menu option:** Again, you can take advantage of the touchscreen or use the Multi Selector:

  ● *Touchscreen:* If you see a scroll bar on the right side of the window, as in Figure 1-12, swipe up or down to scroll to the next page of menu options. Tap the option you want to adjust. Settings available for the selected item then appear. Tap the setting you want to use. Or to exit without making any changes, tap the exit arrow in the upper-right corner of the screen.

  ● *Multi Selector/OK button:* Press the Multi Selector up or down to scroll the menu until the option you want to change is highlighted. Press OK to display the available settings. Repeat the old up-and-down scroll routine until the choice you prefer is highlighted. Then press OK.

  In some cases, a right-pointing triangle appears next to a menu item. That's your cue to tap that item or to press the Multi Selector right to display a submenu. You may also see an Adjust symbol at the bottom of some screens; again, tap the symbol or press the Multi Selector right to access additional options.

During shooting, items that are dimmed in a menu aren't available in the current exposure mode. When you open the Retouch menu, the camera dims options that can't be used with the currently selected photo. Additionally, some menu options are unavailable when you use certain Image Quality settings, which I explain in Chapter 2.

>> **To select items from the Custom Setting menu:** Displaying the Custom Setting menu, represented by the Pencil icon, takes you to a screen that contains six submenus that carry the labels A through F, as shown in Figure 1-13. Each submenu holds clusters of options related to a specific aspect of the camera's operation. To get to those options, tap the submenu name or highlight it with the Multi Selector and press OK.

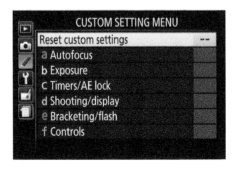

FIGURE 1-13:
The Custom Setting menu contains six submenus of advanced options.

In the Nikon manual, instructions reference the Custom Setting menu items by a menu letter and number. For example, "Custom Setting a1" refers to the first option on the a (Autofocus) submenu. I try to be more specific, so I use the actual setting names. (Really, we all have enough numbers to remember, don't you think?)

After you jump to the first submenu, you can simply scroll up and down the list to view options from other submenus. You don't have to keep going back to the initial menu screen and selecting a submenu.

>> **Create a custom menu or view your 20 most recently adjusted menu items:** The sixth menu is actually two menus that share an apartment: Recent Settings and My Menu, both shown in Figure 1-14. Each menu contains a Choose Tab option as the last item on the menu; select this option to shift between the two menus.

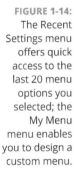

FIGURE 1-14:
The Recent Settings menu offers quick access to the last 20 menu options you selected; the My Menu menu enables you to design a custom menu.

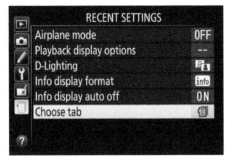

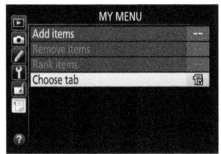

Here's what the two menus offer:

- *Recent Settings:* This screen lists the 20 menu items you ordered most recently. To adjust those settings, you don't have to wade through all the other menus to look for them — head to the Recent Settings menu instead.

  To remove an item from the Recent Settings menu, use the Multi Selector to highlight the item and press the Delete button. Press Delete again to confirm your decision. (If you tap the item in the menu, you pull up that item's options screen.)

- *My Menu:* From this screen, you can create a custom menu that contains your favorite options. Chapter 10 details the steps.

Viewing Critical Picture Settings

Your D5600 gives you the following ways to monitor important picture-taking settings:

>> **Information display:** The left screen in Figure 1-15 gives you a look at this display, which appears during viewfinder shooting. You can turn it on and off by pressing the Info button.

Battery status

Vibration Reduction on

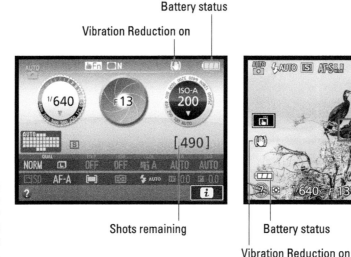

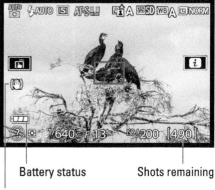

FIGURE 1-15: Press the Info button to view picture-taking settings on the monitor.

Shots remaining

Battery status

Shots remaining

Vibration Reduction on

If your Information screen appears different from the ones shown in this book, don't freak out. The camera offers a variety of Information screen display styles; the screen in Figure 1-15 is the default design used when the Mode dial is set to one of the fully automatic exposure modes (Auto, Effects, Scene, and Flash Off). In the P, S, A, and M exposure modes, a darker background is used. You can alter the look of the Information screens via the Info Display Format option on the Setup menu; Chapter 10 has details.

» **Live View display:** In Live View mode, the Information display is disabled, and the camera instead displays shooting data atop the live preview, as shown on the right in Figure 1-15. To switch to Live View mode, rotate the LV switch (top of the camera, next to the Mode dial).

You can vary the type of data displayed on the Live View screen by pressing the Info button. See the last section of this chapter for more about this feature.

» **Viewfinder:** You also can view some settings at the bottom of the viewfinder, as shown in Figure 1-16. The information that appears depends on the exposure mode; the figure shows the data you see when using Auto mode.

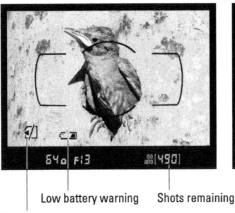 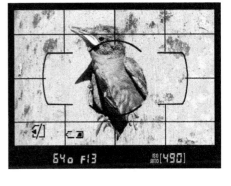

FIGURE 1-16: Picture settings also appear at the bottom of the viewfinder (left); enable the grid for help with aligning objects in the frame (right).

No memory card warning   Low battery warning   Shots remaining

TIP

You can display gridlines in the viewfinder, as shown on the right in the figure. The gridlines help you ensure the alignment of objects in your photo — for example, to make sure that the horizon is level in a landscape. When your eye is up to the viewfinder and the touchscreen is enabled, tap the right half of the monitor to toggle the grid on and off. (If the monitor is swung to the side of the camera, you can tap anywhere on the screen.) This trick works only if you stick with the default Touch Function setting on the Setup menu, however. You also can hide and display the grid via the Viewfinder Grid Display option, found on the Shooting/Display section of the Custom Setting menu.

If what you see in Figures 1-15 and 1-16 looks like a confusing mess, don't worry. Many settings relate to options that won't mean anything to you until you explore the advanced exposure modes (P, S, A, and M). But make note of the following bits of data that are helpful in any exposure mode:

>> **Battery status indicator:** A full-battery icon (refer to Figure 1-15) shows that the battery is fully charged; if the icon appears empty, look for your battery charger.

Just for good measure, the camera also displays a low-battery symbol in the viewfinder (refer to Figure 1-16). If the symbol blinks, the camera won't take more pictures until you charge the battery.

>> **Shots remaining:** Labeled in Figures 1-15 and 1-16, this value indicates how many more pictures you can store on the memory card. If the number exceeds 999, the initial *K* appears, to indicate that the value is in the thousands. For example, 1.0K means that you can store 1,000 more pictures. (*K* is a universally accepted symbol indicating 1,000 units.) The number is rounded down to the nearest hundred. So if the card has room for, say, 1,230 more pictures, the value reads 1.2K.

>> **Memory card warning:** If the memory-card slot is empty, you see the no-card symbol in the viewfinder, as shown in Figure 1-16. The Information screen and Live View display offer a text reminder to insert a card.

>> **Vibration Reduction symbol:** The shaky hand symbol that you see in both displays in Figure 1-15 tells you that Vibration Reduction is enabled. This feature is designed to help you get sharper pictures when you handhold the camera. Camera movement during the exposure can cause image blurring, and Vibration Reduction attempts to compensate for a small amount of camera shake. Not all lenses offer this feature, and you implement it differently depending on the type of lens. Look for the full story in Chapter 4. (Spoiler alert: The 18–55mm AF-P lens featured in this book does offer the feature, and it's turned on by default.) Turn the feature off and on via the Optical VR setting on the Shooting menu.

REMEMBER

The viewfinder display, Live View screen, and Information screen automatically shut off after a specific period of inactivity to preserve battery power. To wake up the displays and return to shooting mode, press the shutter button halfway and release it or press the Info button. To turn the monitor back on so you can view your pictures, press the Playback button. See Chapter 10 for details about altering the auto-shutdown times for the monitor and viewfinder displays.

Adjusting Settings via the Control Strip

TIP

The Information display isn't just for checking current picture-taking settings; it also gives you quick access to some of the most critical of those settings. Specifically, you can adjust the options that appear on the two rows of data near the bottom of the screen — what I refer to as the control strip.

Here's how it works for viewfinder photography:

1. **Display the Information screen by pressing the Info button or pressing the shutter button halfway and releasing it.**

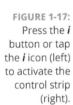

2. **Press the *i* button or tap the *i* symbol on the screen, labeled on the left in Figure 1-17.**

   The top part of the display dims, and the control strip becomes accessible, as shown on the right in Figure 1-17. The currently selected setting appears highlighted, and its name is displayed above the control strip. For example, in Figure 1-17, the Image Quality option is selected.

FIGURE 1-17:
Press the *i*
button or tap
the *i* icon (left)
to activate the
control strip
(right).

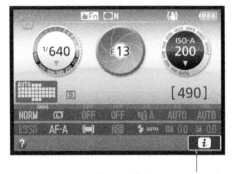

Tap to display control strip

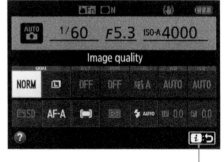

Tap to exit control strip

3. **Select the option that you want to change.**

   Either tap the option or use the Multi Selector to highlight it and then press OK. Either way, the next screen displays available settings.

4. **Adjust the setting as desired.**

   Again, you can tap the setting or use the Multi Selector to highlight it and then press OK. The camera returns you to the initial control strip screen. You can then adjust another setting, if needed.

5. **To exit the control strip, press the _i_ button or tap the strip's exit symbol, labeled on the right in Figure 1-17.**

TIP

You also can just give the shutter button a quick half-press and release it to exit the control strip.

During Live View shooting, things work the same way, but the touchscreen's _i_ symbol appears halfway down the right side of the screen. (Refer to Figure 1-15.) If you don't see the symbol, you may need to press the Info button to change the type of data displayed on the Live View display. Of course, you must also enable the Touch Controls option on the Setup menu to use the touchscreen for view-finder or Live View photography.

Familiarizing Yourself with the Lens

Because I don't know which lens you're using, I can't give you full instructions on its operation. But the following basics apply to most Nikon AF-P and AF-S lenses as well as to certain other lenses that support autofocusing — you should explore the lens manual for specifics, of course:

REMEMBER

>> **Extending/retracting the lens:** If you have a retractable lens like the AF-P kit lens, press the lens lock button while rotating the lens barrel to extend and retract the lens (see Figure 1-18). The camera won't take a picture with the lens in the retracted position.

>> **Zooming:** A zoom lens has a movable _zoom barrel_. The location of the zoom barrel on the kit lens is shown in Figure 1-18. To zoom in or out, rotate the barrel. Some lenses instead use a push/pull setup, where you push and pull the lens away from you or toward you to zoom.

TIP

You can determine the current focal length of the lens by looking at the number that's aligned with the dot labeled _focal-length indicator_ in Figure 1-18. (If you're new to the term _focal length,_ the sidebar "Focal length and the crop factor," later in this chapter, explains the subject.)

>> **Setting the focus method (automatic or manual focusing):** You can find out which focus method is in force by looking at the Focus Mode symbol that appears in the Information and Live View displays. I labeled the setting in Figure 1-19. The letters MF represent manual focusing; anything else repre-sents one of the camera's autofocusing options.

Which autofocus options are available depends on your exposure mode and whether Live View is enabled. Figure 1-19 shows the default autofocus settings, which are AF-A for viewfinder photography and AF-S for Live View photography and movie recording.

Focal-length indicator

Lens lock button

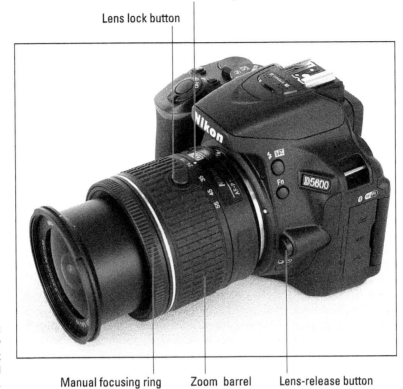

FIGURE 1-18:
Here are a few
features that
may be found
on your lens.

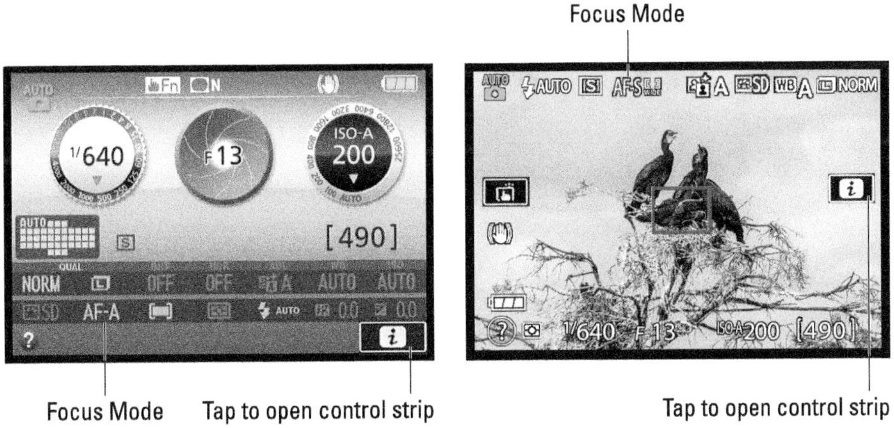

Manual focusing ring   Zoom barrel   Lens-release button

Focus Mode

FIGURE 1-19:
The letters AF
indicate that
the camera is
using one of
its autofocus
options.

Focus Mode   Tap to open control strip   Tap to open control strip

I offer complete focusing details in Chapter 4; for now, I just want to offer a quick primer on how you switch between automatic and manual focusing. The steps differ depending on whether you're using an AF-P or AF-S lens. Here's the scoop:

- *AF-P lens:* Press the *i* button or tap the onscreen *i* symbol to access the control strip and then choose the Focus Mode option to access the available settings. Figure 1-20 illustrates the process for viewfinder photography; Figure 1-21 shows you how things look when Live View is enabled.

FIGURE 1-20:
For viewfinder photography, use the Focus Mode option on the control strip to set an AF-P lens to automatic or manual focusing.

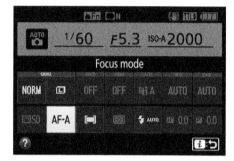
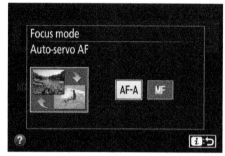

FIGURE 1-21:
You also set the focusing method in Live View mode via the control strip, but the autofocusing options are different than for viewfinder photography.

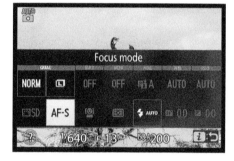
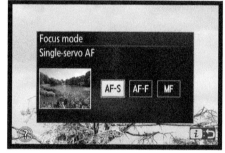

- *AF-S lens:* These lenses typically offer an exterior switch for shifting from automatic to manual focusing. Move the switch to the A position for autofocusing and to M for manual focusing. On some lenses, the switches may instead be marked AF and MF; some lenses have a switch position labeled AF/M, which means that you can use autofocusing to set initial focus and then fine-tune focus manually without changing the position of the switch.

- Even though you set the basic focus method via the switch, you may be able to choose from several autofocusing settings, depending on which exposure mode you use. As is the case with AF-P lenses, establish your preference via the Focus Mode option on the control strip.

By default, the camera also offers autofocusing with manual override for AF-P lenses. The potential issue with this feature, whether you use an AF-P or AF-S lens, is that you can accidentally move the focusing ring, changing the focus point without realizing that you did so. To disable the feature for AF-P lenses, open the Custom Setting menu, head for the Autofocus section of the menu, and change the Manual Focus Ring in AF Mode option to Off, as shown in Figure 1-22. If the menu option is dimmed, your lens doesn't support this feature.

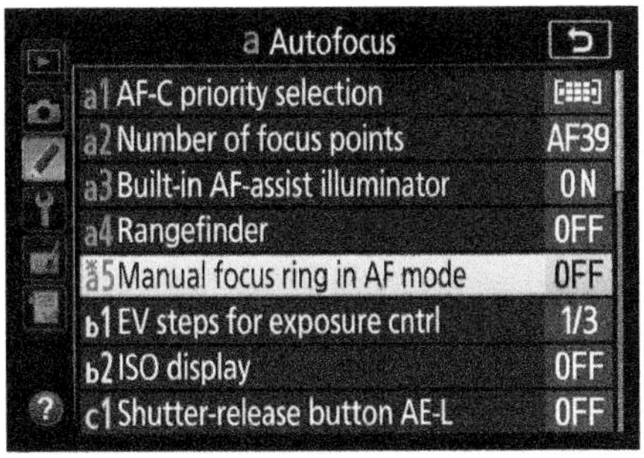

a Autofocus	
a1 AF-C priority selection	⊡
a2 Number of focus points	AF39
a3 Built-in AF-assist illuminator	ON
a4 Rangefinder	OFF
a5 Manual focus ring in AF mode	OFF
b1 EV steps for exposure cntrl	1/3
b2 ISO display	OFF
c1 Shutter-release button AE-L	OFF

FIGURE 1-22:
To disable automatic focusing with manual override for an AF-P lens, set this Custom Setting menu option to Off, as shown here.

» **Focusing:** With either type of lens, use these techniques to set focus:

- *Autofocusing:* Frame your shot and press and hold the shutter button halfway down to establish the focusing distance. During Live View shooting, you also can tap the screen to focus. If the Touch Shutter is enabled, the camera takes a picture immediately after you lift your finger.

- *Manual focusing:* Rotate the focusing ring on the lens barrel. The position of the focusing ring varies depending on the lens; I labeled the one found on the AF-P 18–55mm kit lens in Figure 1-18.

» **Removing a lens:** If you use a retractable lens such as the 18–55mm kit lens, collapse the lens before you remove it. With any type of lens, turn the camera off before removing the lens. Then press the lens-release button (refer to Figure 1-18), and turn the lens toward that button until the lens detaches from the camera's lens mount. Put the rear protective cap onto the back of the lens and, if you aren't putting another lens on the camera, cover the lens mount with its cap, too.

Always switch lenses in a clean environment to reduce the risk of getting dust, dirt, and other contaminants inside the camera or lens. Changing lenses on a sandy beach, for example, isn't a good idea. For added safety, point the camera body slightly down when performing this maneuver; doing so helps prevent any flotsam in the air from being drawn into the camera by gravity.

FOCAL LENGTH AND THE CROP FACTOR

The angle of view that a lens can capture is determined by its *focal length*, or in the case of a zoom lens, the range of focal lengths it offers. Focal length is measured in millimeters. The shorter the focal length, the wider the angle of view. As focal length increases, the angle of view narrows, and the subject occupies more of the frame.

Generally speaking, lenses with focal lengths shorter than 35mm are considered *wide angle lenses,* and lenses with focal lengths greater than 80mm are considered *telephoto* lenses. Anything in the middle is a "normal" lens, suitable for shooting scenes that don't require either a wide or narrow angle of view.

Note, however, that the focal lengths stated in this book and elsewhere are *35mm equivalent focal lengths.* Here's the deal: When you put a standard lens on most dSLR cameras, including the D5600, the available frame area is reduced, as if you took a picture on a camera that uses 35mm film negatives and cropped it. This *crop factor* varies depending on the camera, which is why the photo industry adopted the 35mm-equivalent measuring stick as a standard.

With the D5600, the crop factor is roughly 1.5x. When shopping for a lens, it's important to remember this crop factor to make sure that you get the focal length designed for the type of pictures you want to take. Just multiply the lens focal length by 1.5 to determine the actual angle of view.

Not sure which focal length to choose? Nikon offers a Lens Simulator tool that shows exactly how different focal length lenses capture the same scene. To find it, enter the term *Nikon Lens Simulator* in your browser's search engine.

Working with Memory Cards

As the medium that stores your picture files, the memory card is a critical component of your camera. See the steps at the start of this chapter for help installing a card; follow these tips for buying and maintaining cards:

>> **Buying SD cards:** Again, you can use regular SD cards, which offer less than 4GB of storage space; SDHC cards (4GB–32GB); and SDXC cards (more than 32GB). Aside from card capacity, the other specification to note is *SD speed class,* which indicates how quickly data can be moved to and from the card (the *read/write speed*).

Card speed is indicated in several ways. The most common spec is called SD Speed Class, which rates cards with a number between 2 and 10, with 10 being the fastest. Most cards also carry another designation, UHS-1, -2, or -3; UHS (Ultra High Speed) refers to a new technology designed to boost data transmission speeds above the normal Speed Class 10 rate. The number 1, 2, or 3 inside a little U symbol tells you the UHS rating; UHS-3 is fastest. Note that your camera can use UHS-2 and -3 cards, but you won't get any extra speed benefit; the speed advantage with the D5600 tops out at UHS-1.

Some SD cards also are rated in terms of how they perform when used to record video — specifically, how many frames per second the card can handle. As with the traditional Speed Class rating and UHS rating, a higher video-speed number indicates a faster card.

>> **Formatting a card:** The first time you use a new memory card or insert a card that's been used in other devices, you need to *format* it to prepare it to record your pictures. You also need to format the card if you see the blinking letters *FOR* in the viewfinder or if the monitor displays a message requesting formatting.

Formatting erases everything on your memory card. So before you format a card, be sure that you've copied any data on it to your computer. After doing so, get the formatting job done by selecting Format Memory Card, which is the first option on the Setup menu.

>> **Removing a card:** After you make sure that the memory card access light is off, indicating the camera has finished recording your most recent photo, turn off the camera. Open the memory card door, push down on the card slightly, and then let go. The card pops halfway out of the slot, enabling you to grab it by the tail and remove it.

If you turn on the camera when no card is installed, the symbol [-E-] blinks in the lower-right corner of the viewfinder. A message on the monitor also nudges you to insert a memory card. If you have a card in the camera and you get these messages, try taking out the card and reinserting it.

>> **Handling cards:** Don't touch the gold contacts on the back of the card. (See the right card in Figure 1-23.) When cards aren't in use, store them in the protective cases they came in or in a memory card wallet. Keep cards away from extreme heat and cold as well.

Lock switch   Don't touch!

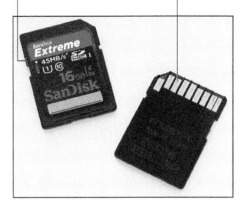

FIGURE 1-23:
Avoid touching the gold contacts on the card.

>> **Locking cards:** The tiny switch on the side of the card, labeled *Lock switch* in Figure 1-23, enables you to lock your card, which prevents any data from being erased or recorded to the card. If you insert a locked card into the camera, a message on the monitor alerts you, and the symbol Cd blinks in the viewfinder.

>> **Using Eye-Fi memory cards:** Your camera works with *Eye-Fi memory cards,* which are special cards that enable you to transmit your files wirelessly to your computer. I don't cover these cards in this book because they're more expensive than regular cards.

Taking a Few Final Setup Steps

Your camera offers scads of options for customizing its performance, some of which I discuss earlier in this chapter. Later chapters explain settings related to actual picture-taking, such as those that affect flash behavior and autofocusing, and Chapter 10 talks about some options that are better left at their default settings until you're fully familiar with your camera. That leaves just the handful of options covered in the next two sections that I recommend you consider at the get-go.

Cruising the Setup menu

The following options live on the Setup menu, which is the one marked with the wrench icon. The menu, which appears in Figure 1-24, is a three-page affair (only Page 1 is visible in the figure). Drag up and down the touchscreen or use the Multi Selector to scroll through the menu and access these settings:

>> **Beep Options:** By default, your camera beeps after certain operations, such as after it sets focus when you shoot in autofocus mode. When the touchscreen is enabled, you also hear a little "boop" every time you tap a screen item. If you need the camera to shut up, silence it via the Beep Options menu item, highlighted in Figure 1-24.

You get two sound controls: For the Beep On/Off option, select Off

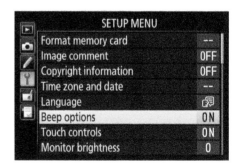

FIGURE 1-24:
Visit the Setup menu to customize the camera's basic operations.

(Touch Controls Only) to silence just touchscreen sounds; choose Off to disable the beep for all operations. The Pitch option lets you set the volume to High or Low.

>> **Monitor Brightness:** This option makes the display brighter or darker. But if you take this step, what you see on the monitor may not be an accurate rendition of the picture exposure. I recommend that you keep the brightness at the default setting (0).

>> **Clean Image Sensor:** By default, an internal sensor-cleaning mechanism runs every time you turn the camera on or off. You also can perform a cleaning at any time by selecting this option and choosing Clean Now. (Nikon recommends that you set the camera upright, on a solid surface, when you perform the cleaning.) Don't try to perform the cleaning several times in a row — if you do, the camera temporarily disables the function to protect itself. The Clean At Startup/Shutdown option enables you to specify whether you want the camera to change from the default setting to clean only at startup, only at shutdown, or never. I suggest that you stick with the default.

>> **Lock Mirror Up for Cleaning:** This option relates to cleaning the camera's image sensor; it moves the camera's internal mirror out of the way to allow access to the sensor. I don't recommend that you tackle this operation yourself because you can easily damage the camera if you don't know what you're doing. Instead, take the camera to a good camera store or repair shop for cleaning.

>> **Slot Empty Release Lock:** This feature determines whether the camera lets you take a picture when no memory card is installed. If you set it to Enable Release, you can take a temporary picture that appears briefly on the monitor with the word *Demo* but isn't recorded anywhere. The feature is provided mainly for use in camera stores, enabling salespeople to demonstrate the camera without having to keep a memory card installed. I can think of no good reason why anyone else would change the setting from the default, Release Locked.

WARNING

>> **Airplane Mode:** Your camera offers two forms of wireless connectivity: regular Wi-Fi and Bluetooth. When these options are enabled, you can upload pictures wirelessly to a smartphone or tablet, as well as use your smart device as a wireless remote control. To take advantage of these features, you must install the Nikon SnapBridge app (it's free).

I cover wireless functions in the appendix of this book, but take a moment now to check the Airplane Mode option, found on the third page of the Setup menu. Like the Airplane Mode on a smartphone or tablet, this setting shuts down the camera's wireless transmissions, which your flight crew will politely ask you to do before takeoff. Even when you're not in an environment that prohibits wireless signals, enabling Airplane Mode saves battery power, so I recommend keeping the option set to On until you're ready to use the wireless functions. (The default setting is Off.) An airplane symbol appears on the Information display and Live View screen when Airplane Mode is on.

>> **Conformity Marking:** I bring this one up just so that you know you can ignore it: When you select the option, you see logos indicating the camera conforms with certain camera-industry standards. I know you'll sleep better at night with that information.

>> **Firmware Version:** Select this option to view which version of the camera *firmware,* or internal software, your camera runs. You see the firmware items C and L. At the time this book was written, C was version 1.01; L was 2.015.

Keeping your camera firmware up to date is important, so visit the Nikon website (www.nikon.com) regularly to find out whether your camera sports the latest version. You can find detailed instructions at the site on how to download and install any firmware updates.

If you use an Apple iOS device to run the camera's wireless functions, the update from 1.00 to 1.01 is a must. The update fixes issues that caused problems when using those functions on devices running certain versions of the iOS.

Custom Setting options

Check the status of these Custom Setting menu options before you shoot your first pictures, too:

>> **File Number Sequence:** This option, found on the Shooting/Display submenu and highlighted in Figure 1-25, controls how the camera names your picture files. When the option is set to Off, as it is by default, the camera restarts file numbering at 0001 every time you format the memory card or insert a new memory card. Numbering is also restarted if a new image-storage folder is created. (Chapter 10 explains folders.)

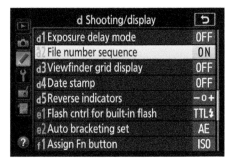

FIGURE 1-25:
Danger, Will Robinson! Change the File Number Sequence option to On to avoid winding up with multiple pictures that have the same filename.

This setup can cause problems over time, creating a scenario where you wind up with multiple images that have the same filename — not on the current memory card, but when you download images to your computer. So set the option to On. Note that when you get to picture number 9999, file numbering is still reset to 0001, however. The camera automatically creates a new folder to hold your next 9,999 images.

In addition to On and Off, the option offers a Reset setting. This option enables you to assign the first file number (which ends in 0001) to the next picture you shoot. Then the camera behaves as if you selected the On setting.

Should you be a really, *really* prolific shooter and snap enough pictures to reach image 9999 in folder 999, the camera will refuse to take another photo until you choose that Reset option and either format the memory card or insert a brand-new one.

» **Date Stamp:** Using this option, you can imprint on the photo the shooting date, the date and time, or the number of days between the day you took the picture and another date that you specify. This feature works only with pictures that you shoot in the JPEG file format; see the Chapter 2 section related to the Image Quality setting for details about file formats.

TIP

The default Date Stamp setting, Off, is the way to go; you don't need to permanently mar your photos to find out when you took them. Every picture file includes a hidden vat of text data, or *metadata,* that records the shooting date and time as well as all the camera settings you used — f-stop, shutter speed, and lots more. You can view this data during playback and, after downloading, in the free software provided with your camera as well as in many photo programs.

Restoring default settings

Should you want to return your camera to its original, out-of-the-box state, the camera manual contains a complete list of most of the default settings. Look on the pages that introduce each of the menus.

You can also partially restore default settings by taking these steps:

» **Reset all Shooting Menu options:** Open the Shooting menu and select Reset Shooting Menu. Note that resetting the menu does not affect the Storage Folder option, which is a concern only if you create custom folders, as outlined in Chapter 10.

» **Reset all Custom Setting Menu options:** Choose Reset Custom Settings at the top of the Custom Setting menu.

WARNING

Resetting the Custom Setting menu restores the File Number Sequence option to its default, Off, which is most definitely Not a Good Thing. If you restore the menu defaults, be sure that you revisit that option and return it to the On setting. See the preceding section for details.

>> **Restore critical picture-taking settings *without* affecting all options on the Custom Setting menu:** Use the two-button reset method: Press and hold the Menu button and the Info button simultaneously for longer than 2 seconds. (The little green dots near these two buttons are a reminder of this function.) See the camera manual for a list of exactly which settings are restored.

Shooting Pictures in Auto Mode

Your camera is loaded with features for the advanced photographer, enabling you to exert precise control over options such as f-stop, shutter speed, ISO, flash power, and much more. But you don't have to wait until you master those topics to take great pictures, because your camera also offers point-and-shoot simplicity through its Auto exposure mode.

The next two sections walk you through the process of taking a picture in Auto mode, starting with normal (viewfinder) photography and then moving on to Live View photography. Both sets of steps assume that you're using autofocusing and the default picture settings. If you need help switching to autofocusing, see the earlier section "Familiarizing Yourself with the Lens." For information on how to reset the camera to its default settings, see the preceding section.

Viewfinder photography in Auto mode

When you use the viewfinder to compose photos, follow these steps to take a picture:

1. **Set the Mode dial to Auto, as shown in Figure 1-26.**

2. **Looking through the viewfinder, frame your subject so that it appears within the autofocus brackets, labeled in Figure 1-27.**

3. **Press and hold the shutter button halfway down.**

   At this point, the following occurs:

   - *Exposure metering begins.* The autoexposure meter analyzes the light and selects the initial exposure settings. The camera continues monitoring the light up to the

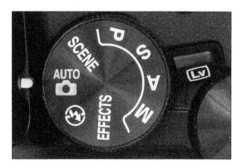

FIGURE 1-26:
Set the Mode dial to Auto for point-and-shoot simplicity.

time you take the picture, however, and may adjust the exposure settings if lighting conditions change.

- *The built-in flash pops up if the camera thinks additional light is needed.* If you're in a situation where flash is prohibited, return to Step 1 and change the Mode dial setting from Auto to Auto Flash Off, which is the setting between Auto and Effects (refer to Figure 1-26). This shooting mode does the same thing as Auto but disables flash.

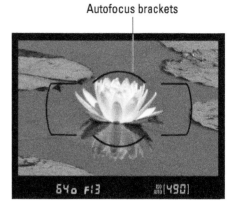

Autofocus brackets

FIGURE 1-27:
Frame your subject so that it's within the area surrounded by the autofocus brackets.

- *The autofocus system begins to do its thing.* In dim light, the AF-assist lamp may shoot out a beam of light to help the camera measure the distance between your subject and the lens so that it can better establish focus.

TECHNICAL STUFF

- *The shots remaining value changes to display the buffer capacity, as shown in Figure 1-28.* The buffer is a temporary storage tank where the camera stores picture data until it has time to record that data to the memory card. This system exists so you can take a continuous series of pictures without waiting between shots until each image is written to the card. When the buffer is full, you can't take another picture until the camera catches up with its recording work.

Selected focus point

Focus indicator light   Buffer value

FIGURE 1-28:
The green light indicates that the camera locked focus on the object under the focus point.

4. **Check the focus indicators in the viewfinder.**

When the camera has established focus, one or more of the focus points turns red for a split second. The red focus points represent the areas of the frame used to set the focusing distance. (Typically, the camera focuses on the object closest to the camera.) Then a single black focus point appears, as shown in Figure 1-28. At the bottom of the viewfinder, the focus indicator, labeled in the figure, lights to give you further notice that focus has been achieved.

If the subject isn't moving, autofocus remains locked as long as you hold the shutter button halfway down. But if the camera detects subject motion, it automatically switches to continuous autofocusing and adjusts focus as needed up to the time you take the picture. (In order for the camera to adjust focus properly, you must reframe as needed to keep your subject within the autofocus brackets.)

5. **Press the shutter button the rest of the way to record the image.**

TIP

If the camera refuses to take the picture, don't panic: This error is likely related to autofocusing. By default, the camera insists on achieving focus before it releases the shutter to take a picture. You can press the shutter button all day, and the camera just ignores you if it can't set focus.

Try backing away from your subject a little — you may be exceeding the minimum focusing distance of the lens. If that doesn't work, the subject just may not be conducive to autofocusing. Highly reflective objects, scenes with very little contrast, and subjects behind fences are some of the troublemakers. The easiest solution? Switch to manual focusing and set focus yourself.

WARNING

While the camera sends the image data to the memory card, the memory card access lamp lights. Don't turn off the camera or remove the memory card while the lamp is lit or else you may damage both camera and card.

When the recording process is finished, the picture appears briefly on the camera monitor. If the picture doesn't appear or you want to take a longer look at the image, see Chapter 8, which covers picture playback.

Live View photography in Auto mode

Most aspects of shooting in Live View are the same as for viewfinder photography. Autofocusing, however, works quite differently. Here are the steps to take a picture in Auto mode using the default Live View settings:

1. **Set the Mode dial to Auto, as shown in Figure 1-29.**

    Or, if you need to ensure that the camera's flash doesn't fire, choose the Auto Flash Off mode (the setting between Auto and Effects on the Mode dial).

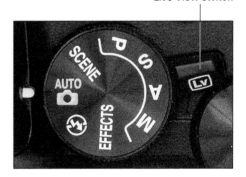

Live View switch

FIGURE 1-29:
Rotate the Live View switch once to enter Live View mode; rotate a second time to return to viewfinder shooting.

2. **Rotate the Live View switch (refer to Figure 1-29).**

The viewfinder goes dark, and the scene in front of the lens appears on the monitor, along with some shooting data, as shown in Figure 1-30. The figures show the default Live View display; see the tips at the end of this step list for other display options.

Exposure-mode symbol   Selected face

Face detection box   Standard focus frame

FIGURE 1-30:
For portraits, a focus box appears automatically over each subject's face (left); otherwise, you see a focus box in the center of the screen (right).

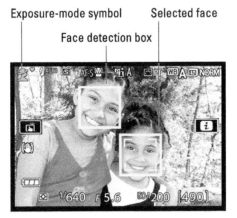
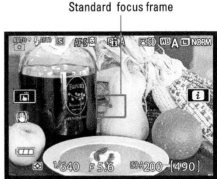

3. **Compose your shot.**

4. **Check the position of the focusing frame; if necessary, adjust the frame so it's over your subject.**

REMEMBER

The frame that appears depends on your subject:

- *Portraits:* By default, the camera uses an autofocusing option called Face Priority AF-area mode. In that mode, yellow focus frames appear over any faces the camera detects, as shown on the left side of Figure 1-30. In a group portrait, the frame that includes the interior corner marks indicates the face that will be used to set the focusing distance. To select a different face as the focus point, use the Multi Selector to move the focus box over it.

- *Other subjects:* Anytime the camera can't detect a face, it switches to Wide Area AF-area mode, and you see a red focus frame in the center of the screen (refer to the right side of Figure 1-30). Again, use the Multi Selector to move the focus box over your subject. Press the OK button to move the focus box quickly to the center of the frame.

TIP

You also can set focus by tapping your subject on the screen, but if the Touch Shutter feature is enabled, the camera immediately takes the picture after you tap. See the list at the end of this section for details. For now, stick with using the Multi Selector to position the focus box.

5. **Press the shutter button halfway to set focus and initiate exposure metering.**

When focus is set, the focus frame turns green and you hear a beep (assuming you didn't disable it via the Setup menu). In dim lighting, the built-in flash pops up unless you selected the Auto Flash Off setting in Step 1.

REMEMBER

In Live View mode, the camera always locks focus when you press the shutter button halfway, even if the subject is moving. If you want the camera to track focus on a moving subject, you must shift from the default Focus Mode setting — AF-S (for single-servo autofocus) — to AF-F (full-time servo) mode. Chapter 4 has details.

6. **Press the shutter button all the way down to record the picture.**

The photo appears briefly on the monitor, and then the live preview reappears.

TIP

After you press the shutter button halfway in Step 5, the camera may shift automatically to one of four Scene modes that are designed to capture specific types of subjects. The exposure-mode symbol labeled in Figure 1-30 is your cue that this switch was made. For example, in the left screen in the figure, the camera shifted to Portrait mode, represented by the symbol of a lady with a hat. The other three Scene modes that the camera may select are Landscape (mountain symbol), Close Up (flower symbol), and Night Portrait (head-and-shoulders with a star). If you see the word *Auto* with a heart, as on the right screen of the figure, the camera is sticking with ordinary Auto mode. If you prefer to select a Scene type directly, see the first section of Chapter 2.

To close out this chapter, here are a few important pointers to remember when you use Live View mode:

info

>> **Press the Info button to change the type of data that's displayed on the monitor.** You can choose from five displays:

- *Detailed Photo Indicators:* Reveals extensive shooting data for still photography (refer to Figure 1-30). The display uses this mode by default.

- *Movie Indicators:* Displays data related to movie recording, as shown on the upper-left screen in Figure 1-31. The black bars along the top and bottom of the screen show how much of the vertical image area is excluded from the frame because of the 16:9 aspect ratio of movies.

- *Hide Indicators:* Displays only the markings shown in the upper-right corner in Figure 1-31.

TIP

In this display mode, as well as in the two described next, the four horizontal markers near the corners of the display take the place of the bars that indicate the 16:9 movie frame area when you use the Show Movie Indicators display.

Movie Indicators

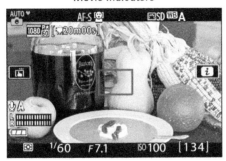

Hide Indicators

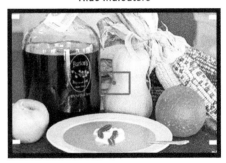

Framing Grid

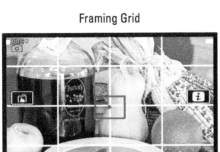

Basic Photo Indicators

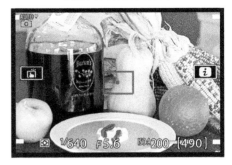

FIGURE 1-31:
Press the Info button to change the Live View display style.

- *Framing Grid:* Adds a grid, the 16:9 framing marks, and a limited assortment of still photo capture settings (refer to the lower-left corner of Figure 1-31).

- *Basic Photo Indicators:* Presents the same data as the Framing Grid display, minus the grid, as shown in the lower-right corner in the figure.

>> **If you enable the Touch Shutter feature, you can tap anywhere on the screen to set focus and snap the picture.** When the feature is turned on, as it is by default, you see the symbol labeled in Figure 1-32. Tap the symbol to turn off the Touch Shutter; the word *Off* then appears with the symbol.

Even when the Touch Shutter is disabled, you can still tap the screen to set focus when using autofocus. Then use the shutter button to take the picture.

Touch Shutter   Tap to display control strip

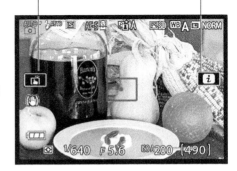

FIGURE 1-32:
These symbols relate to the Touch Shutter and Information display control strip.

REMEMBER

>> **To access the Live View control strip, press the *i* button or tap the icon labeled in Figure 1-32.** See the earlier section "Adjusting Settings via the Control Strip" for help with using this time-saving feature.

>> **Cover the viewfinder to prevent light from seeping into the camera and affecting exposure.** Nikon sells a cover designed for this purpose: the DK-5 Eyepiece Cap, which sells for about $4. To use it, first slide the rubber eyecup that surrounds the viewfinder up and out of the groove that holds it in place. Then slide the Eyepiece Cap down into the groove. (Orient the cover so that the Nikon label faces the viewfinder.)

>> **In Live View mode, the monitor turns off by default after 10 minutes of inactivity.** When monitor shutdown is 30 seconds away, a countdown timer appears in the upper-left corner of the screen. You can adjust the shutdown timing via the Auto Off Timers option; Chapter 10 has details.

>> **Using Live View for an extended period can harm your pictures and the camera.** In Live View mode, the camera's innards heat up more than usual, and that extra heat can create the proper electronic conditions for *noise,* a defect that gives your pictures a speckled look. Perhaps more importantly, the increased temperatures can damage the camera. For that reason, Live View is automatically disabled if the camera detects a critical heat level.

>> **Aiming the lens at the sun or another bright light can damage the camera.** Of course, you can cause problems by doing this even during viewfinder shooting, but the possibilities increase when you use Live View. You can harm not only the camera's internal components but also the monitor (not to mention your eyes).

>> **Some lights may interfere with the Live View display.** The operating frequency of some types of lights, including fluorescent and mercury-vapor lamps, can create electronic interference that causes the monitor display to flicker or exhibit odd color banding. Changing the Flicker Reduction option on the Setup menu may resolve this issue. At the default setting, Auto, the camera gauges the light and chooses the right setting for you. But you also can choose from two specific frequencies: 50 Hz and 60 Hz. (In the United States and Canada, the standard frequency is 60 Hz; in Europe, it's 50 Hz.)

IN THIS CHAPTER

» Selecting an exposure mode

» Changing the shutter-release mode

» Choosing the right Image Size (resolution) setting

» Understanding the Image Quality setting: JPEG or Raw?

» Adding flash

Chapter 2

Reviewing Five Essential Picture-Taking Options

E very camera manufacturer strives to ensure that your initial encounter with the camera is a happy one. To that end, the D5600's default settings are designed to make it easy to take a good picture the first time you press the shutter button. The camera is set to the Auto exposure mode, so all you need to do is frame, focus, and shoot, as outlined at the end of Chapter 1.

Although the default settings deliver acceptable pictures in many cases, they don't produce optimal results in every situation. You may be able to take a decent portrait in Auto mode, for example, but by tweaking a few settings, you can turn that decent portrait into a stunning one.

This chapter helps you start fine-tuning the camera settings by explaining five basic picture-taking options: exposure mode, shutter-release mode, image size, image quality, and flash. They're not the most exciting features (don't think I didn't notice you stifling a yawn), but they make a big difference in how easily you can capture the photo you have in mind.

Choosing an Exposure Mode

The first setting to consider is exposure mode, which you select via the Mode dial, shown in Figure 2-1. Your choices fall into two categories: beginner modes that offer point-and-shoot simplicity, and advanced modes that enable you to precisely control exposure, focus, color, and other picture qualities. The next several sections offer details to help you choose the best mode for your level of experience.

Auto Flash Off

Beginner exposure modes

My guess is that you bought this book for help with using the camera's advanced exposure modes, so they receive the majority of the page space. But until you have time to digest that information — or if you just need a break from thinking about the advanced options — you can take advantage of the beginner modes outlined in the next three sections.

WARNING

Because these modes are designed to make picture-taking simple, they prevent you from accessing many of the camera's features. You can't use the White Balance control, for example, to tweak picture colors. Options that are off-limits appear dimmed on camera menus, Information and Live View displays, and the control strip.

Auto and Auto Flash Off modes

In both modes, the camera analyzes the scene and selects what it considers the most appropriate settings to capture the image. The only difference between the two modes is that Auto Flash Off (labeled in Figure 2-1) disables flash. In Auto mode, you can choose from a few Flash modes, which I detail later in this chapter. For step-by-step instructions on taking pictures in these modes, see the last part of Chapter 1.

Effects mode

This mode works like Auto except that the camera applies one of ten special effects to the picture. Chapter 11 provides details on Effects mode and also explains how you can apply effects to existing pictures via the Retouch menu.

Scene modes

Setting the Mode dial to Scene provides access to automatic exposure modes designed to capture specific subjects in ways deemed best according to photography tradition. For example, in Portrait mode, skin tones are manipulated to appear warmer and softer, and the background appears blurry to bring attention to your subject. In Landscape mode, greens and blues are intensified, and the camera tries to maintain sharpness in both near and distant objects. Figure 2-2 offers examples of both modes.

Portrait mode

Landscape mode

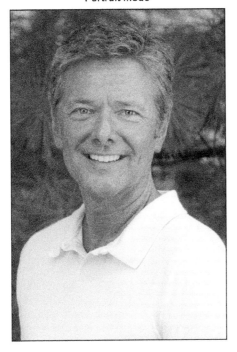
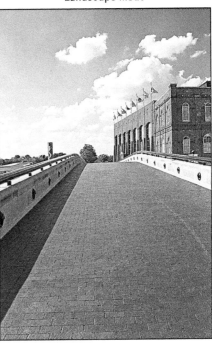

FIGURE 2-2:
Portrait mode produces pleasant skin tones and a soft background; Landscape mode delivers vivid colors and keeps both foreground and background objects sharp.

An icon representing the current Scene type appears in the upper-left corner of the monitor, as shown in Figure 2-3. (In Live View mode, you may need to press the Info button to cycle through the various Live View displays until you reach one that shows the icon.)

To access other Scene modes, rotate the Command dial to display a selection screen, as shown in Figure 2-4. Keep rotating the dial or tap the scroll arrows labeled in the figure to advance through the available scenes. When you land on a scene you want to try, exit the selection screen by pressing the shutter button halfway and releasing it. Then just compose, focus, and shoot.

Current scene mode symbol

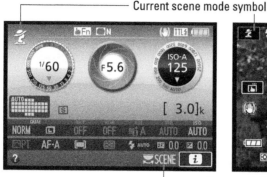

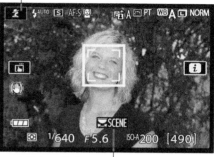

Current scene mode symbol

FIGURE 2-3:
After setting the Mode dial to Scene, the exposure mode icon changes to indicate the currently selected scene (Portrait, in these screens).

Command dial symbol

The names of the Scene modes are pretty self-explanatory, but if you need a hint as you scroll through your options, press the Zoom Out button to display a brief description of the mode currently selected. Unfortunately, this trick works only for viewfinder photography and not during Live View shooting.

For the most part, the process of taking pictures in the Scene modes is the same as for shooting in Auto mode, a process I outline at the end of Chapter 1. A few Scene modes, however, use different default settings for Release mode, flash, and autofocusing. I provide details when discussing Release mode and flash later in this chapter; see Chapter 4 for help with autofocusing.

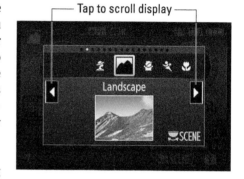

Tap to scroll display

Landscape

FIGURE 2-4:
To scroll through the available scenes, rotate the Command dial or tap the left or right scroll arrows.

REMEMBER

Finally, understand that in very dim or very bright light, the camera may not be able to produce the results promised by the Scene mode. For example, Sports mode can't freeze action unless the scene is very brightly lit. The focal length and range of aperture settings on your lens, which affect how much of a scene appears in focus, also may limit the camera's ability to produce the look you expect. Chapters 3 and 4 explain these issues, so I won't get into them here; for now, just know that moving up to the advanced modes described next gives you a greater chance of success.

Advanced exposure modes: P, S, A, and M

To get the most out of your camera, step up to P (programmed autoexposure), S (shutter-priority autoexposure), A (aperture-priority autoexposure), or M (manual) exposure mode. You then gain access to settings you can't control in the beginner modes.

Here's a brief preview of those settings and how they affect your picture:

>> **Aperture and shutter speed:** These two settings affect exposure as well as other important picture characteristics. The aperture setting (f-stop) affects *depth of field* (the distance over which focus appears sharp). Shutter speed determines whether moving objects appear sharp or blurry and whether any movement of the camera during the exposure blurs the image. Chapter 3 explains these exposure issues as well as the differences between the P, S, A, and M modes.

>> **Autofocusing:** Most beginner modes limit your access to options that modify the behavior of the autofocusing system. To discover the additional possibilities available in the advanced modes, visit Chapter 4.

>> **Color:** If colors appear incorrect — perhaps skin tones are *too* warm (overly reddish-yellow) or a freshly groomed putting green appears a little blue — you can use the White Balance setting and other color options to produce the colors you have in mind. These options are off-limits in the beginner modes. See Chapter 5 for ways to correct and enhance colors.

>> **Flash:** Advanced exposure modes also provide more control over the camera's built-in flash. For example, you can manually control the amount of light the flash emits instead of relying on the camera to set that value. Refer to the last part of this chapter for a flash primer.

Setting the Release Mode

The Release mode setting determines whether the camera captures a single image each time you press the shutter button; records a burst of photos as long as you hold down the shutter button; or uses Self-Timer mode, which delays the image capture until a few seconds after you press the shutter button. In addition, the camera offers Quiet Shutter mode, which dampens the normal shutter-release sounds.

Why *Release mode?* It's short for *shutter-release mode.* The shutter is a barrier between the lens and the image sensor; when you press the shutter button, the camera opens (releases) the shutter so that light can strike the sensor, creating the photograph. (Chapter 3 explains this aspect of your camera in detail.)

On the Information screen and Live View display, the current Release mode is indicated in the areas highlighted by red circles in Figure 2-5. (If your Live View screen shows a different assortment of data, press the Info button to cycle through the available display modes.)

FIGURE 2-5:
The highlighted symbols represent the Release Mode setting; here, the Single Frame (S) is selected.

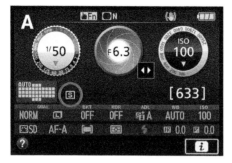
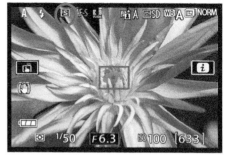

Upcoming sections describe each mode. First, familiarize yourself with the ways you can change the Release mode. You can use these methods:

>> **Release Mode button:** For fastest results, press and hold the Release Mode button, labeled in Figure 2-6, to display the selection screen shown in Figure 2-7. Keep pressing the button and rotate the Command dial to scroll through the settings. When the one you want to use is highlighted, release the button.

Alternatively, you can let up on the Release Mode button after the settings screen appears. If you go this route, use the Multi Selector to scroll through the settings. To select a setting, highlight it and press OK. Or just tap the setting.

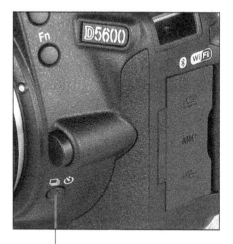

Release Mode button

FIGURE 2-6:
The Release Mode button offers the fastest access to the setting.

>> **Shooting menu:** Scroll to the second page of the menu to access the setting, as shown in Figure 2-8.

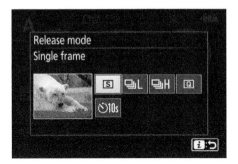

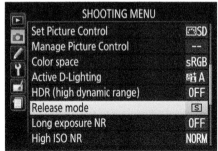

FIGURE 2-7:
While holding down the Release Mode button, rotate the Command dial to cycle through the available options.

FIGURE 2-8:
The Release Mode option is also found on the Shooting menu.

With those basics out of the way, the next few sections explain how each Release mode works.

Single Frame and Quiet Shutter modes

 Single Frame Release mode captures one picture each time you release the shutter, whether you're using the touch shutter in Live View mode or the plain old shutter button. Single Frame is the default setting for all exposure modes except the Sports and Pet Portrait Scene modes.

 Quiet Shutter mode works just like Single Frame mode but makes less noise as it goes about its business. First, the camera disables the beep that it emits by default when it achieves focus. Additionally, if you keep the shutter button depressed after you take a picture, you can delay the sound the camera makes at the end of an image capture. The idea is that you can delay the final sounds to a moment when the noise won't be objectionable — say, after the groom says "I do."

 Even in Quiet mode, the camera beeps when you tap the touchscreen. To turn that sound effect off, set the Beep Options setting on the Setup menu to Off (touch controls only). To disable the beep for all functions, choose the Off setting instead.

WARNING

USING THE TOUCH SHUTTER

When Live View is enabled, you can set focus by simply tapping your subject on the monitor. But for still photography, you can take things one step further: You can tell the camera to release the shutter button as soon as you lift your finger off the monitor. Nikon calls this feature the *touch shutter*. You can use the touch shutter to record only one photo at a time; the burst mode options (Continuous High and Continuous Low) don't play well with this feature.

An icon in the Live View display tells you whether the touch shutter is enabled or not. When the feature is enabled, as it is by default, you see the icon shown on the left in the figure here. To disable the touch shutter, tap the icon so that it looks like the one shown on the right side of the figure. You can still set focus by tapping the screen; you just have to use the shutter button to actually take the picture.

Touch shutter on

Touch shutter off

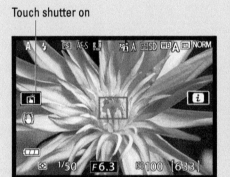
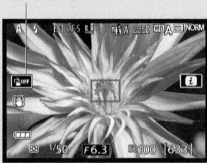

Continuous (burst mode) shooting

Continuous Low and Continuous High enable *burst mode* shooting. That is, the camera records a continuous series of images for as long as you hold down the shutter button, making it easier to capture fast-paced action. Here's how the two modes differ:

>> **Continuous Low:** The camera can capture as many as 3 frames per second (fps).

>> **Continuous High:** Records as many as 5 fps, depending on the Image Quality setting, which I cover later in this chapter. If you select the Image Quality setting that produces 14-bit RAW (NEF) files, the maximum frame rate is 4 fps.

A few critical details about these two Release modes:

>> **You can't use flash.** If flash is enabled, you get one shot per each press of the shutter button, as in Single Frame mode.

Pet Portrait Scene mode uses the Continuous High Release mode by default. Problem is, that mode also sets the flash to fire automatically in dim lighting. If the flash pops up when you press the shutter button halfway, you need to disable flash, as outlined later in this chapter, or forego burst mode shooting.

>> **Images are stored temporarily in the memory buffer.** The camera has a small amount of internal memory — called a *buffer* — where it stores picture data until it has time to record all the photos in a burst of shots to the memory card. The number of pictures the buffer can hold depends on certain camera settings, such as Image Quality. When you press the shutter button halfway, the shots remaining value in the lower-right corner of the viewfinder and Live View display changes to show an estimate of how many pictures will fit in the buffer.

After shooting a burst of images, wait for the memory card access light to go out before turning off the camera. (The light is in the lower-right corner of the camera back.) That's your signal that the camera has moved all data from the buffer to the memory card. Turning off the camera before that happens may corrupt the image file.

>> **Your mileage may vary.** The number of frames per second depends on several factors, including shutter speed. To achieve the highest rate, the shutter speed must be 1/250 second or faster. Additionally, although you can capture as many as 100 frames in a single burst, the frame rate can drop if the buffer gets full.

>> **Continuous Low is enough for all but the fastest action.** Unless you're shooting a subject that's moving at a really fast pace, not too much changes between frames when you shoot at 5 fps. So, when you use Continuous High, you typically wind up with lots of shots that show the exact same thing, wasting space on your memory card. Continuous Low usually gives you plenty of frames to capture the shot without the unnecessary file bloat.

>> **The touch shutter isn't compatible with burst-mode shooting.** The Touch Shutter feature enables you to both set focus and trigger the shutter release by simply tapping your subject on the monitor. But as mentioned in the sidebar devoted to this feature, you get only one photo per tap even if the Release mode is set to one of the Continuous options.

Self-timer shooting

You're no doubt familiar with Self–Timer mode, which delays the shutter release for a few seconds after you release the shutter button or, in Touch Shutter mode, when you lift your finger from the monitor. After you take that step, the AF–assist lamp on the front of the camera starts to blink, and the camera emits a series of beeps (assuming you didn't disable its voice via the Beep Options setting on the Setup menu). A few seconds later, the camera captures the image.

TIP

By default, the camera waits 10 seconds after you press the shutter button and then records a single image. But you can tweak the delay time and capture as many as nine shots at a time. Set your preferences by using the Self–Timer option, found in the Timers/AE Lock section of the Custom Setting menu and shown in Figure 2–9. Here's what you need to know about the two settings:

>> **Self-Timer Delay:** Choose a delay time of 2, 5, 10, or 20 seconds. The selected delay time appears with the Self-Timer symbol in the Information and Live View displays.

>> **Number of Shots:** Specify how many frames you want to capture with each press of the shutter button; the maximum is nine. When you record multiple frames, shots are taken at 4-second intervals.

FIGURE 2-9:
You can adjust the self-timer capture delay and the number of frames taken with each press of the shutter button.

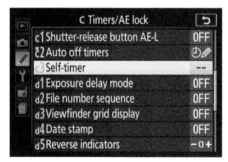
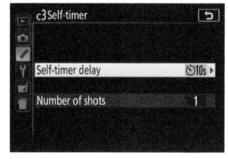

WARNING

Two more points about self–timer shooting:

>> **You must reselect the Self-Timer setting for each picture (or series of frames) you want to shoot.** After the specified number of shots are captured, the camera exits Self-Timer Release mode and then returns to the Release mode you used before your Self-Timer shot(s). Turning off the camera also resets the Release mode.

>> **Cover the viewfinder during self-timer shooting.** Otherwise, light may seep into the camera through the viewfinder and affect exposure. You can purchase the Nikon viewfinder cover (DK-5 Eyepiece Cap, about $4) or just use the camera strap or anything else that's convenient.

Investigating other shutter-release options

In addition to the Release mode setting, your camera offers a few other features related to triggering the shutter release. Check 'em out in the next four sections.

Remote control shooting

You have two ways to release the shutter via remote control:

>> **Wired remote control:** Plug the optional Nikon MC-DC2 remote cord into the accessory terminal (top connection port under the cover on the left side of the camera). The remote costs about $25.

>> **Wireless remote control:** If you own a smart phone or other device that's compatible with the Nikon SnapBridge app, you can use that device as a wireless remote. The appendix of this book offers more information about that option.

    You also can purchase dedicated Nikon wireless remote control units. That's not an inexpensive proposition, however: At the least, you need the WR-R10 transceiver unit, which plugs into the camera's accessory terminal, and the WR-T10 controller, the handheld device that houses the remote shutter button. Together, they'll set you back about $200. There's also the even more spendy WR-1 remote controller (about $650), which offers advanced features such as the ability to trigger the shutters of multiple cameras at the same time. To read more about these products, head for the Nikon website (www.nikon.com).

Whether you go wired or wireless, take note of the Remote Control item on the Setup menu, shown on the left in Figure 2-10. Select the Remote Shutter Release option, as shown on the right in the figure, to specify whether you want to use the remote to take a still photo or to stop and start movie recording. If the remote you use has a Fn (Function button), select Assign Fn Button to change the purpose of that button. By default, the Fn button locks autoexposure and autofocus when you press the remote's shutter button.

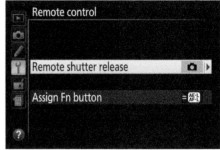

FIGURE 2-10:
Through this
Setup menu
option, you
can specify
whether you
want to use the
remote control
to trigger the
shutter release
or start and
stop movie
recording.

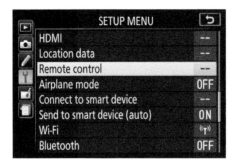

SETUP MENU	↩
HDMI	--
Location data	--
Remote control	--
Airplane mode	OFF
Connect to smart device	--
Send to smart device (auto)	ON
Wi-Fi	((ᵀ))
Bluetooth	OFF

Remote control	
Remote shutter release	📷 ▶
Assign Fn button	=⬛

Exposure Delay Mode

TECHNICAL
STUFF

One component of a dSLR camera is a mirror that moves every time you press the shutter button. The vibration caused by the mirror action can cause a small amount of blur when you use a very slow shutter speed, shoot with a long tele-photo lens, or take extreme close-ups.

To cope with that issue, some cameras offer *mirror-lockup* shooting, which delays opening the shutter until after the mirror movement is complete. Although the D5600 doesn't offer mirror-lockup shooting, it does provide another solution: Exposure Delay Mode. When you enable this feature, the camera waits about 1 second after the mirror is raised to release the shutter, ensuring the mirror movement is complete before the image is recorded.

Look for the Exposure Delay Mode option in the Shooting/Display section of the Custom Setting menu. You can use Exposure Delay Mode with any Release mode. Just don't forget that you enabled the feature or else you'll drive yourself batty trying to figure out why the camera isn't responding to your shutter-button finger. I say this from experience. . . .

Interval Timer Shooting

With Interval Timer Shooting, you can set the camera to automatically release the shutter at intervals ranging from seconds to hours apart. This feature enables you to capture a subject as it changes over time — a technique commonly known as *time-lapse photography* — without having to stand around pressing the shutter button the whole time.

WARNING

You can't take advantage of this feature when Live View is engaged. You also must disable autobracketing and HDR, two features I cover in Chapter 3.

Here's how to set up the camera for time-lapse photography:

1. **Set the Release mode to Single Frame (S) or Quiet Shutter (Q).**

   The fastest way to adjust the setting is to hold down the Release Mode button while rotating the Command dial.

2. **Display the Shooting menu and select Interval Timer Shooting, as shown on the left in Figure 2-11.**

   The screen on the right in Figure 2-11 appears.

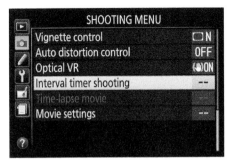
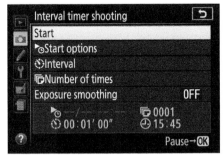

FIGURE 2-11: The Interval Timer Shooting feature enables you to do time-lapse photography.

3. **To begin setting up your capture session, select Start Options, as shown on the left in Figure 2-12.**

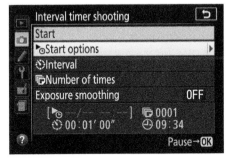
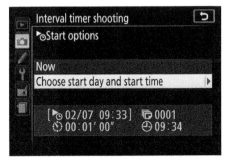

FIGURE 2-12: Choose this option to delay the start of the interval captures until a later time.

This setting determines when the camera begins capturing frames. You get two choices, as shown on the right in Figure 2-12:

- *Now:* Capture begins immediately after you complete the rest of the interval-timing setup steps.

- *Choose start day and start time:* Delays capture until a time you specify. If you select this option, you see a screen that enables you to set the date, hour, and minute that you want the interval captures to begin. After setting the start time, press OK or tap the OK icon to return to the main setup screen.

REMEMBER

The Start Time option is based on a 24-hour clock, as is the Interval option (explained next). The current time appears in the lower-right corner of the screen and is based on the date/time information you entered when setting up the camera.

4. **Set the Interval and Number of Times options.**

Look for these options on the main setup screen, directly below the Start Options item (see Figure 2-13). A few points to note:

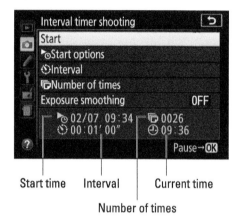

- *Interval:* Determines how long the camera pauses between frames. Make sure the delay time you specify is longer than the shutter speed you plan to use.

- *Number of times:* Determines how many frames the camera records during the interval-timing shooting session.

Tap OK or press the OK button after adjusting each setting to return to the main setup screen. You can view your selected settings at the bottom of the screen, as shown in Figure 2-13.

Start time   Interval   Current time

Number of times

FIGURE 2-13:
Your chosen capture settings appear at the bottom of the main setup screen.

5. **Enable or disable Exposure Smoothing.**

Exposure Smoothing tells the camera to try to match the exposure of each shot to the one taken previously. Obviously, if your goal is a series of frames that show how the subject appears as the sun rises and falls, you should turn this option off, as it is by default. You may want to enable it, however, if you're shooting a subject that will be illuminated with a consistent light source throughout the entire shooting time or if the light may change only slightly, such as when recording a hummingbird at a feeder during an afternoon.

WARNING

The Exposure Smoothing option doesn't work in the M (manual) exposure mode unless you enable Auto ISO Sensitivity, which gives the camera permission to increase the ISO setting as necessary to maintain a consistent exposure. (The next chapter explains this setting.)

6. **Select the Start option at the top of the setup screen, as shown in Figure 2-13.**

   If you selected Now as the Start Time option in Step 3, the first shot is recorded about 3 seconds after you select Start. If you set a delayed start time, the camera displays the message *Interval Timer Shooting* for a few seconds.

A few additional points about the Interval Timer Shooting feature:

REMEMBER

>> **The card access light blinks while Interval Timer Shooting is in progress.** It's the little light just above the Delete button on the back of the camera.

>> **You can't adjust camera settings while the interval sequence is in progress.** Make sure everything is set up to your liking before you begin the interval-shooting session.

>> **If you're autofocusing, be sure the camera can focus on your subject.** The camera initiates focusing before each shot. See Chapter 4 for details about autofocusing.

>> **To pause or cancel interval timing, press the OK button between shots.** On the screen that appears, you can choose from three actions:

   • *Restart shooting immediately:* Select Restart.

   • *Restart at a later date/time:* Select Start Options. Then choose Start Day and Start Time and enter the date and time that you want to resume interval shooting. Return to the initial screen and choose Restart.

   • *Exit interval shooting:* Select Off. Or just turn the camera off or change the Mode dial setting.

>> **To prevent exposure miscues, cover the viewfinder.** This prevents light from entering the viewfinder and fooling the exposure meter.

>> **When the interval sequence is complete, the Interval Timer Shooting menu option is reset to Off.** The card access light stops blinking shortly after the final image is recorded to the memory card.

Time-Lapse Movie

Just like Interval Timer Shooting, the Time-Lapse Movie option on the Shooting menu records a series of photographs over a period of time, at specified intervals. Then it takes things one step further, stitching the photos together to create a silent movie.

You can shoot a time-lapse movie in any exposure mode except the Effects modes. A few other critical points to note:

>> **The quality and maximum recording time of the movie depends on settings that you select from the Movie Settings option, found at the end of the Shooting menu.** By default, the camera uses a frame size of 1920 x 1080, frame rate of 60 frames per second, and the lower of the two Movie Quality settings (Normal). That results in a maximum recording time of 20 minutes, assuming your camera memory card has enough free space to hold a movie file of that length. (The maximum size of a movie file is 4GB.) To find out more these and other movie settings, check out Chapter 7.

>> **Compose the scene using Live View movie mode.** Because the end result is a movie, your photos are cropped to fit the 16:9 aspect ratio of a movie frame. So rotate the LV switch to engage Live View and then press the Info button until you see the Movie Indicators display. Black bars appear across the top and bottom of the screen to indicate the available frame area. After setting up the shot, rotate the LV switch again to exit Live View; the Time-Lapse Movie menu option isn't available in Live View mode.

>> **Time-Lapse Movie isn't available when the camera is connected to an HDMI display, either** — which, unfortunately, means I can't show you the menu screens for this feature because I create those screens by connecting the camera to an HDMI video-capture card. Luckily, most of the options are the same or similar to the Interval Timer Shooting screens, which you can see in the preceding section.

After you choose Time-Lapse Movie from the Shooting menu, you see a setup screen similar to the one shown on the right in Figure 2-11. Two options, Interval and Exposure Smoothing, work as described in the preceding section. The Shooting Time setting determines how long the camera records photographs after you start the capture session. By default, pictures are taken every 5 seconds for 25 minutes, which results in a finished movie length of 5.1 minutes. As you change the Shooting Time value, the camera updates the movie length value, shown in blue near the bottom of the screen.

To exit the Shooting Time screen, tap OK or press the OK button. Then choose Start to begin the capture session. If you need to interrupt shooting, press the OK button. When the camera finishes shooting all the pictures, it stitches the frames and presents you with a movie file. You can't access the individual frames. See Chapter 7 for details on playing movies.

Checking Image Size and Image Quality

Your preflight camera check should also include a look at the Image Size and Image Quality settings. The first option sets picture resolution; the second, file type.

The names of these settings are a little misleading, though, because the Image Size setting also contributes to picture quality, and the Image Quality setting affects the file size of the picture. Because the two work in tandem to determine quality and size, it's important to consider them together. The next few sections explain each option; following that, I offer a few final tips and show you how to select the settings you want to use.

Also check out the section related to ISO in Chapter 3; very high ISO settings can also reduce image quality. In this case, a defect known as *noise* can give the picture a speckled appearance.

Considering the Image Size setting (resolution)

The Image Size setting determines how many pixels are used to create your photo. *Pixels* are the square tiles from which digital images are made; you can see some pixels close up in the right image in Figure 2-14, which shows a greatly magnified view of the eye area in the left image.

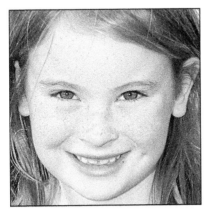
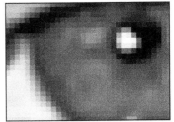

Pixels are the building blocks of digital photos.

Pixel is short for *picture element.*

The number of pixels in an image is referred to as *resolution.* You can define resolution in terms of either the *pixel dimensions* — the number of horizontal pixels and vertical pixels — or total resolution, which you get by multiplying those two values. This number is usually stated in *megapixels* (or MP, for short), with one megapixel equal to 1 million pixels.

Your camera offers three Image Size options: Large, Medium, and Small. Table 2-1 lists the resolution values for each setting. (Megapixel values are rounded off.)

TABLE 2-1

Image Size (Resolution) Options

Setting	Resolution
Large	6000 x 4000 (24.0 MP)
Medium	4496 x 3000 (13.5 MP)
Small	2992 x 2000 (6.0 MP)

REMEMBER

However, if you select Raw (NEF) as the Image Quality setting, images are captured at the Large setting. You can vary the resolution only for pictures taken in the JPEG format. The upcoming section "Understanding Image Quality options (JPEG or Raw)" explains file formats.

To choose the right Image Size setting, you need to understand the three ways that resolution affects your pictures:

>> **Print size**: Pixel count determines the size at which you can produce a high-quality print. When an image contains too few pixels, details appear muddy, and curved and diagonal lines appear jagged. Such pictures are said to exhibit pixelation.

Depending on your photo printer, you typically need anywhere from 200 to 300 pixels per linear inch, or ppi, for good print quality. To produce an 8 x 10 print at 200 ppi, for example, you need a pixel count of 1600 x 2000, or about 3.2 megapixels.

WARNING

Even though many photo-editing programs enable you to add pixels to an existing image — known as *upsampling* — doing so doesn't enable you to successfully enlarge your photo. In fact, upsampling typically makes matters worse.

To give you a better idea of the impact of resolution on print quality, Figures 2-15, 2-16, and 2-17 show you the same image at 300 ppi, at 50 ppi, and then resampled from 50 ppi to 300 ppi (respectively). As you can see, there's no way around the rule: If you want quality prints, you need the right pixel count from the get-go.

300 ppi

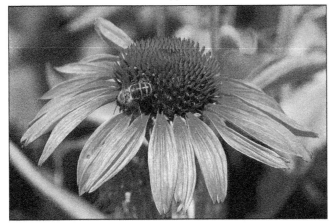

FIGURE 2-15:
A high-quality
print depends
on a high-
resolution
original.

50 ppi

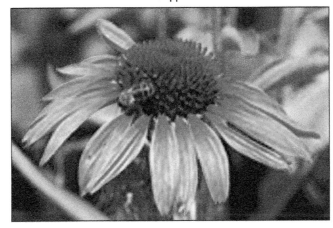

FIGURE 2-16:
At 50 ppi,
the image
has a jagged,
pixelated look.

50 ppi resampled to 300ppi

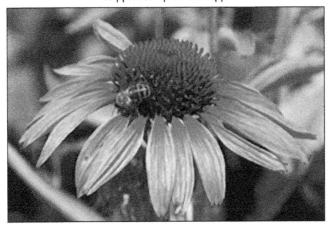

FIGURE 2-17:
Adding pixels
in a photo
editor doesn't
rescue a low-
resolution
original.

>> **Screen display size:** Resolution doesn't affect the quality of images viewed on a monitor, TV, or other screen device the way it does printed photos. Instead, resolution determines the *size* at which the image appears. I explain this issue in a bit more detail in Chapter 9; for now, just know that you need way fewer pixels for onscreen photos than you do for prints.

>> **File size:** Every pixel increases the amount of data required to create the picture file. So a higher-resolution image has a larger file size than a low-resolution image.

WARNING

Large files present several problems:

>> You can store fewer images on the memory card, your computer's hard drive, an online storage site, and other storage media, such as a DVD.

>> The camera needs more time to process and store the image data on the memory card after you press the shutter button. This extra time can hamper fast-action shooting.

>> When you share photos online, larger files take longer to upload and download.

>> When you edit photos in your photo software, your computer needs more resources and time to process large files.

TIP

As you can see, resolution is a bit of a sticky wicket. What if you aren't sure how large you want to print your images? What if you want to print your photos *and* share them online? I take the better-safe-than-sorry route, which leads to the following recommendations:

>> **Always shoot at a resolution suitable for print.** You then can create a low-resolution copy of the image for use online. In fact, your camera offers a built-in resizing option that I cover in Chapter 9.

>> **For everyday images, Medium is a good choice.** I find Large to be overkill for casual shooting, creating huge files for no good reason. Keep in mind that even at the Small setting, the pixel count (2992 x 2000) gives you enough resolution to produce an 8 x 10-inch print at 200 ppi.

TIP

>> **Choose Large for an image that you plan to crop or print very large, or both.** The benefit of maxing out the resolution is that you have the flexibility to crop your photo and still generate a decently sized print of the remaining image. Figure 2-18 offers an example. When I was shooting this photograph, I couldn't get close enough to fill the frame with my main interest — the two

juvenile herons at the center of the scene. But because I had the resolution cranked up to Large, I could later crop the shot to the composition you see on the right and still produce a great-looking print. In fact, I could have printed the cropped image at a much larger size than fits on the page here.

FIGURE 2-18:
A high-resolution original (left) enabled me to crop the photo and still have enough pixels to produce a quality print (right).

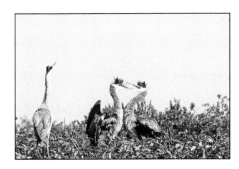

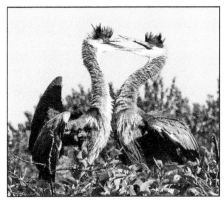

Understanding Image Quality options (JPEG or Raw)

If I had my druthers, the Image Quality option would instead be called File Type because that's what the setting controls. Here's the deal: The file type, sometimes also known as a file *format*, determines how your picture data is recorded and stored. Your choice does affect picture quality, but so does the Image Size setting, as described in the preceding section, and the ISO setting, covered in the next chapter. In addition, your choice of file type has ramifications beyond picture quality.

At any rate, your camera offers two file types: JPEG and Camera Raw — or Raw, for short, which goes by the specific moniker NEF (Nikon Electronic Format) on Nikon cameras. The next sections explain the pros and cons of each format. If your mind is already made up, skip ahead to the section "Setting Image Size and Image Quality" to find out how to make your selection.

WARNING

Don't confuse *file format* with the Format Memory Card option on the Setup menu. That option erases all data on your memory card.

JPEG: The imaging (and web) standard

Pronounced "jay-peg," this format is the default setting on your D5600, as it is on most digital cameras. JPEG is popular for two main reasons:

>> **Immediate usability:** All web browsers and e-mail programs can display JPEG files, so you can share pictures online immediately after you shoot them. You also can get a JPEG file printed at any retail photo outlet. The same can't be said for Raw (NEF) files, which must be converted to JPEG for online sharing and to JPEG or another standard format, such as TIFF, for retail printing.

>> **Small files:** JPEG files are smaller than Raw files. And smaller files consume less room on your camera memory card and in your computer's storage tank.

The downside (you knew there had to be one) is that JPEG creates smaller files by applying *lossy compression*. This process actually throws away some image data. Too much compression produces a defect called *JPEG artifacting*. Figure 2-19 compares a high-quality original (left photo) with a heavily compressed version that exhibits artifacting (right photo).

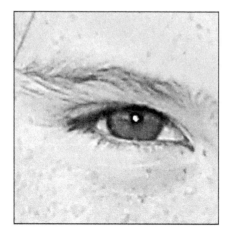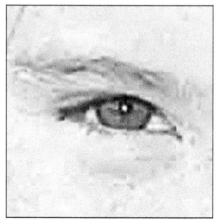

FIGURE 2-19: The reduced quality of the right image is caused by excessive JPEG compression.

Fortunately, your camera enables you to specify how much compression you're willing to accept. You can choose from three JPEG settings, which produce the following results:

>> **JPEG Fine:** The compression ratio is 1:4 — that is, the file is four times smaller than it would otherwise be. Because very little compression is applied, you shouldn't see many compression artifacts, if any.

>> **JPEG Normal:** The compression ratio rises to 1:8. The chance of seeing some artifacting increases as well. This setting is the default.

>> **JPEG Basic:** The compression ratio jumps to 1:16. That's a substantial amount of compression that brings with it a lot more risk of artifacting.

Note, though, that even the Basic setting doesn't result in anywhere near the level of artifacting you see in the right image in Figure 2-19. I've exaggerated the defect in that example to help you recognize artifacting and understand how it differs from the quality loss that occurs when you have too few pixels (refer to Figures 2-15 through 2-17). In fact, if you keep the image print or display size small, you aren't likely to notice a great deal of quality difference between the Fine, Normal, and Basic compression levels. It's only when you greatly enlarge a photo that the differences become apparent.

TIP

Given that the differences between the compression settings aren't that easy to spot until you enlarge the photo, is it okay to stick with the default setting — Normal — or even drop down to Basic to capture smaller files? Well, only you can decide what level of quality your pictures demand. For me, the added file sizes produced by the Fine setting aren't a huge concern, given that the prices of memory cards fall all the time. Long-term storage is more of an issue; the larger your files, the faster you fill your hard drive, online storage account, or whatever other digital closet you may be using to archive your files. But in the end, I prefer to take the storage hit in exchange for the lower compression level of the Fine setting. You never know when a casual snapshot will be so great that you want to print or display it large enough that even minor quality loss becomes a concern. And of all the defects that you can correct in a photo editor, artifacting is one of the hardest to remove.

If you don't want *any* risk of artifacting, change the file type to Raw (NEF). Or consider your other option, which is to record two versions of each file — one Raw and one JPEG. The next section offers details.

Raw (NEF): The purist's choice

The other picture file type you can create is *Camera Raw*, or just *Raw* (as in uncooked), for short.

TECHNICAL
STUFF

Each manufacturer has its own flavor of Raw. Nikon's is NEF, for Nikon Electronic Format, so you see the three-letter extension NEF at the end of Raw filenames.

Raw is popular with advanced, very demanding photographers for three reasons:

>> **Greater creative control:** With JPEG, internal camera software tweaks your images, adjusting color, exposure, and sharpness as needed to produce the results that Nikon believes its customers prefer. With Raw, the camera simply records the original, unprocessed image data. The photographer then copies the image file to the computer and uses special software known as a Raw converter to produce the actual image, making decisions about color, exposure, and so on at that point. Nikon Capture NX-D, available for free download from the Nikon website, offers a Raw converter, and the D5600 also has a built-in Raw converter. I cover both options in Chapter 9.

>> **Higher bit depth:** Bit depth is a measure of how many distinct color values an image file can contain. JPEG files restrict you to 8 bits each for the red, blue, and green color components, or *channels,* that make up a digital image, for a total of 24 bits. That translates to roughly 16.7 million possible colors. On the D5600, you can set the camera to capture either 12 or 14 bits per channel when you shoot in the Raw format.

Although jumping from 8 to 12 or 14 bits sounds like a huge difference, you may never notice any difference in your photos — that 8-bit palette of 16.7 million values is more than enough for superb images. Where the extra bits can come in handy is if you adjust exposure, contrast, or color in your photo-editing program. When you apply extreme adjustments, the extra bits sometimes help avoid a problem known as banding or posterization, which creates abrupt color breaks where you should see smooth, seamless transitions. (A higher bit depth doesn't always prevent this problem, however.)

>> **Best picture quality:** Because Raw doesn't apply the destructive compression associated with JPEG, you don't run the risk of the artifacting that can occur with JPEG.

But Raw isn't without its disadvantages:

>> **You can't do much with your pictures until you process them in a Raw converter.** You can't share them online or put them into a text document or multimedia presentation. You can view and print them immediately if you use Nikon NX-D or the other free Nikon photo program, ViewNX-i. (I cover this program in Chapter 9 as well.) But most other programs require you to convert the Raw files to a standard format first, such as JPEG or TIFF. Ditto for retail photo printing.

>> **Raw files are larger than JPEGs. Unlike JPEG, Raw doesn't apply lossy compression to shrink files.** In addition, Raw files are always captured at the

maximum resolution. For both reasons, Raw files are significantly larger than JPEGs, so they take up more room on your memory card and on your computer's hard drive or other picture-storage device.

Whether the upside of Raw outweighs the down is a decision you need to ponder based on your photographic needs and on whether you have the time to, and interest in, converting Raw files.

TIP

You do have the option to capture a picture in the Raw and JPEG formats at the same time. In this scenario, you wind up with two files: one in the Raw format and one in the JPEG format. The JPEG file can be set to either Fine, Normal, or Basic. I often take this route when I'm shooting pictures I want to share right away with people who don't have software for viewing Raw files. I upload the JPEGs to a photo-sharing site where everyone can view them, and then I process the Raw versions when I have time.

My take: Choose JPEG Fine or Raw (NEF)

At this point, you may be finding all this technical goop a bit overwhelming, so allow me to simplify things for you. Until you have the time or energy to completely digest all the ramifications of JPEG versus Raw, here's a quick summary of my thoughts on the matter:

>> If you require the absolute best image quality and have the time and interest in doing the Raw conversion, shoot Raw.

>> If great photo quality is good enough and you don't have time to spend processing images, stick with JPEG Fine.

>> If you don't mind the added file-storage space requirement and want the flexibility of both formats, choose a Raw+JPEG option, which stores one copy of the image in each format. Set the JPEG version to Fine, Normal, or Basic depending on how you plan to use the JPEG image. Again, for top quality, choose Fine.

>> If you go with JPEG only, stay away from JPEG Normal and Basic. (Remember, Normal is the default setting on your camera.) The trade-off for smaller files isn't, in my opinion, worth the risk of compression artifacts.

Setting Image Size and Image Quality

REMEMBER

Now for the lowdown on how to check and adjust these settings: First, to see which options are currently in force, check the Information screen or Live View display. The Image Size and Image Quality settings appear next to each other, in the areas labeled in Figure 2-20.

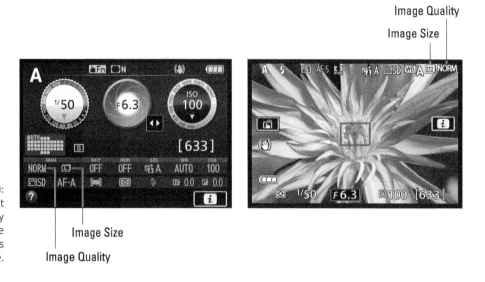

FIGURE 2-20:
The current
Image Quality
and Image
Size settings
appear here.

Image Quality

Image Size

Image Size

Image Quality

To adjust the settings, you have two choices:

>> **Control strip:** Press the *i* button or tap the *i* icon on the display to access the control strip. Choose the option you want to change — Image Size or Image Quality — to display a screen showing the available settings. For example, choosing the Image Quality option, as shown on the left in Figure 2-21, takes you to the screen shown on the right, where you can select the setting you want to use. Figure 2-22 illustrates the process of setting the Image Size option through the control strip. (The figures show the Information screen control strip, but things work the same way in Live View mode.)

Shots remaining

File size (megabytes)

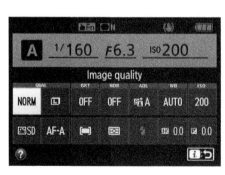
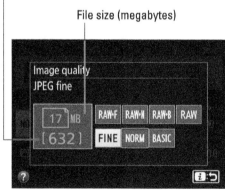

FIGURE 2-21:
You can adjust
the Image
Quality setting
quickly via the
control strip.

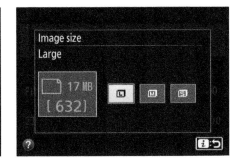

TIP

Notice that in the screens shown on the right in Figures 2-21 and 22, the display indicates the file size in MB (megabytes) that will result from the currently selected combination of Image Size and Image Quality settings — 17MB, in the figures. You also see the number of pictures that will fit on the memory card at that file size (632, in the figures). Keep in mind that certain other factors also affect the file size, such as the level of detail and color in the subject.

» **Shooting menu:** You also can adjust both settings via the Shooting menu. If you select the Image Size setting, as shown on the left in Figure 2-23, the options screen shows the pixel counts for each setting, as shown on the right. The number in parentheses (24M, in the figure) shows the image size as measured in *megapixels* — the number of horizontal pixels times the number of vertical pixels. This value is different from the size of the *file* needed to hold all those pixels, which is measured in *megabytes* (MB). You can view that number only when changing the settings through the control strip.

File size (megapixels)

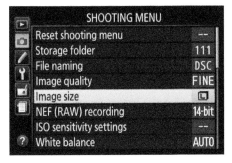

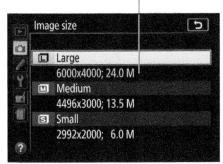

When you choose the Raw (NEF) option, all pictures are automatically captured at the Large resolution setting. However, if you choose one of the Raw+JPEG settings, the JPEG version is captured at the selected Image Size setting.

REMEMBER

In addition, you can specify the bit depth of Raw files. Make the call through the NEF (RAW) Recording option on the Shooting menu, as shown in Figure 2-24. You can choose from 12 or 14 bits. If you stick with 14 bits, which is the default setting, the file can contain more color data, but at the price of an increase in file size. A 12-bit Raw file has a size of 21.3MB; a 14-bit file, 26.3 MB. See the earlier section "Raw (NEF): The purist's choice" for more information about bit depth.

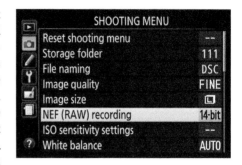

FIGURE 2-24:
For Raw files, you can specify how many bits of color data you want to record.

Adding Flash

Another basic picture-taking option to consider is whether you want to use the built-in flash to illuminate your subject.

REMEMBER

However, whether you can use the built-in flash depends on your exposure mode. The flash isn't available in Auto Flash Off mode and the following Scene modes: Landscape, Sports, Night Landscape, Beach/Snow, Sunset, Dusk/Dawn, Candlelight, Blossom, and Autumn Colors. All Effects modes except Super Vivid, Pop, Photo Illustration, and Toy Camera Effect also disable the built-in flash.

TIP

If you do a lot of flash photography, you may want to invest in an external flash head, which attaches to the hot shoe on top of your camera. When you use an external flash head, you *can* use flash in exposure modes that disable the built-in flash, with the exception of Auto Flash Off mode.

The rest of this chapter concentrates on taking advantage of the built-in flash. For help with an external flash, I need to point you to the flash manual because different flash units provide different flash settings.

Enabling and disabling flash

In certain exposure modes, flash is set by default to fire automatically if the camera thinks the ambient light is insufficient; in other modes, you have to manually enable flash. Here's the breakdown:

>> **Auto mode, all Scene modes that permit flash except Food mode, and Toy Camera Effect mode:** Flash is set to Auto by default. After you press the shutter button, the camera assesses the available light and automatically pops up the built-in flash if it finds that light is lacking.

TIP

If you don't want to use flash, you may be able to disable it via the Flash mode setting. See the next section for how-tos.

>> **Photo Illustration Effects mode:** Flash is disabled by default, but you can override that setting by changing the Flash mode setting.

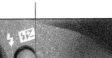

>> **P, S, A, and M modes and the Food Scene mode:** There's no such thing as automatic flash in these modes. Instead, if you want to use the built-in flash, press the Flash button on the side of the camera, labeled in Figure 2-25. Don't want flash? Just press down gently on the top of the flash to close the unit.

The camera does give you a little flash input, though: If the camera thinks you need to use flash, you see a blinking question mark, a flash symbol, or both, in the displays. If you tap the question mark symbol on the display or press the Zoom Out button, a message appears recommending that you use flash.

Flash button

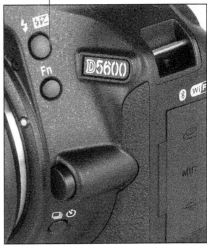

FIGURE 2-25:
In P, S, A, and M modes (and the Food Scene mode), raise the built-in flash by pressing the Flash button.

Choosing a Flash mode

The Flash mode setting determines how and when the flash fires. The next section introduces the various options; following that, you can find details on how to adjust the setting.

Sorting through your Flash mode options

Your camera offers the following flash modes, represented in the Information and Live View displays by the symbols you see in the margins here. (Skip to Figure 2-29 to see where to find the symbols in the displays.)

» **Auto:** The camera decides whether the flash fires. This mode isn't available in the P, S, A, and M modes or the Food Scene mode.

 » **Flash Off:** In Auto exposure mode or the Scene and Effects modes that permit flash, choose this Flash mode to prevent the flash from firing. (In the P, S, A, and M modes and the Food Scene mode, simply close the flash unit if you don't want to use flash.)

 » **Fill Flash:** Think of this mode, available in the P, S, A, M, and Food Scene modes, as normal flash. You may also hear this mode called force *flash* because the flash fires no matter the amount of available light.

TIP

Although most people think of flash as an indoor lighting option, adding flash can improve outdoor photos, too. After all, your main light source — the sun — is overhead, so although the top of the subject may be adequately lit, the front typically needs additional illumination.

As an example, Figure 2-26 shows a floral image taken both with and without a flash. The small pop of light provided by the built-in flash is also beneficial when shooting subjects that happen to be slightly shaded. Flash can also enhance outdoor portraits, especially if your subject is standing in front of a very bright or very dark background. The section on shooting portraits in Chapter 6 offers examples of portrait settings that call for flash.

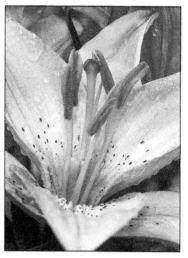

Shooting with flash in bright light involves a couple of complications, however; see the sidebar "Using flash outdoors," later in this chapter, for help.

WARNING

No flash   With flash

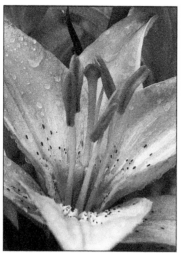

FIGURE 2-26:
Adding flash
resulted
in better
illumination
and a slight
warming
effect.

>> **Red-Eye Reduction:** Red-eye is caused when flash light bounces off a subject's retinas and is reflected back to the camera lens, making the subject appear possessed by a demon. This flash mode is designed to reduce the chances of red-eye.

When you use Red-Eye Reduction mode, the AF-assist lamp on the front of the camera lights briefly before the flash fires. The subject's pupils constrict in response to the light, allowing less flash light to enter the eye and cause that glowing red reflection. Be sure to warn your subjects to wait for the flash, or else they may step out of the frame or stop posing after they see the light from the AF-assist lamp.

REMEMBER

In Auto exposure mode as well as in certain other Scene and Effects modes that permit flash, red-eye reduction flash is just a variation of the regular Auto flash setting. That is, if the camera sees the need for flash, it fires the flash with red-eye reduction engaged. In this case, you see the word Auto next to the red-eye symbol. Additionally, a few Scene modes use a variation of red-eye reduction, combining that feature with a slow shutter speed. This flash mode displays the little eye icon plus the words Auto Slow. It's important to use a tripod and ask your subject to remain still during the exposure to avoid a blurry picture.

>> **Slow-Sync and Rear-Sync:** In the flash modes listed so far, the flash and shutter are synchronized so that the flash fires at the exact moment the shutter opens.

TECHNICAL
STUFF

Technical types call this flash arrangement *front-curtain sync,* which refers to how the flash is synchronized with the opening of the shutter. Here's the deal: The camera uses a type of shutter involving two curtains that move across the frame. When you press the shutter button, the first curtain opens, allowing light to strike the image sensor. At the end of the exposure, the second curtain draws across the frame to once again shield the sensor from light. With front-curtain sync, the flash fires when the front curtain opens.

Your camera also offers these four special sync modes:

- *Slow-Sync:* This mode, available only in the P and A exposure modes, also uses front-curtain sync, but allows a shutter speed slower than the 1/60 second minimum that's in force when you use Fill Flash and Red-Eye Reduction flash. Because of the longer exposure, the camera has time to absorb more ambient light, which has two benefits: Background areas that are beyond the reach of the flash appear brighter; and less flash power is needed, resulting in softer lighting.

The downside of the slow shutter speed is, well, the slow shutter speed. Any movement of your camera or subject during the exposure can blur the picture, and the slower the shutter speed, the greater the chances of camera or subject motion. A tripod is essential to a good outcome, as are subjects that can hold very, very still. I find that the best practical use for this mode is shooting nighttime still-life subjects like the one you see in Figure 2-27. However, if you're shooting a nighttime portrait and you have a subject that can maintain a motionless pose, slow-sync flash can produce softer, more flattering light.

Regular flash

Slow-sync flash

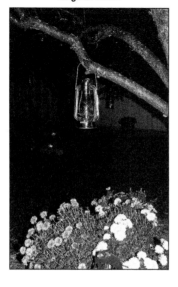 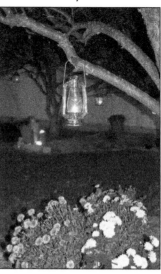

FIGURE 2-27:
Slow-sync flash produces softer, more even lighting than normal flash in nighttime pictures.

TIP

Even though the official Slow-Sync mode appears only in the P and A exposure modes, you can get the same result in the M and S modes by simply using a slow shutter speed and the normal, Fill Flash mode. You can use a shutter speed as slow as 30 seconds when using flash in those modes. In fact, I prefer using those modes when I want the slow-sync look because I can directly control the shutter speed.

 REAR

- *Rear-Curtain Sync:* In this mode, available only in shutter-priority (S) and manual (M) exposure modes, the flash fires at the end of the exposure, just before the shutter closes. The classic use of this mode is to combine the flash with a slow shutter speed to create trailing-light effects like the one you see in Figure 2-28. With Rear-Curtain Sync, the light trails extend behind the moving object (my hand, and the match, in this case), which makes visual sense. If instead you use slow-sync flash, the light trails appear in front of the moving object.

You can set the shutter speed as low as 30 seconds and as high as 1/200 second in this Flash mode.

SLOW REAR

- *Slow-Rear:* Hey, not confusing enough for you yet? This mode enables you to produce the same motion trail effects as with Rear-Curtain Sync, but in the P and A exposure modes. The camera automatically chooses a slower shutter speed than normal after you set the f-stop, just as with regular Slow-Sync mode.

- *Slow-Sync with Red-Eye Reduction:* In P and A exposure modes, you can also combine a slow-sync flash with the red-eye reduction feature. The symbol that represents this mode is the normal red-eye eyeball combined with the word Slow.

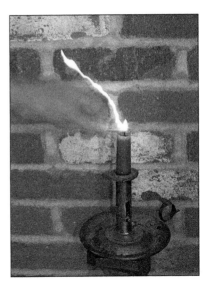

FIGURE 2-28:
I used Rear-Curtain Sync Flash to create this candle-lighting image.

IN SYNC: FLASH TIMING AND SHUTTER SPEED

TIP

To properly expose flash pictures, the camera has to synchronize the firing of the flash with the opening and closing of the shutter. For this reason, the range of available shutter speeds is limited when you use flash. The maximum shutter speed is 1/200 second; the minimum shutter speed varies, depending on the exposure mode:

- Auto, all Effects modes that permit flash, and all Scene modes except Portrait and Night Portrait: 1/60 second

- Nighttime Portrait: 1 second

- Portrait: 1/30 second

- P, A: 1/60 second (unless you use one of the Slow-Sync Flash modes, which permit a shutter speed as slow as 30 seconds)

- S: 30 seconds

- M: 30 seconds (for Fill Flash mode, you can exceed that limit if the shutter speed is set to Bulb or Time, which are two special shutter speeds I discuss in Chapter 3)

Setting the Flash mode

You can view the current Flash mode in the Information and Live View displays, as shown in Figure 2-29. (In Live View mode, press the Info button to cycle through the display modes to get to the one shown in the figure.) The white lightning bolt, labeled *Flash mode* in the figures, represents the standard, Fill Flash setting.

Through-the-lens flash metering   Flash mode

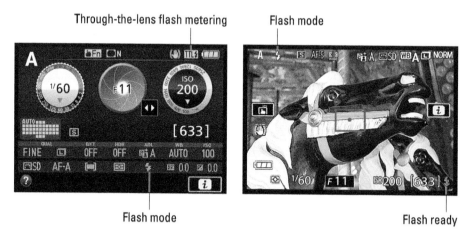

Flash mode   Flash ready

In the viewfinder as well as in the lower-right corner of the Live View display, you see a single lightning bolt. This symbol simply tells you that the flash is ready to fire. (You can't view the Flash mode in the viewfinder.) The symbol blinks if the camera thinks you need to add flash.

TECHNICAL STUFF

As for the TTL symbol, highlighted on the left in Figure 2-29, it represents the current setting of the Built-in Flash Cntrl (Control) option on the Custom Setting menu. TTL, which stands for *through the lens*, represents the normal flash metering operation: The camera measures the light coming through the lens and sets the flash output accordingly. Your other option is to set the flash output manually, as explained in the last section of this chapter. If you take that route, the letter *M* appears in place of *TTL*. You can choose between the two settings only when the Mode dial is set to P, S, A, or M.

When the flash is raised, you can use these techniques to change the Flash mode:

>> **Flash button + Command dial:** As soon as you press the Flash button, the Flash mode option in the display becomes selected, as shown in Figure 2-30. The same thing happens in the Live View display, but the related symbol is at the top of the screen (refer to Figure 2-29). Either way, keep the Flash

button pressed while rotating the Command dial to cycle through the Flash modes.

» **Control strip:** Press the *i* button or tap the *i* icon on the monitor to activate the control strip in the Information and Live View displays. Select the Flash mode option, as shown on the left in Figure 2-31, to display a screen listing the mode settings, as shown on the right in the figure.

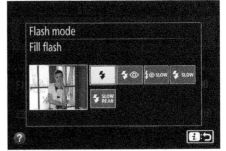

FIGURE 2-30:
The fastest way to change the Flash mode is to hold down the Flash button and rotate the Command dial.

Either way, remember that which Flash mode settings are available depends on your exposure mode.

FIGURE 2-31:
You also can adjust the Flash mode by using the normal control-strip method; press the *i* button or tap the on-screen *i* symbol to activate the control strip.

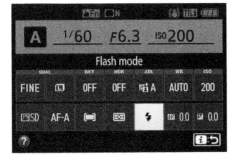 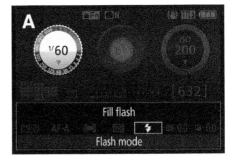

Adjusting flash output

TIP

In the P, S, A, or M exposure modes, as well as in certain other modes that permit flash, you have some control over flash power, even if you stick with the default, TTL (through the lens) automatic flash metering. If you want more or less flash light than the camera thinks is appropriate, you can adjust flash output by using *Flash Compensation.*

Flash Compensation settings are stated in terms of *exposure value (EV)* numbers. A setting of EV 0.0 indicates no flash adjustment; you can increase the flash power to EV +1.0 or decrease it to EV −3.0.

USING FLASH OUTDOORS

TIP

Contrary to what you might expect, adding flash can often improve outdoor photos taken during the daytime, even when the sun is bright. But be aware of two potential issues:

- **Colors may need tweaking.** When you combine multiple light sources, such as flash and daylight, colors may appear warmer or cooler than neutral. If you prefer a neutral color rendition, see the Chapter 5 section related to the White Balance control to find out how to address this issue.

- **Keep an eye on shutter speed.** Because of the way the camera needs to synchronize the firing of the flash with the opening of the shutter, the fastest shutter speed you can use with the built-in flash is 1/200 second. In bright sun, you may need to stop down the aperture significantly or lower the ISO, if possible, to avoid overexposing the image even at 1/200 second. As another option, you can place a neutral density filter over the lens; this accessory reduces the light that comes through the lens without affecting colors. Of course, you can simply move your subject into the shade.

On the flip side, the camera may select a shutter speed as slow as 1/60 second in the P and A modes, depending on the lighting conditions. If your subject is moving, it's a good idea to work in the S or M modes so that you control the shutter speed, the exposure setting that determines whether moving subjects appear blurry. See the next chapter for more information on that subject.

As an example of the benefit of this feature, look at the carousel images in Figure 2-32. The first image shows a flash-free shot. Clearly, I needed a flash to compensate for the fact that the horses were shadowed by the roof of the carousel. But at normal flash power, as shown in the middle image, the flash was too strong, creating glare in some spots and blowing out the highlights in the white mane. By dialing the flash power down to EV –1.0, I got a softer flash that straddled the line perfectly between no flash and too much flash.

As for boosting the flash output, you may find it necessary on some occasions, but don't expect the built-in flash to work miracles even at a Flash Compensation of +1.0. The reach of the built-in flash is limited, so it simply can't illuminate objects that are very far from the camera. In other words, don't even try taking flash pictures of a darkened recital hall from your seat in the balcony — all you'll wind up doing is annoying everyone.

| No flash | Flash EV 0.0 | Flash EV -1.0 |

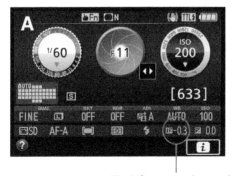

FIGURE 2-32:
When normal flash output is too strong, dial in a lower Flash Compensation setting.

REMEMBER

The current Flash Compensation setting appears in the Information display, in the area highlighted on the left in Figure 2-33. If this readout is dimmed, Flash Compensation isn't available in your current exposure mode. In the Live View display, you see only a symbol indicating that Flash Compensation is enabled, as shown on the right side of Figure 2-33. Note that if the feature is turned off (set to EV 0.0), the symbol doesn't appear in the Live View display.

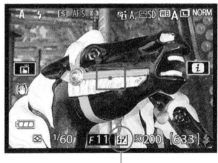

FIGURE 2-33:
These symbols represent Flash Compensation.

Flash Compensation setting   Flash Compensation enabled

One quirk: Some modes that disable the built-in flash make the Flash Compensation setting available. What gives? The option is provided solely for use with an external flash head. Any adjustment you make to the camera's flash-exposure setting is added to flash-power changes you make using the controls on the flash head. The built-in flash won't fire no matter what Flash Compensation value you select.

To adjust the amount of Flash Compensation, use either of these tricks:

>> **Two-button-plus-Command-dial maneuver:** First, press the Flash button to pop up the built-in flash. Then press and hold the Flash button and the Exposure Compensation button simultaneously. When you press the buttons, the Flash Compensation value becomes highlighted in the display, as shown in Figure 2-34. In the viewfinder, the current setting takes the place of the usual Frames Remaining value. While keeping both buttons pressed, rotate the Command dial to adjust the setting. I find that any technique that involves coordinating this many fingers a little complex, but you may find it easier than I do.

>> **Control strip:** After pressing the *i* button or tapping the onscreen *i* symbol to display the strip, select the Flash Compensation setting, as shown in Figure 2-35. The camera then displays a screen where you can set the compensation amount. Press OK or tap the OK symbol to lock in the new setting.

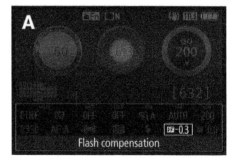

FIGURE 2-34:
Rotate the Command dial while pressing the Flash and Exposure Compensation buttons to adjust the flash power.

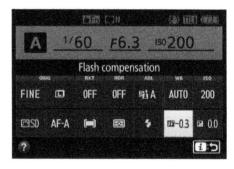

FIGURE 2-35:
You also can adjust the setting by using the control strip.

WARNING

In Scene modes that permit flash, the Flash Compensation setting is reset to 0.0 when you turn off the camera or switch to a different Scene mode. In other exposure modes, the flash-power adjustment remains in force until you reset the value, even if you turn off the camera. So be sure to check the setting before you next use the flash.

Controlling flash output manually

If you're experienced in the way of the flash, you can manually set flash output via the Flash Cntrl for Built-in Flash option, found in the Bracketing/Flash section of the Custom Setting menu and shown on the left in Figure 2-36. The normal setting is TTL (for automatic, through-the-lens metering), but if you select Manual, as shown on the right in Figure 2-36, you can choose specific flash power settings ranging from Full to 1/32 power.

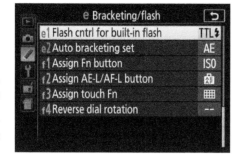 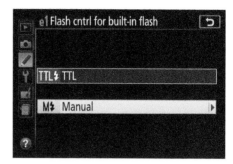

FIGURE 2-36: Using this option, you can control the flash output manually.

When flash is set to manual control, the TTL icon that normally appears in the upper-right corner of the Information display (refer to Figure 2-29) is replaced by the letter *M*. In the viewfinder, an icon that looks like the Information screen's Flash Compensation icon (a lightning bolt with a +/– sign) blinks.

2

Taking Creative Control

Find out how to control exposure and shoot in the advanced exposure modes (P, S, A, and M).

Master the focusing system and discover how to manipulate depth of field.

Adjust color by using white balance and Picture Control settings.

Get pro tips for shooting portraits, action shots, landscapes, close-ups, and more.

Take advantage of your camera's HD movie-recording features.

IN THIS CHAPTER

» **Understanding the basics of exposure**

» **Choosing the right exposure mode: P, S, A, or M?**

» **Reading meters and other exposure cues**

» **Solving exposure problems**

» **Creating a safety net with automatic bracketing**

Chapter **3**

Taking Charge of Exposure

U nderstanding exposure is one of the most intimidating challenges for a new photographer. Discussions of the topic are loaded with technical terms — *aperture, metering, shutter speed, ISO,* and the like. Add the fact that your camera offers many exposure controls, all sporting equally foreign names, and it's no wonder that many people decide to stick with Auto exposure mode and let the camera take care of all exposure decisions.

I fully relate to the confusion you may be feeling — I've been there. But I can also promise that when you take things nice and slow, digesting a piece of the exposure pie at a time, the topic is *not* as complicated as it seems on the surface. I guarantee that the payoff will be worth your time, too. You'll not only gain the know-how to solve just about any exposure problem but also discover ways to use exposure to put your creative stamp on a scene.

To that end, this chapter provides everything you need to know about controlling exposure, from a primer in exposure terminology (it's not as bad as it sounds) to tips on using the P, S, A, and M exposure modes, which are the only ones that offer access to all exposure features. *Note:* The one exposure-related topic not covered in this chapter is flash; I discuss flash in Chapter 2 because it's among the options you can access even in Auto mode. Also, this chapter deals with still photography; Chapter 7 covers movie recording.

Introducing the Exposure Trio: Aperture, Shutter Speed, and ISO

Any photograph is created by focusing light through a lens onto a light-sensitive recording medium. In a film camera, the film negative serves as that medium; in a digital camera, it's the *image sensor,* which is a sophisticated electrical component that measures the light in a scene and then passes that information to the camera's data-processing center so that an image can be created. (Yes, a digital camera is essentially a computer with a lens.)

Between a digital camera's lens and sensor are two barriers — the aperture and shutter — which work in concert to control how much light makes its way to the sensor. In the digital world, the design and arrangement of the aperture, shutter, and sensor vary depending on the camera; Figure 3-1 offers an illustration of the basic concept.

The aperture and shutter, along with a third feature — ISO — determine *exposure,* which is basically the picture's overall brightness and contrast. This three-part exposure formula works as follows:

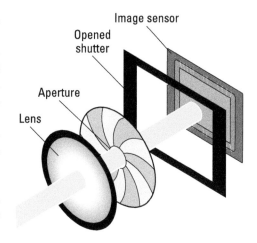

FIGURE 3-1:
The aperture size and shutter speed determine how much light strikes the image sensor.

>> **Aperture (controls amount of light):** The *aperture* is an adjustable hole in a diaphragm inside the lens. You change the aperture size to control the size of the light beam that can enter the camera.

Aperture settings are stated as *f-stop numbers,* or simply *f-stops,* and are expressed by the letter *f* followed by a number: f/2, f/5.6, f/16, and so on. The lower the f-stop number, the larger the aperture, and the more light is permitted into the camera, as illustrated by Figure 3-2. (If it seems backward to use a higher number for a smaller aperture, think of it this way: A higher value creates a bigger light barrier than a lower value.) The range of available aperture settings varies from lens to lens.

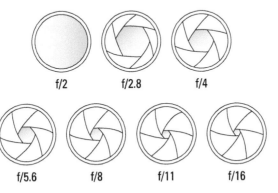

FIGURE 3-2: A lower f-stop number means a larger aperture, allowing more light into the camera.

f/2   f/2.8   f/4

f/5.6   f/8   f/11   f/16

>> **Shutter speed (controls duration of light):** The shutter works something like, er, the shutters on a window. The camera's shutter stays closed, preventing light from striking the image sensor (just as closed window shutters prevent sunlight from entering a room) until you press the shutter button. Then the shutter opens briefly to allow light that passes through the aperture to hit the sensor. The exception to this scenario is when you compose in Live View mode: When you enable Live View, the shutter opens and remains open so that the image can form on the sensor and be displayed on the monitor. When you press the shutter button, the shutter first closes and then reopens for the actual exposure.

Either way, the length of time that the shutter is open is the *shutter speed,* which is measured in seconds: 1/60 second, 1/250 second, 2 seconds, and so on.

>> **ISO (controls light sensitivity):** *ISO,* which is a digital function rather than a mechanical structure on the camera, enables you to adjust how responsive the image sensor is to light.

TECHNICAL STUFF

The term *ISO* is a holdover from film days, when an international standards organization rated each film stock according to light sensitivity: ISO 200, ISO 400, ISO 800, and so on. On a digital camera, the sensor itself doesn't actually get more or less sensitive when you change the ISO. Instead, the light "signal" that hits the sensor is either amplified or dampened through electronics wizardry, sort of like how raising the volume on a radio boosts the audio signal. The upshot is the same as changing to a more light-reactive film stock. Using a higher ISO means that less light is needed to produce the image, enabling you to use a smaller aperture, faster shutter speed, or both.

Distilled to its essence, the image-exposure formula is this simple:

>> Together, aperture and shutter speed determine how much light strikes the image sensor.

>> ISO determines how much the sensor reacts to that light and thus how much light is needed to expose the picture.

REMEMBER

The tricky part of the equation is that aperture, shutter speed, and ISO settings affect pictures in ways that go beyond exposure:

>> Aperture affects *depth of field,* or the distance over which focus remains acceptably sharp.

>> Shutter speed determines whether moving objects appear blurry or sharply focused.

>> ISO affects the amount of image *noise,* which is a defect that looks like specks of colored sand.

Understanding these side effects is critical to choosing the combination of aperture, shutter speed, and ISO that will work best for your subject, so the next three sections explore each issue. If you're already familiar with this stuff and just want to know how to adjust exposure settings, skip ahead to the section "Setting Aperture, Shutter Speed, and ISO."

Aperture affects depth of field

The aperture setting, or f-stop, affects *depth of field,* which is the distance over which focus appears acceptably sharp. With a shallow depth of field, your subject appears more sharply focused than faraway objects; with a large depth of field, the sharp-focus zone spreads over a greater distance.

REMEMBER

As you reduce the aperture size by choosing a higher f-stop number — *stop down the aperture,* in photo lingo — you increase the depth of field. As an example, see Figure 3-3. For both shots, I established focus on the fountain statue. Notice that the background in the first image, taken at f/13, is sharper than in the right example, taken at f/5.6. Aperture is just one contributor to depth of field, however; the focal length of the lens and the distance between that lens and your subject also affect how much of the scene stays in focus. See Chapter 4 for the complete story.

f/13, 1/25 second, ISO 200   f/5.6, 1/125 second, ISO 200

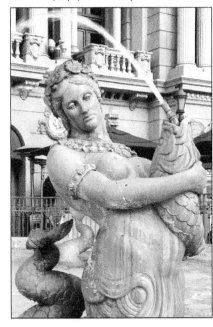 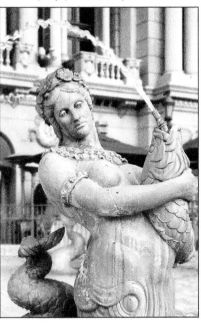

FIGURE 3-3:
Widening
the aperture
(choosing a
lower f-stop
number)
decreases
depth of field.

TIP

One way to remember the relationship between f-stop and depth of field is to think of the *f* as standing for *focus*. A higher f-stop number produces a larger depth of field, so to extend the zone of sharp focus, use a higher f-stop. Higher *f*-stop number, greater zone of *focus*. (Please *don't* share this tip with photography elites, who will roll their eyes and inform you that the *f* in *f-stop* most certainly does *not* stand for focus but for the ratio between the aperture size and lens focal length — as if *that's* helpful to know if you're not an optical engineer. Chapter 1 explains focal length, which *is* helpful to know.)

Shutter speed affects motion blur

At a slow shutter speed, moving objects appear blurry; a fast shutter speed captures motion cleanly. This phenomenon has nothing to do with the actual focus point of the camera but rather on the movement occurring — and being recorded by the camera — while the shutter is open.

Compare the photos in Figure 3-3, for example. The static elements are perfectly focused in both images although the background in the left photo appears sharper because I shot that image using a higher f-stop, increasing the depth of field. But how the camera rendered the moving portion of the scene — the fountain water — was determined by shutter speed. At 1/25 second (left photo), the water blurs, giving it a misty look. At 1/125 second (right photo), the droplets appear more sharply focused, almost frozen in mid-air. How high a shutter speed you need to freeze action depends on the speed of your subject.

If your picture suffers from overall blur, as in Figure 3-4, the camera itself moved during the exposure, which is always a danger when you handhold a camera. The slower the shutter speed, the longer the exposure time and the longer you have to hold the camera still to avoid the blur that's caused by camera shake.

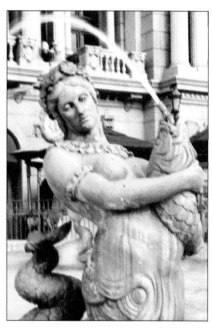

How slow a shutter speed can you use before camera shake becomes a problem? The answer depends on a couple factors, including your physical abilities and your lens — the heavier the lens, the harder it is to hold steady. Camera shake also affects your picture more when you shoot with a lens that has a long focal length. You may be able to use a slower shutter speed with a 55mm lens than with a 200mm lens, for example. Finally, it's easier to detect slight blurring in an image that shows a close-up view of a subject than in one that captures a wider area. Moral of the story: Take test shots to determine the slowest shutter speed you can use with each of your lenses.

FIGURE 3-4:
If both stationary and moving objects are blurry, camera shake is the usual cause.

Of course, to avoid the possibility of camera shake altogether, mount your camera on a tripod. Also investigate whether your lens offers Vibration Reduction, a feature that helps compensate for small amounts of camera shake. Chapter 4 covers that handy option along with other solutions for blurry pictures, which aren't always the result of camera shake.

Freezing action isn't the only way to use shutter speed to creative effect. When shooting waterfalls, for example, many photographers use a slow shutter speed to give the water even more of a blurry, romantic look than you see in my fountain example. With colorful subjects, a slow shutter can produce some cool abstract effects and create a heightened sense of motion. Chapter 6 offers examples of both effects.

ISO affects image noise

As ISO increases, making the image sensor more reactive to light, you increase the risk of producing noise. *Noise* is a defect that looks like sprinkles of sand and is similar in appearance to film *grain*, a defect that often mars pictures taken with high ISO film. Figure 3-5 offers an example.

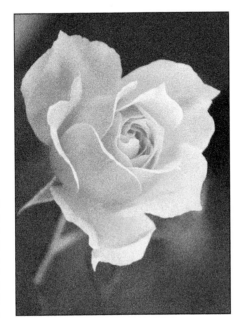
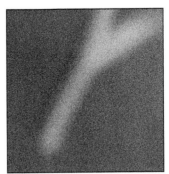

FIGURE 3-5:
Caused by
a very high
ISO or long
exposure time,
noise becomes
more visible
as you enlarge
the image.

Ideally, then, you should always use the lowest ISO setting on your camera to ensure top image quality. Sometimes, though, the lighting conditions don't permit you to do so and still use the aperture and shutter speeds you need.

Take my rose image as an example. When I shot these pictures, I didn't have a tripod, so I needed a shutter speed fast enough to allow a sharp handheld image. I opened the aperture to f/5.6, which was the widest setting on the lens I was using, to allow as much light as possible into the camera. At ISO 100, I needed a shutter speed of 1/40 second to expose the picture, and that shutter speed wasn't fast enough for a successful handheld shot. You see the blurred result on the left in Figure 3-6. By raising the ISO to 200, I was able to use a shutter speed of 1/80 second, which enabled me to capture the flower cleanly, as shown on the right in the figure.

ISO 100, f/5.6, 1/40 second

ISO 200, f/5.6, 1/80 second

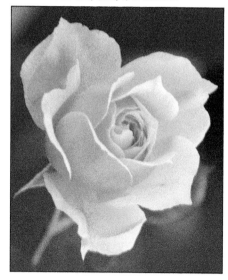
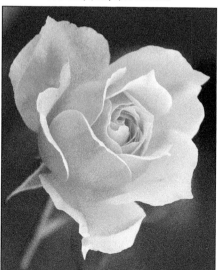

FIGURE 3-6:
For this image, raising the ISO allowed me to bump up the shutter speed enough to capture a blur-free shot while handholding the camera.

Fortunately, you don't encounter serious noise on the D5600 until you really crank up the ISO. In fact, you may even be able to get away with a fairly high ISO if you keep the print or display size small: Noise becomes more apparent as you enlarge the photo, as shown on the right in Figure 3-5. Noise is also easier to spot in shadow areas of the picture and in large areas of solid color.

How much noise is acceptable — and, therefore, how high of an ISO is safe — is your choice. Even a little noise isn't acceptable for pictures that require the highest quality, such as images for a product catalog or a travel shot that you want to blow up to poster size.

WARNING

A high ISO isn't the only cause of noise: A long exposure time (slow shutter speed) can also produce the defect. So, how high you can raise the ISO before the image gets ugly varies depending on shutter speed.

Doing the exposure balancing act

REMEMBER

As you change any of the three exposure settings — aperture, shutter speed, and ISO — one or both of the other two must also shift to maintain the same image brightness. Say that you're shooting a soccer game and you notice that although the overall exposure looks great, the players appear slightly blurry at the current shutter speed. If you raise the shutter speed, you have to compensate with a larger aperture (to allow in more light during the shorter exposure) or a higher ISO setting (to make the camera more sensitive to the light) — or both.

Again, changing these settings impacts the image in ways beyond exposure:

» Aperture affects depth of field, with a higher f-stop number increasing the distance over which objects appear sharp.

» Shutter speed affects whether motion of the subject or camera results in a blurry photo. A faster shutter "freezes" action and also helps safeguard against all-over blur that can result from camera shake when you're hand-holding the camera.

» ISO affects the camera's sensitivity to light. A higher ISO makes the camera more responsive to light but also increases the chance of image noise.

Returning to the soccer situation, then, if you want to increase shutter speed to freeze the action, you have to decide whether you prefer the shorter depth of field that comes with a larger aperture or the increased risk of noise that accompanies a higher ISO.

TIP

Different photographers use different approaches to finding the right combination of aperture, shutter speed, and ISO, and you'll no doubt develop your own system as you become more familiar with these concepts. In the meantime, here's how I handle things:

» I use ISO 100, the lowest setting on the camera, unless the lighting conditions are so poor that I can't use the aperture and shutter speed I want without raising the ISO.

» If my subject is moving, I give shutter speed the next highest priority in my exposure decision. I might choose a fast shutter speed to ensure a blur-free photo or, on the flip side, select a slow shutter to intentionally blur that moving object, an effect that can create a heightened sense of motion.

» For nonmoving subjects, I make aperture a priority over shutter speed, setting the aperture according to the depth of field I have in mind. For portraits, for example, I use a large aperture — say, in the range of f/2.8 to f/5.6 — so that I get a short depth of field, creating a nice, soft background for my subject. For landscapes, I usually go the opposite direction, stopping down the aperture as much as possible to capture the subject at the greatest depth of field. (Again, remember that the range of f-stops you can choose depends on your lens.)

Keeping all this straight is a little overwhelming at first, but the more you work with your camera, the more the whole exposure equation will make sense to you. You can find tips for choosing exposure settings for specific types of pictures in Chapter 6; keep moving through this chapter for details on how to actually adjust aperture, shutter speed, and ISO.

TIP

EXPOSURE STOPS: HOW MANY DO YOU WANT TO SEE?

In photo lingo, the word *stop* refers to an increment of exposure. To increase exposure by one stop means to adjust the aperture or shutter speed to allow twice as much light into the camera as the current settings permit. To reduce exposure a stop, you use settings that allow half as much light. Doubling or halving the ISO value also adjusts exposure by one stop.

By default, most exposure settings on your camera are based on one-third stop adjustments. If you prefer, you can tell the camera to present adjustments in half-stop increments so that you don't have to cycle through as many settings each time you want to make a change. Make your preferences known through the EV Steps for Exposure Cntrl setting, found in the Exposure section of the Custom Setting menu. This setting affects the shutter speed, aperture, Exposure Compensation, Flash Compensation, and exposure bracketing settings. It also determines the increment used to indicate the amount of under- or overexposure in the meter.

Obviously, the default setting provides the greatest degree of exposure fine-tuning, so I stick with that option. In this book, instructions assume that you're using the defaults as well.

Stepping Up to Advanced Exposure Modes (P, S, A, and M)

In the Auto, Auto Flash Off, Scene modes, and Effects exposure modes, you have little control over exposure. You may be able to choose from one or two Flash modes, and you can adjust ISO in some modes. But to gain full control over exposure, set the Mode dial to one of the advanced modes highlighted in Figure 3-7. You also need to use these modes to take advantage of many other camera features, including some of its color and autofocus options.

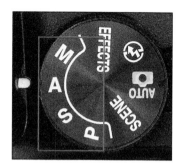

FIGURE 3-7:
You can control exposure and certain other picture properties fully only in P, S, A, or M mode.

The major difference between the four modes is the level of control you have over aperture and shutter speed. Here's how things shake out:

>> **P (programmed autoexposure):** The camera selects an initial aperture setting and shutter speed that it thinks will deliver a good exposure at the current ISO setting. But you can choose from different combinations of the two for creative flexibility. For example, if you're shooting action, you can pick the combo that offers the fastest shutter speed. Or, if you taking a portrait, you can choose the pairing that offers the lowest f-stop number in order to blur the background as much as possible.

>> **S (shutter-priority autoexposure):** You set the shutter speed, and the camera chooses the aperture setting that produces a good exposure at that shutter speed and the current ISO setting.

>> **A (aperture-priority autoexposure):** The opposite of shutter-priority autoexposure, this mode asks you to select the aperture setting. The camera then selects the appropriate shutter speed — again, based on the selected ISO setting.

>> **M (manual exposure):** In this mode, you specify both shutter speed and aperture. The brightness of your photo depends on the settings you select and the current ISO setting.

REMEMBER

To sum up, the first three modes are semiautomatic modes that are designed to offer exposure assistance while still providing you with some creative control. Note one important point about P, S, and A modes, however: In extreme lighting conditions, the camera may not be able to select settings that will produce a good exposure, and it doesn't stop you from taking a poorly exposed photo. You may be able to solve the problem by using features designed to modify autoexposure results, such as Exposure Compensation (explained later in this chapter) or by adding flash, but you get no guarantees.

Manual mode puts all exposure control in your hands. If you're a longtime photographer who comes from the days when manual exposure was the only game in town, you may prefer to stick with this mode. If it ain't broke, don't fix it, as they say. And in some ways, manual mode is simpler than the semiautomatic modes — if you're not happy with the exposure, you just change the aperture, shutter speed, or ISO setting and shoot again. By contrast, when you use the P, S, and A modes, you have to experiment with features that modify autoexposure results, such as the aforementioned Exposure Compensation.

So which mode should you use? Well, P mode is useful when you're first starting out because it automates exposure but gives you access to the camera's other controls (color options, focus options, and so on). But after you understand aperture and shutter speed and know what settings you want to use, I recommend leaving P mode behind. It's just too time consuming to work your way through a batch of shutter speed and aperture combinations to find one that is appropriate.

My choice is to use aperture-priority autoexposure when I'm shooting stationary subjects and want to control depth of field — aperture is my *priority* — and to switch to shutter-priority autoexposure when I'm shooting a moving subject and I'm most concerned with controlling shutter speed. Frankly, my brain is taxed enough by all the other issues involved in taking pictures — what my Release mode setting is, what resolution I need, where I'm going for lunch as soon as I make this shot work — that I appreciate having the camera do some of the exposure "lifting."

However, when I know exactly what aperture and shutter speed I want to use or I'm after an out-of-the-ordinary exposure, I use manual exposure. For example, sometimes when I'm doing a still life in my studio, I want to create a certain mood by underexposing a subject or even shooting it in silhouette. The camera will always fight you on that result in the P, S, and A modes because it so dearly wants to provide a good exposure. Rather than dial in all the autoexposure tweaks that could eventually force the result I want, I simply set the mode to M, adjust the shutter speed and aperture directly, and give the autoexposure system the afternoon off.

But even when you use the M exposure mode, you're never really flying without a net: The camera assists you by displaying the exposure meter, explained next.

Checking the Exposure Meter

Before explaining how to adjust aperture, shutter speed, and ISO, I want to introduce you to the *exposure meter*, which tells you whether your picture will be properly exposed at your chosen exposure settings.

If and when the meter appears depends on whether you shoot in the M, P, S, or A exposure mode:

>> **M mode:** The meter is always present in the Information and Live View displays, as shown in Figure 3-8. You also can see a simplified version of the meter in the viewfinder data display; Figure 3-9 offers a close-up look at that meter design.

REMEMBER

>> **P, S, and A modes:** The meter doesn't appear unless the camera anticipates an exposure problem — for example, if you're shooting in S (shutter-priority autoexposure) mode, and the camera can't select an f-stop that will properly expose the image at your chosen shutter speed and ISO. The meter also shows up if you enable Exposure Compensation. Through this feature, which I detail toward the end of this chapter, you can request a brighter or darker exposure on your next shot. The meter indicates the level of adjustment you request through the Exposure Compensation setting.

FIGURE 3-8:
In M exposure
mode, the
exposure
meter
appears in the
Information
and Live View
displays.

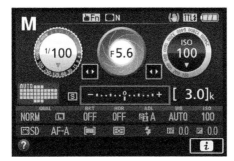
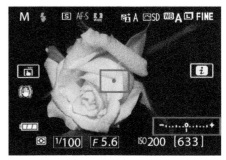
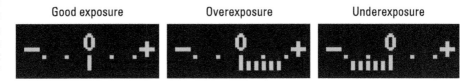

FIGURE 3-8:
In M exposure
mode, the
exposure
meter
appears in the
Information
and Live View
displays.

FIGURE 3-9:
The bars
under the
meter indicate
the amount
of under- or
overexposure.

Good exposure   Overexposure   Underexposure

Here's what you need to know about using the meter:

>> **Waking up the meter:** By default, the meter appears when you press the shutter button halfway and then turns off automatically after 8 seconds of inactivity to save battery power. To wake up the meter, just give the shutter button another half-press. (You can adjust the meter's auto shutdown timing via the Auto Off Timers option on the Custom Setting menu. Chapter 10 has details.)

>> **Reading the meter:** The minus-sign end of the meter represents underexposure; the plus sign, overexposure. If you see a single vertical bar under the 0 on the meter, as in Figure 3-8 and the left example in Figure 3-9, you're good to go. If small bars appear to the left or right of the zero mark, you have a problem. Bars appearing to the right of 0, as shown in the middle example in Figure 3-9, indicate that the image will be overexposed. Bars appear to the left of zero, as in the right example in Figure 3-9, indicate underexposure.

A couple other details to note:

TECHNICAL
STUFF

● *The markings on the meter indicate exposure stops.* The squares on either side of the 0 in the viewfinder display represent one full stop each. The small lines below, which appear only when the meter needs to indicate over- or underexposure, break each stop into thirds. So the middle readout in Figure 3-9, for example, indicates an overexposure of 1 and 2/3 stop. The right readout indicates the same amount of underexposure.

On the Information and Live View meters (refer to Figure 3-8), the concept is the same, but because these screens have room for a larger meter display, the third-stop meter positions appear along with the full-stop markings. The taller bars on the meter represent the full-stop position; the smaller bars between, the third-stop positions. Again, if the camera anticipates an exposure problem, bars appear *under* the meter to indicate the amount of under- or overexposure.

- *If a triangle appears at the end of the meter, the amount of over- or underexposure exceeds the range of the meter.* In other words, you have a serious exposure problem.

- *Don't forget that when Exposure Compensation is enabled, the meter indicates how much exposure adjustment is in force.* For example, if you ask the camera for a brighter picture on your next shot and you request a one-stop adjustment, the meter will indicate an overexposure of one stop. That's because the camera thinks its original exposure settings were dead on — and you're overriding that decision through Exposure Compensation.

- *You can reverse the meter orientation.* For photographers used to a camera that orients the meter with the positive (overexposure) side appearing on the left and the negative (underexposure) side on the right — the design that Nikon used for years — the D5600 offers the option to flip the meter to that orientation. Make that adjustment via the Reverse Indicators option, found in the Shooting/Display section of the Custom Setting menu.

>> **Understanding how exposure is calculated:** The information the meter reports is based on the *metering mode,* which determines which part of the frame the camera considers when calculating exposure. At the default setting, exposure is based on the entire frame, but you can select two other metering modes. See the next section for details.

REMEMBER

In Live View mode, metering may be calculated differently for some scenes than when you use the viewfinder, even if the same metering mode is in force. The rationale is to produce an exposure that's close to what you see in the live preview, which gets darker or lighter as you change exposure settings in an attempt to simulate the final exposure. However, I don't recommend that you trust the preview because it can be deceiving depending on the ambient light in which you're viewing the monitor. In addition, when you apply Exposure Compensation, an option that produces a brighter or darker image in the P, S, and A modes, the monitor can't adjust itself to accommodate the full range of Exposure Compensation settings. Long story short: The meter is a more accurate indication of exposure than the live preview.

REMEMBER

Finally, keep in mind that the meter's suggestion on exposure may not always be the one you want to follow. For example, you may want to shoot a backlit subject in silhouette, in which case you *want* that subject to be underexposed. In other words, the meter is a guide, not a dictator.

Choosing an Exposure Metering Mode

REMEMBER

To interpret the exposure meter, you need to know the current *metering mode*, which determines which part of the frame the camera analyzes to calculate exposure. The Information screen and Live View display contain a symbol representing the current metering mode; look in the areas labeled in Figure 3-10. (In Live View mode, press the Info button as needed to shift to a display that includes the symbol.)

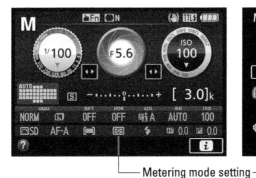 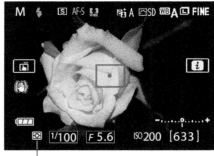

Metering mode setting

FIGURE 3-10: This symbol represents the Matrix metering mode.

You can choose from three metering modes, described in the following list and represented in the displays by the icons shown in the margins:

>> **Matrix:** The camera analyzes the entire frame and then selects an exposure that's designed to produce a balanced exposure.

>> **Center-weighted:** The camera bases exposure on the entire frame but puts extra emphasis — or *weight* — on the center of the frame. Specifically, the camera assigns 75 percent of the metering weight to an 8mm circle in the center of the frame.

>> **Spot:** In this mode, the camera bases exposure entirely on a circular area that's about 3.5mm in diameter, or about 2.5 percent of the frame.

For viewfinder photography, the location used for this pinpoint metering depends on an autofocusing option called the AF-area mode. Detailed in Chapter 4, this option determines which of the camera's focus points the autofocusing system uses to establish focus. Here's how the setting affects exposure metering:

- *If you choose the Auto Area mode,* in which the camera chooses the focus point for you, metering is based on the center focus point.

- *If you use any of the other AF-area modes,* which enable you to select a specific focus point, the camera bases metering on that point.

Because of this autofocus/autoexposure relationship, it's best to switch to one of the AF-area modes that allow focus-point selection when you want to use spot metering. In Auto Area mode, exposure may be incorrect if you compose your shot so that the subject isn't at the center of the frame.

In Live View mode, the area under the focus frame is used to calculate exposure when you use spot metering. Chapter 4 explains how the Live View focus frame works.

As an example of how the metering mode affects exposure, Figure 3-11 shows the same image captured in each mode. In the matrix example, the bright background caused the camera to select an exposure that left the statue dark. Switching to center-weighted metering helped somewhat but didn't quite bring the statue out of the shadows. Spot metering produced the best result as far as the statue goes, although the resulting increase in exposure left the sky a little washed out.

Matrix metering   Center-weighted metering   Spot metering

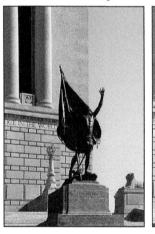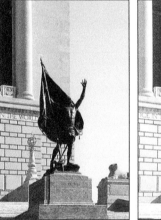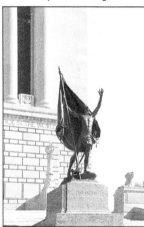

FIGURE 3-11:
The metering mode determines which area of the frame the camera considers when calculating exposure.

 Matrix metering is the default setting, and you can change the metering mode only in the P, S, A, and M exposure modes. The only way to adjust the setting is via the Information display or Live View control strip, as shown in Figure 3-12. Remember: Activate the strip by pressing the *i* button or tapping the *i* symbol on the touchscreen.

TIP

In theory, the best practice is to check the metering mode before you shoot and choose the one that best matches your exposure goals. But that's a bit of a pain, not just in terms of having to adjust yet one more capture setting but also in terms of having to *remember* to adjust one more capture setting. Here's my advice: Until you're really comfortable with all the other controls on your camera, just stick with the default setting, which is matrix metering. That mode produces good results in most situations, and after all, you can see in the monitor whether you disagree with how the camera metered or exposed the image and simply reshoot after adjusting the exposure settings to your liking. This option, in my mind, makes the whole Metering mode issue a lot less critical than it is when you shoot with film.

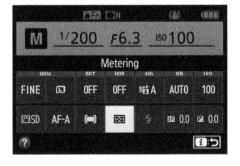 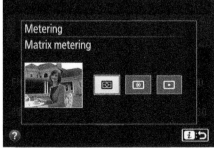

FIGURE 3-12:
Change the metering mode setting via the control strip.

The one exception might be when you're shooting a series of images in which a significant contrast in lighting exists between subject and background. Then, switching to center-weighted metering or spot metering may save you the time spent having to adjust the exposure for each image. (Don't worry about the background coming out too bright or too dark in those metering modes if your subject is properly exposed.)

Setting Aperture, Shutter Speed, and ISO

The next sections detail how to view and adjust these critical exposure settings. For a review of how each setting affects your pictures, check out the first part of this chapter.

Adjusting aperture and shutter speed

You can view the current aperture (f-stop) and shutter speed in the Information display and Live View display, as well as in the viewfinder, as shown in Figures 3-13 and 3-14. During viewfinder photography, you may need to give the shutter button a quick half-press and release to wake up the exposure meter. In Live View mode, you may need to press the Info button to cycle to a display that includes the aperture and shutter speed settings.

Shutter speed   Aperture (f-stop)

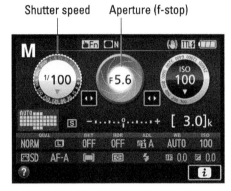

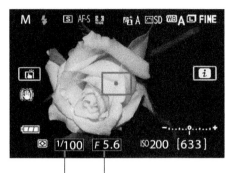

FIGURE 3-13:
You can view
the current
f-stop and
shutter speed
on the
Information
display and
Live View
screen.

Shutter speed   Aperture (f-stop)

REMEMBER

In the viewfinder, shutter speeds are presented as whole numbers, even if the shutter speed is set to a fraction of a second. For example, the number 100 indicates a shutter speed of 1/100 second. When the shutter speed slows to 1 second or more, quote marks appear after the number — 1″ indicates a shutter speed of 1 second, 4″ means 4 seconds, and so on.

You adjust the settings differently depending on the exposure mode, as follows:

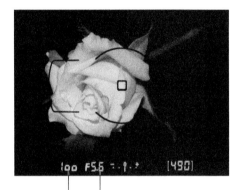

Shutter speed   Aperture (f-stop)

FIGURE 3-14:
The settings also appear in the viewfinder.

TIP

>> **P (programmed autoexposure):** The camera displays its recommended f-stop and shutter speed when you press the shutter button halfway. But you can rotate the Command dial to select a different combination of settings. The number of possible combinations depends on the aperture settings the camera can select, which depends on your lens.

An asterisk (*) appears next to the P symbol in the upper-left corner of the Information and Live View displays if you adjust the aperture/shutter speed settings. You see a tiny P* symbol at the left end of the viewfinder display as well. To get back to the initial combo of shutter speed and aperture, rotate the Command dial until the asterisk disappears from the displays and the P* viewfinder symbol turns off.

>> **S (shutter-priority autoexposure):** In this mode, you take control over shutter speed. The fastest way to set shutter speed is to rotate the Command dial. As you do, the camera automatically adjusts the aperture as needed to maintain proper exposure.

You can also use the touchscreen to adjust the shutter speed, as follows:

- *Information screen (viewfinder photography):* Tap the box highlighted on the left in Figure 3-15. You then see the screen shown on the right, with a box on either side of the shutter-speed display. Tap *those* boxes to change the shutter speed. Tap the exit arrow in the upper right corner of the display to lock in the setting and exit to the Information display.

FIGURE 3-15:
You can use these touchscreen controls to adjust shutter speed.

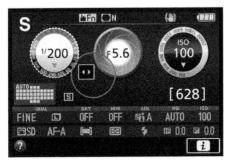
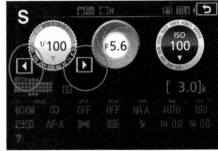

- *Live View photography:* Tap the shutter speed value (bottom of the display) to bring up adjustment arrows. Tap those arrows to increase or decrease the shutter speed and then tap the exit arrow in the upper-right corner of the screen.

Available shutter speeds range from 30 seconds to 1/4000 second *except* when flash is enabled. When you use flash, the top shutter speed is 1/200 second; minimum shutter speeds vary depending on the exposure mode. (See Chapter 2 for flash details.) This limitation is due to the way the camera must time the flash with the opening of the shutter.

WARNING

Even though you're working in shutter-priority mode, keep an eye on the f-stop, too, if depth of field is important to your photo. Remember that a low f-stop value produces shallow depth of field; a high value, long depth of field. Also note that in extreme lighting conditions, the camera may not be able to adjust the aperture enough to produce a good exposure at the current shutter speed. So you may need to compromise on shutter speed or ISO.

» **A (aperture-priority autoexposure):** Again, you can change the f-stop setting by rotating the Command dial or by using the touchscreen. In A mode, the touchscreen controls appear under the aperture readout on the Information display, and you can simply tap the f-stop setting value on the Live View display. The camera automatically selects the appropriate shutter speed needed to expose the image at your chosen aperture.

The range of available f-stop settings depends on your lens. For zoom lenses, the range typically also changes as you zoom in and out. For example, a lens may offer a maximum aperture of f/3.5 when set to its widest angle (shortest focal length) but limit you to f/5.6 when you zoom in to a longer focal length. Check your lens manual for details on the minimum and maximum aperture settings.

TIP

The circular graphic that displays the f-stop value in the Information display is designed to resemble an actual aperture. The center of the graphic grows or shrinks as you change the f-stop value, which indicates the setting is opening or closing the aperture, allowing in more or less light, respectively. Note that this graphic disappears if you switch from the default Information display style (called Graphic) to a simpler display (Classic). You adjust this setting via the Info Display Format option on the Setup menu; Chapter 10 has details.

WARNING

Again, just because you're controlling the f-stop doesn't mean you can ignore the shutter speed. After you set the f-stop, check the shutter speed that the camera chose to make sure you can handhold the camera at that speed without the risk of camera shake. And if your scene contains moving objects, verify the shutter speed is fast enough to stop action (or slow enough to blur it, if that's your creative goal). These same warnings apply when you use P mode.

» **M (manual exposure):** Set aperture and shutter speed like so:

- *Adjust shutter speed:* Rotate the Command dial or use the touchscreen controls, just as you do in shutter-priority mode.

  In Manual mode, you can access two shutter speed settings not available in the other modes: Choose the value one notch past the slowest speed (30 seconds) to access the *Bulb* setting, which keeps the shutter open as long as the shutter button is pressed. Rotate the dial one more time to access the *Time* setting. In that mode, you press the shutter button and release it to start the exposure and then depress the button again to end the exposure. The maximum exposure time is 30 minutes.

WARNING

  When you use Bulb and Time modes — or any time you select a slow shutter speed — using a tripod is also essential to ensuring a steady shot. But even the pressure of your finger on the shutter button may create enough vibration to blur the photo. So for best results, use a remote control to trigger the shutter release in these modes. No remote? Set the camera to Self-Timer Release mode, depress the shutter button, and then take your hands away from the camera.

- *Adjust aperture:* Press the Exposure Compensation button (on top of the camera) while rotating the Command dial. Notice the little aperture-like symbol that lies next to the button? That's your reminder of the button's role in setting the f-stop in M mode.

Fortunately for those of us who have a hard time remembering our phone number, let alone which button to press to access the f-stop in Manual mode, the camera also provides touchscreen access to the setting. For viewfinder shooting, tap the arrow box under the f-stop readout to access the adjustment arrows; during Live View shooting, just tap the f-stop value at the bottom of the screen.

In P, S, or A mode, the settings that the camera selects are based on what it thinks is the proper exposure. If you don't agree, you can switch the camera to manual exposure mode and dial in the aperture and shutter speed that deliver the exposure you want. Or, if you want to stay in P, S, or A mode, you can tweak exposure using the features explained in the section "Solving Exposure Problems," later in this chapter.

Controlling ISO

REMEMBER

The ISO setting adjusts the camera's sensitivity to light. A higher ISO enables you to use a faster shutter speed or a smaller aperture (higher f-stop number) because less light is needed to expose the image. But a higher ISO also increases the possibility of noise (refer to Figure 3-5).

You can't adjust ISO in the Auto and Auto Flash Off exposure modes and the Night Vision Effects mode. In other exposure modes, you can choose ISO values ranging from 100 to 25600. You also have the option of sticking with Auto ISO and letting the camera select the ISO it feels is appropriate for your chosen aperture and shutter speed. To see the current ISO setting, look in the Information and Live View displays, in the areas highlighted in Figure 3-16. The viewfinder reports the ISO value only when the option is set to Auto. The value appears on the right end of the viewfinder, just to the left of the Shots Remaining value. Otherwise, the ISO area of the viewfinder is empty.

FIGURE 3-16:
The ISO setting appears in the Information and Live View displays.

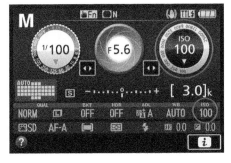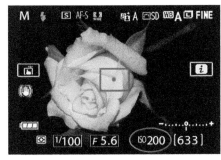

If you want to view the ISO setting in the viewfinder, you can tell the camera to display that number in the area normally reserved for the Shots Remaining value. Open the Custom Setting menu, select the Exposure submenu, and set the ISO Display option to On. You then must rely on the Information and Live View displays to check the Shots Remaining value. (All figures and instructions in this book assume that you stick with the default arrangement, which is to keep the Shots Remaining value visible in the viewfinder.)

To adjust ISO, you have these options:

>> **Fn (Function) button:** By default, pressing the Fn button (left-front side of the camera) highlights the ISO setting in the displays. Keep pressing the button while rotating the Command dial to change the setting.

>> **Information display or Live View control strip:** You also can adjust the setting via the control strip, as illustrated in Figure 3-17. Press the *i* button or tap the onscreen *i* icon to access the strip.

If you use the Multi Selector to highlight an ISO setting on the settings screen, you must press OK to lock in your choice. Tapping the return arrow in the lower-right corner exits the screen without changing the setting. For a quicker result, tap the setting you want to use. The camera adjusts the setting and returns you to the control strip screen.

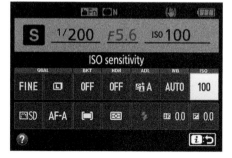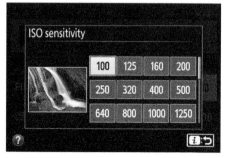

FIGURE 3-17: In the control strip, look for the ISO setting here.

>> **Shooting menu:** Finally, you can change the setting via the ISO Sensitivity Settings option on the Shooting menu, shown on the left in Figure 3-18. After choosing that option, choose ISO Sensitivity on the screen shown on the right to display the menu of available ISO setting. (The other options you see in Figure 3-18 are available only in the P, S, A, and M modes.)

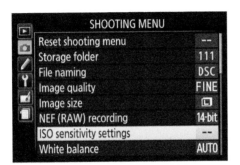
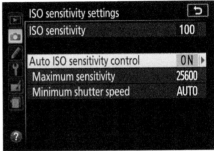

FIGURE 3-18:
Access
advanced ISO
options from
the Shooting
menu.

TIP

So what's up with the special menu options provided for the P, S, A, and M modes? Well, in those modes, Auto ISO doesn't appear as an option when you select an ISO setting. But if you enable the Auto ISO Sensitivity Control option, as shown on the right in Figure 3-18. you can enable Auto ISO as a backup. Here's how it works: You dial in a specific ISO setting — say, ISO 100. The camera uses that ISO if doing so will produce a good exposure. If not, it adjusts ISO as necessary.

After turning on Auto ISO Sensitivity Control, two additional menu items appear, as shown in the figure. Through these options, you can tell the camera when it should step in and offer ISO assistance:

>> **Maximum Sensitivity:** This option sets the highest ISO that the camera can use when it overrides the selected setting — a great feature because it enables you to decide how much noise potential you're willing to accept in order to get a good exposure. Even if the picture can't be properly exposed, the camera won't go any higher than the limit you set.

>> **Minimum Shutter Speed:** Set the minimum shutter speed at which the ISO override engages when you use the P and A exposure modes.

TIP

If you set this option to Auto, the camera selects the minimum shutter speed setting based on the focal length of your lens — the idea is that with a longer lens, you need a faster shutter speed to avoid the blur that camera shake can cause when you handhold the camera. You also have the option to select a specific shutter speed. However, ultimately, exposure trumps camera shake issues: If the camera can't expose the picture at what it thinks is a safe shutter speed for your lens focal length, it uses a slower speed. For this reason, I prefer to select a specific slow-shutter limit.

When the camera is about to override your ISO setting, it alerts you by blinking the ISO Auto label in the viewfinder and in the Live View display. The message "ISO-A" blinks in the Information display as well. When you view your pictures in the monitor, the ISO value appears in red if you use certain playback display modes. (Chapter 8 has details.)

To disable Auto ISO override, set Auto ISO Sensitivity Control to Off.

TIP

DAMPENING NOISE

High ISO settings and long exposure times can result in *noise,* a defect that gives pictures a speckled look. To help solve the problem, your camera offers two noise-removal filters: *Long Exposure Noise Reduction,* which dampens the type of noise that occurs during long exposures; and *High ISO Noise Reduction,* designed to reduce the appearance of ISO-related noise. You enable both filters from the Shooting menu.

If you turn on Long Exposure Noise Reduction, the camera applies the filter to pictures taken at shutter speeds of longer than 1 second. For High ISO Noise Reduction, you can choose from four settings. The High, Normal, and Low settings let you control the strength of the noise-removal effect. At the fourth setting, Off, the camera actually still applies a tiny amount of noise removal "as required." In other words, you can't really disable this function altogether. Nikon does promise that the amount of noise reduction at the Off setting is less than at the Low setting, so that's something.

Why would you want to turn off noise reduction? Because enabling it has disadvantages. First, the filters are applied after you take the picture, as the camera processes the image data. While the Long Exposure Noise Reduction filter is being applied, the message "Job Nr" appears in the viewfinder. The time needed to apply this filter can significantly slow your shooting speed.

Second, although filters that go after long-exposure noise work fairly well, those that attack high ISO noise work primarily by applying a slight blur to the image. Don't expect this process to totally eliminate noise, and do expect some resulting image softness. You may be able to get better results by using the blur tools or noise-removal filters found in many photo editors, because you can blur just the parts of the image where noise is most noticeable.

Solving Exposure Problems

Along with controls over aperture, shutter speed, and ISO, your camera offers a collection of tools designed to solve tricky exposure problems.

If the problem is underexposure due to a lack of ambient light, your camera's built-in flash is at the top of the list of exposure aids to consider. Chapter 2 explains how to get good flash results. But you also have several other exposure-correction features at your disposal, whether your subject appears under- or over-exposed. The next several sections introduce you to these features. Also check out

Chapter 11, which shows you how to tweak exposure of existing photos by applying tools found on the Retouch menu.

Applying Exposure Compensation

REMEMBER

In the P, S, and A exposure modes, you have some input over exposure. In P mode, you can rotate the Command dial to choose from different combinations of aperture and shutter speed; in S mode, you can dial in the shutter speed; and in A mode, you can select the aperture setting. But because these are semiautomatic modes, the camera ultimately controls the final exposure. If your picture turns out too bright or too dark in P mode, you can't simply choose a different f-stop/shutter speed combo because they all deliver the same exposure — which is to say, the exposure that the camera has in mind. And changing the shutter speed in S mode or adjusting the f-stop in A mode won't help either because as soon as you change the setting that you're controlling, the camera automatically adjusts the other setting to produce the same exposure it initially delivered. What about changing the ISO? Nope, that won't do the trick. The camera just recalculates the f-stop or shutter speed (or both) it needs to maintain the "proper" exposure at that ISO.

Not to worry: You actually do have final say over exposure in P, S, and A modes. The secret is Exposure Compensation, a feature that tells the camera to produce a brighter or darker exposure on your next shot, whether or not you change the aperture or shutter speed (or both, in P mode).

As an example of what Exposure Compensation can do, take a look at the first image in Figure 3-19. The initial exposure selected by the camera left the balloon too dark; I used Exposure Compensation to produce the brighter image on the right.

How the camera arrives at the brighter or darker image depends on the exposure mode. In A mode, the camera adjusts the shutter speed but leaves your selected f-stop in force. In S mode, the camera adjusts the f-stop and keeps its hands off the shutter speed control. In P, the camera decides whether to adjust aperture, shutter speed, or both. In all three modes, the camera may also adjust ISO if you enable Auto ISO Sensitivity Control. Keep in mind, though, that the camera can adjust f-stop only so much, according to the aperture range of your lens. And the range of shutter speeds, too, is limited by the camera itself. So there's no guarantee that the camera can actually deliver a better exposure when you dial in Exposure Compensation. If you reach the end of the f-stop or shutter speed range, you either have to adjust ISO or compromise on your selected f-stop or shutter speed.

EV 0.0   EV +1.0

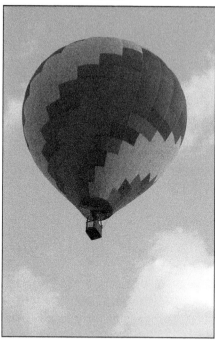 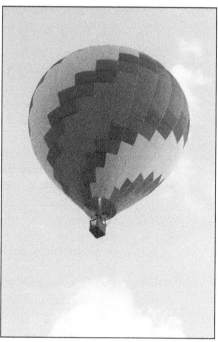

FIGURE 3-19:
For a brighter
exposure
in P, S, or A
mode, raise
the Exposure
Compensation
value.

With that background info out of the way, here are the details about this feature:

TIP

» **You also can apply Exposure Compensation in the Scene modes and Night Vision Effects mode.** In these modes, the camera decides which exposure setting to adjust to produce a brighter or darker picture.

» **Exposure Compensation is also available for shooting movies.** Chapter 7 details the art of cinematography with your D5600.

» **Exposure Compensation affects the meter in M exposure mode.** Although the camera doesn't change your selected exposure settings in M (manual) exposure mode if Exposure Compensation is enabled, the exposure *meter* is affected: It indicates whether your shot will be properly exposed based on the Exposure Compensation setting.

» **Exposure Compensation settings are stated in terms of EV numbers, as in EV +2.0.** Possible values range from EV +5.0 to EV –5.0. (*EV* stands for *exposure value.*) Each full number on the EV scale represents an exposure shift of one stop. A setting of EV 0.0 results in no exposure adjustment. For a brighter image, raise the Exposure Compensation value; for a darker image, lower the value. For my balloon image, I set the value to EV +1.0.

>> **Where and how you check the current setting depends on the display, as follows:**

- *Information display:* This one's straightforward: The setting appears in the control-strip area labeled on the left in Figure 3-20. In addition, the meter shows the amount of compensation being applied. In Figure 3-20, for example, the meter indicator appears one stop toward the positive end of the meter, reflecting the EV +1.0 setting.

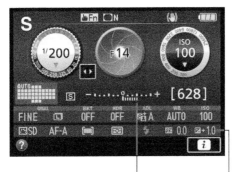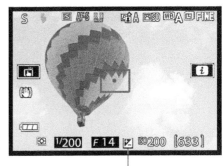

FIGURE 3-20:
These indicators tell you whether Exposure Compensation is enabled.

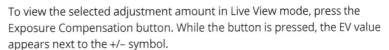

Meter showing EV +1.0 adjustment

Exposure Compensation enabled

Exposure Compensation setting

- *Live View display:* If Exposure Compensation is turned on, you see the +/– symbol labeled on the right in the figure; otherwise, that area of the display appears empty.

 To view the selected adjustment amount in Live View mode, press the Exposure Compensation button. While the button is pressed, the EV value appears next to the +/– symbol.

- *Viewfinder:* The viewfinder also displays the plus/minus symbol only, but again, you can press the Exposure Compensation button to temporarily view the EV setting. Or just look at the exposure meter: As in the Information display, the exposure meter tells you how much exposure shift is in force.

>> **You can change the Exposure Compensation setting in two ways:**

 - *Press the Exposure Compensation button while rotating the Command dial.* Pressing the button automatically activates the setting, and you can spin the Command dial to enter the amount of adjustment you want to apply.

- *Use the control strip.* You know the drill: Press the *i* button or tap the *i* symbol on the touchscreen to activate the strip. Then select the Exposure Compensation option, as shown on the left in Figure 3-21, to display the screen shown on the right, where you can set the amount of adjustment. Be sure to tap OK or press the OK button to lock in the new setting.

FIGURE 3-21:
One way
to adjust
Exposure
Compensation
is via the
control strip.

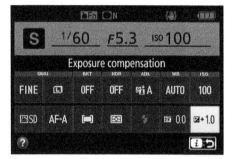
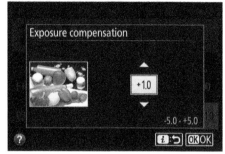

>> **As you adjust the setting in Live View mode, the monitor brightness updates to show you how the change will affect exposure.** However — and this is a biggie, so stop texting and pay attention — the preview can only show an adjustment up to +/– EV 3.0, even though you can set the adjustment as high as +/– EV 5.0. Also, if you don't see a change in the screen brightness as you adjust the Exposure Compensation value, check the shutter speed and aperture values. If one or the other is blinking, the camera is telling you that it can't provide you with the brighter or darker exposure because it's reached the limit of the available shutter speeds or f-stop settings.

>> **When you use flash, the Exposure Compensation setting affects both background brightness and flash power.** But you can further modify the flash power through a related option, Flash Compensation. You can find out more about that feature at the end of Chapter 2.

WARNING

>> **In the P, S, A, and M exposure modes, your Exposure Compensation setting remains in force until you change it, even if you power off the camera.** So always set the value back to EV 0.0 after taking the last shot for which you want to apply compensation. It's easy to forget that the feature is turned on, which can lead to over- or underexposed images when there is a change in lighting conditions.

For the Scene and Effects modes that allow you to set Exposure Compensation, the adjustment is reset to zero compensation when you turn the camera off or choose a different exposure mode.

Expanding tonal range

A scene like the one in Figure 3-22 presents the classic photographer's challenge: Choosing exposure settings that capture the darkest parts of the subject appropriately causes the brightest areas to be overexposed. And if you instead *expose for the highlights* — that is, set the exposure settings to capture the brightest regions properly — darker areas are underexposed.

Active D-Lighting Off

Active D-Lighting Auto

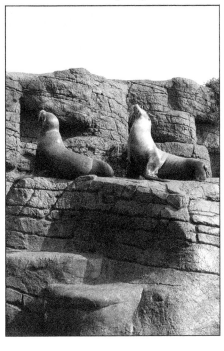 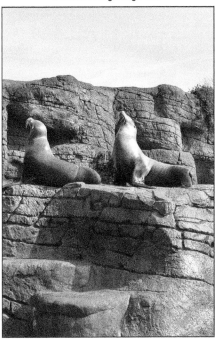

FIGURE 3-22: Active D-Lighting captured the shadows without blowing out the highlights.

In the past, you had to choose between favoring highlights or shadows. But with the D5600, you can expand *tonal range* — the range of brightness values in an image — through two features: Active D-Lighting and HDR (high dynamic range). The next two sections explain both options.

Applying Active D-Lighting

One way to cope with a high-contrast scene like the one in Figure 3-23 is to turn on Active D-Lighting. The *D* is a reference to *dynamic range,* the term used to describe the range of brightness values that an imaging device can capture. By turning on this feature, you enable the camera to produce an image with a slightly greater dynamic range than usual.

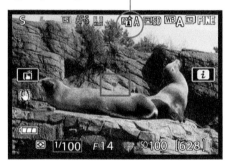
Active D-Lighting setting

REMEMBER

Specifically, Active D-Lighting gives you a better chance of keeping highlights intact while better exposing the darkest areas. In my seal scene, Active D-Lighting produced a brighter rendition of the darkest parts of the rocks and the seals, yet the color in the sky didn't get blown out, as it did when I captured the image with Active D-Lighting turned off. The highlights in the seal and in the rocks in the lower-right corner of the image also are toned down a tad in the Active D-Lighting version.

Active D-Lighting does its thing in two stages. First, it selects exposure settings that result in a slightly darker exposure than normal, which helps to retain highlight details. After you snap the photo, the camera brightens the darkest areas of the image to rescue shadow detail.

Symbols representing the current Active D-Lighting setting appear in the Information and Live View displays, in the areas circled in Figure 3-23. The symbol in the figures represents the Auto setting, which tells the camera to select the amount of exposure adjustment. I used this setting for my seal image. Note that when Active D-Lighting is turned off, the symbol disappears from the Live View display.

In Auto, Auto Flash Off, Scene, and Effects exposure modes, you're stuck with Auto Active D-Lighting; you can't disable the feature or vary the extent of the adjustment. In the P, S, A, and M modes, Auto is the default Active D-Lighting setting, but you can choose from five other settings: H* (extra high), H (high), N (normal), L (low), and Off.

TIP

I usually keep this option set to Off so I can decide for myself whether I want any adjustment instead of having the camera apply it to every shot. Even with a high-contrast scene that's designed for the Active D-Lighting feature, you may decide that you prefer the "contrasty" look that results from disabling the option.

To select the setting you want to use — again, available only in P, S, A, and M exposure modes — take either of these paths:

>> **Control strip:** Press the *i* button or tap the *i* symbol in the display to activate the control strip, and then select the Active D-Lighting option, as shown on the left in Figure 3-24. You're escorted to the screen shown on the right in the figure, where you can specify the adjustment level.

Remember that if you use the Multi Selector to highlight a setting, you must press OK to lock in that setting. To save yourself that step, just tap the setting you want to use.

FIGURE 3-24:
The fastest way to adjust the Active D-Lighting setting is via the control strip.

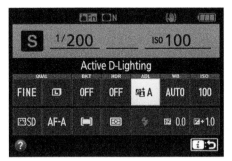
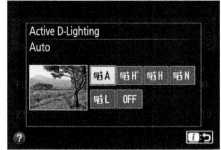

>> **Shooting menu:** You also can change the setting via the Shooting menu, as shown in Figure 3-25.

A few more pointers about using Active D–Lighting:

TIP

>> You get the best Active D-Lighting results in matrix metering mode.

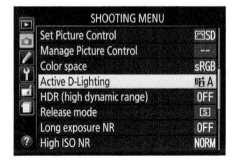

>> Nikon doesn't recommend that you use Active D-Lighting in the M exposure mode, but it's worth trying if you can't get results you like with

FIGURE 3-25:
But you also can change the setting via the Shooting menu.

the feature turned off. In M mode, the camera doesn't change the shutter speed or f-stop to achieve the darker exposure it needs for Active D-Lighting to work; instead, the meter readout guides you to select the right settings unless you have automatic ISO override enabled. In that case, the camera may instead adjust ISO to manipulate the exposure.

>> If you're not sure whether the picture will benefit from Active D-Lighting, try Active D-Lighting bracketing, which automatically records the scene once with the feature disabled and once at a level you select. See the section "Bracketing Exposure" at the end of this chapter for details.

TIP

If you opt out of Active D-Lighting, the Retouch menu offers a D-Lighting filter that applies a similar adjustment to existing pictures. See Chapter 11 for help.

Exploring high dynamic range (HDR) photography

In the past few years, many digital photographers have been experimenting with a technology called HDR photography. HDR stands for *high dynamic range* — again, dynamic range refers to the spectrum of brightness values that a camera or another imaging device can record.

The idea behind HDR is to capture the same shot multiple times, using different exposure settings for each image. You then use special imaging software, called *tone mapping software,* to combine the exposures in a way that uses specific brightness values from each shot. By using this process, you get a shot that contains a much higher dynamic range than the camera can capture in a single image.

TIP

The D5600 offers a feature that provides automated HDR photography. When you enable this option, the camera records two images, each at different exposure settings, and then does the tone-mapping manipulation for you to produce a single HDR image. This feature is available only in the P, S, A, and M exposure modes.

So how is HDR different from Active D-Lighting — other than the fact that it records two photos instead of manipulating a single capture? Well, with the HDR feature, you can request an exposure shift that results in up to three stops difference between the two photos. That enables you to create an image that has a broader dynamic range than you can get with Active D-Lighting.

Figure 3-26 shows an example of a scene that may benefit from the HDR feature. Half of the area is in bright sunshine, and the other is in shadow. When taking the top-left photo in the figure, I exposed for the highlights, which left the right side of the scene too dark. For the top-right image, I set exposure for the shaded area, which blew out the highlights in the sunny areas. By enabling the HDR feature, I was able to produce the bottom image in the figure. The shadows aren't completely eliminated, and some parts of the rose bush on the left side of the shot are a little brighter than I want, but on the whole, the camera balanced out the exposure fairly well.

Before you try the HDR feature, note these important points:

>> **Although the camera shoots two frames, you wind up with just a single HDR photo.** You can't play back or access the original two shots.

>> **Because the camera is recording and merging two photos, the feature works well only on stationary subjects.** If the subject is moving, it appears as two translucent forms in different areas in the merged frame.

Exposed for highlights

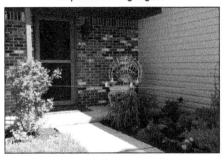

Exposed for shadows

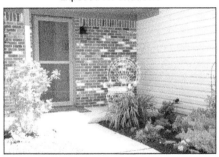

HDR, Extra High

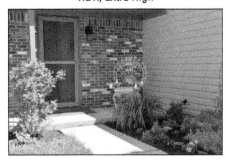

>> **Use a tripod to make sure that you don't move the camera between shots.** Otherwise, the merged shots may not align properly.

>> **When you enable HDR, you can't use flash, the Continuous Release modes, or the Raw (NEF) Image Quality setting.** Chapter 2 explains all three of these settings and how to adjust them.

>> **You can choose from four levels of HDR exposure shift: Low, Normal, High, or Extra High.** I used Extra High to produce the image in Figure 3-26. If you select Auto, the camera chooses what it considers the best adjustment.

WARNING

>> **The camera disables HDR after your first two frames are captured and merged.** That makes experimenting cumbersome because you have to continuously enable the feature each time you want to try different exposure settings or simply shoot another HDR frame. Annoying, to say the least.

I should also explain that if you want to produce the more-extreme type of HDR imagery that you see in photography magazines, you need to go beyond the two-frame, three-stop limitations of the in-camera HDR feature. To give you a point of comparison, Figure 3-27 shows an example I created by blending five frames with a variation of five stops between frames. The first two images show you the brightest and darkest exposures; the last image shows the HDR composite.

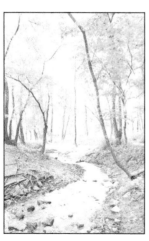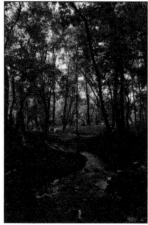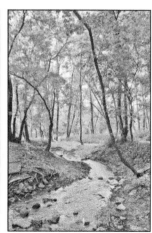

FIGURE 3-27:
Using HDR
software tools,
I merged the
brightest
and darkest
exposures
(left and
middle) along
with several
intermediate
exposures, to
produce the
composite
image (right).

On the other hand, the effect created by the camera's HDR tool looks more real-istic than the one in Figure 3-27. When applied to its extreme limits, HDR pro-duces something of a graphic-novel look. My example is pretty tame; some people might not even realize that any digital trickery has been involved. To me, it has the look of a hand-tinted photo.

And of course, even though the in-camera HDR tool may not be enough to produce the surreal HDR look that's all the rage these days, you can still use your D5600 for HDR work — you just have to adjust the exposure settings yourself between shots and then merge the frames using your own HDR software. You should also shoot the images in the Raw format because HDR tone-mapping tools work best on Raw images, which contain more bits of picture data than JPEG files.

All that said, the HDR feature is worth investigating when you're confronted with a high-contrast scene and you want to see how much you can broaden the dynamic range. Just take one shot with the feature enabled and a second with it turned off, and then compare the results to see which setting works best.

The Information screen and Live View displays indicate the HDR setting in the areas highlighted in Figure 3-28. (In the Live View display, the setting status appears only if you enable HDR.) To adjust the setting, use these options:

» **Control strip:** The fastest way to enable HDR and choose the level of expo-sure shift is via the control strip, as illustrated in Figure 3-29. To activate the control strip, press the *i* button or tap the onscreen *i* icon.

» **Shooting menu:** You also can set up your HDR shot via the Shooting menu, as shown on the right in Figure 3-29.

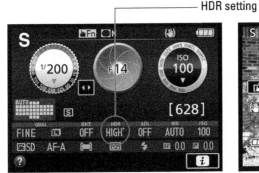

HDR setting

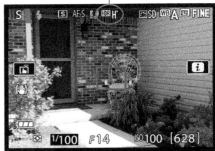

FIGURE 3-28:
These symbols
indicate the
HDR setting.

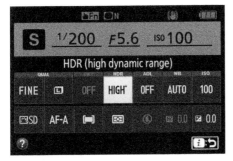

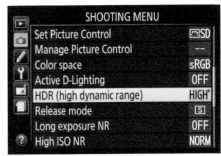

FIGURE 3-29:
Enable HDR
via the control
strip (left) or
Shooting
menu (right).

REMEMBER

Either way, frame your subject a little loosely; the camera may need to trim away the edges of the frame in order to perfectly align the two shots in the HDR image. When you press the shutter button, the camera records two frames in quick succession and then creates the merged HDR image. The message "Job Hdr" appears in the viewfinder as this digital manipulation is being accomplished.

Eliminating vignetting

Because of some optical science principles that are too boring to explore, some lenses produce pictures that appear darker around the edges of the frame than in the center, even when the lighting is consistent throughout. This phenomenon goes by several names, but the two heard most often are *vignetting* and *light fall-off*. How much vignetting occurs depends on the lens, your aperture setting, and the lens focal length.

To help compensate for vignetting, your camera offers a Vignette Control feature, which adjusts image brightness around the edges of the frame. Figure 3-30 shows an example. In the left image, just a slight amount of light fall-off occurs at the corners, most noticeably at the top of the image. The right image shows the same scene with Vignette Control enabled.

Vignette Control Off

Vignette Control, Normal setting

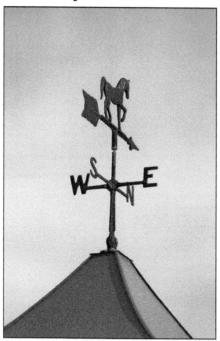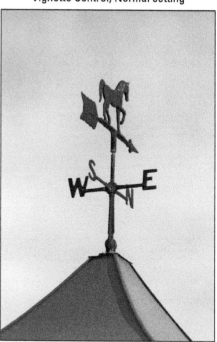

FIGURE 3-30:
Vignette
Control tries
to correct
the corner
darkening that
can occur with
some lenses.

Now, the "before" example hardly exhibits serious vignetting — it's likely that most people wouldn't even notice if it weren't shown next to the "after" example. But if you're a stickler for this sort of thing or your lens suffers from stronger vignetting, it's worth trying the feature. The adjustment is available in all your camera's exposure modes. You can choose from four Vignette Control settings: High, Normal, Low, and Off. Normal is the default.

When the feature is enabled, a symbol indicating the current level of adjustment appears in the Information screen; check the area highlighted in the left screen in Figure 3-31. If no symbol is visible, Vignette Control is turned off. The Live View display doesn't offer any indication about the Vignette Control status.

» **The correction is available only for still photos.** Sorry, video shooters; this feature doesn't apply in Movie mode.

» **Vignette Correction works only with certain lenses.** First, your lens must be Nikon Type G, E, or D (PC lenses excluded). In addition, the feature works only with DX lenses, which are lenses specifically made for the size of the sensor used by the D5600. The feature doesn't work with FX lenses, which are designed for the larger sensors used in so-called *full-frame cameras.*

Vignette Control set to Normal

FIGURE 3-31:
When Vignette
Control is
enabled, the
Information
display shows
the current
setting (left);
adjust the
setting through
the Shooting
menu (right).

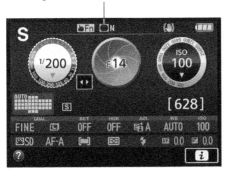

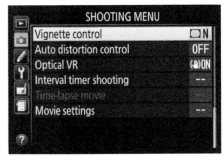

WARNING

>> **In some circumstances, the correction may produce increased noise at the corners of the photo.** This problem occurs because exposure adjustment can make noise more apparent.

Using autoexposure lock

To help ensure a proper exposure, your camera continually meters the light until the moment you depress the shutter button fully. In autoexposure modes, it also keeps adjusting exposure settings as needed to maintain a good exposure.

For most situations, this approach works great, resulting in the right settings for the light that's striking your subject at the moment you capture the image. But on occasion, you may want to lock in a certain combination of exposure settings before you're ready to snap the picture.

The easiest way to lock in exposure settings is to switch to M (manual) exposure mode and simply select the f-stop, shutter speed, and ISO settings that work best for your subject. But if you prefer to stay with an autoexposure mode, you can press the AE-L/AF-L button to lock the current autoexposure settings at any time after you press the shutter button halfway to initiate exposure metering. This feature is known as *autoexposure lock*, or AE Lock for short. You can take advantage of AE Lock in any autoexposure mode except Auto or Auto Flash Off.

A few fine points about using this feature:

>> **While AE Lock is in force, the letters AE-L appear in the displays.** Look for this indicator at the left end of the viewfinder; next to the metering mode icon at the bottom of the Live View display; and just beneath the shutter speed setting in the Information display.

>> **By default, focus is also locked when you press the button if you're using autofocusing.** You can change this behavior by customizing the AE-L/AF-L button function, as outlined in Chapter 10.

>> **For the best results, pair this feature with the Spot Metering mode and autofocus settings that enable to you select a single focus point.** Then, if you frame your subject under that focus point, exposure is set and locked based on your subject. You can find out how to use Spot metering earlier in this chapter; Chapter 4 explains autofocus settings.

>> **Be sure to keep holding down until you release the shutter button.** And if you want to use the same focus and exposure settings for your next picture, keep the AE-L/AF-L button pressed between shots.

Bracketing Exposures

Many photographers use *exposure bracketing* to ensure that at least one shot of a subject is properly exposed. *Bracketing* simply means to shoot the same subject multiple times, slightly varying the exposure settings for each image.

In the P, S, A, and M exposure modes, your camera offers *automatic bracketing.* When you enable this feature, your only job is to press the shutter button to record the shots; the camera automatically adjusts the exposure settings between each image. This feature is especially helpful in situations where you don't have time to review images and adjust exposure settings between shots. The D5600, however, takes things one step further than most cameras that offer automatic bracketing, enabling you to bracket not just basic exposure but also Active D–Lighting or white balance.

REMEMBER

The camera records a three–shot series of bracketed images when you use the autoexposure and white-balance bracketing options. For Active D–Lighting, you get only two shots in the series: one with the feature turned off and one at the setting currently in force for the Active D–Lighting option. (See "Applying Active D–Lighting," earlier in this chapter, for details on changing that setting.)

For exposure bracketing, the camera achieves the shift in exposure differently depending on your exposure mode. In A and M modes, your aperture setting is left alone, and the shutter speed is adjusted between shots. In S mode, the camera instead respects the shutter speed you select and varies the aperture setting between frames. In P mode, the camera may adjust aperture, shutter speed, or both. In all modes, your selected ISO setting remains unchanged. However, if you enable the Auto ISO Sensitivity option, explained earlier in this chapter, the camera may automatically adjust the ISO if it can't achieve the desired exposure shift by varying the f-stop or shutter speed.

Chapter 5 explains how to use the white-balance bracketing option. To try your hand at exposure or Active D-Lighting bracketing, follow these steps:

1. **Set your camera to the P, S, A, or M exposure mode.**

   You can't take advantage of the feature in any other mode.

2. **Display the Custom Setting menu and select Bracketing/Flash.**

   The menu shown on the left in Figure 3-32 appears.

3. **Select Auto Bracketing Set to display the screen shown on the right in the figure.**

   On this screen, you specify whether you want to bracket exposure (AE), white balance (WB), or Active D-Lighting (ADL). Note that even though the first option is called AE (for autoexposure), it enables you to bracket exposure in M (manual exposure) mode just the same.

FIGURE 3-32:
Before
enabling auto
bracketing,
select the
feature you
want the
camera to
adjust between
shots.

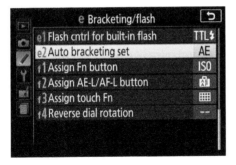
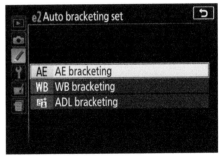

4. **Select the desired bracketing option.**

   If the touchscreen is enabled, just tap the option. If not, use the Multi Selector to highlight the setting and then press OK.

5. **Use the control strip to specify the bracketing increment.**

   After pressing the *i* button or tapping the *i* icon to activate the control strip, select the BKT setting, as shown on the left in Figure 3-33. On the next screen, shown on the right in the figure, choose the desired amount of shift you want the camera to apply when taking your bracketed shots. (Again, if you use the Multi Selector to select an option, press OK to finalize that step.)

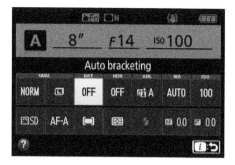 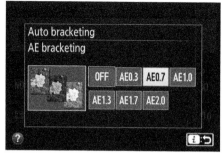

FIGURE 3-33:
Set the
bracketing
amount from
the control
strip.

The available settings depend on the feature you're bracketing, as follows:

- *For exposure bracketing,* the settings control the amount of exposure shift between frames. The settings are based on Exposure Compensation values. For example, if you choose 0.7 for an autoexposure bracketing set, the camera makes three exposures: one with exposure values as metered by the camera, one exposure with EV +0.7, and one exposure with EV –0.7 Your choices are from 0.3 EV to 2.0 EV. Choosing Off disables bracketing.

- *For Active D-Lighting bracketing,* you get only two options: ADL and Off. Select ADL. (This option is a little weird — if you select Off, you just disable bracketing.)

6. **After exiting the settings screen, exit the control strip by pressing the shutter button halfway and releasing it.**

   You also can tap the *i* symbol in the lower-right corner of the display.

7. **Shoot your first bracketed series.**

   Remember: For autoexposure bracketing, a series consists of three shots; for Active D-Lighting, two shots.

REMEMBER

   When bracketing is enabled, the Information and Live View displays offer a *bracketing indicator*. That's a technical way of saying, "Little bars appear under the meter, each one representing one shot in your bracketed series." Figure 3-34 shows the location of the bracketing indicator in the Information screen; in the Live View display, the indicator appears in the lower-right portion of the screen.

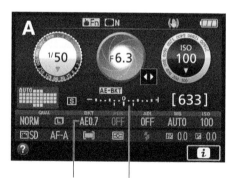

Bracketing amount   Bracketing indicator

FIGURE 3-34:
The bars under the meter tell you which frame of the bracketed series you're about to shoot.

The indicator updates after each picture to show you how many more shots are left in the series. For example, the middle bar represents your first shot; after you take your first picture, it disappears. You then see one or two bars — and thus, one or two shots left to shoot — depending on whether you're bracketing exposure or Active D-Lighting. A label on top of the meter reminds you which feature you're bracketing — AE-BKT (autoexposure) bracketing, in the figure.

8. **To disable bracketing, repeat Step 5 and select Off from the second screen, shown in Figure 3-34.**

   If you want to cancel bracketing in the middle of shooting a bracketed series, rotate the Mode dial to select any setting other than P, S, A, or M.

 If you set the Release mode to Continuous Low or Continuous High, you can save yourself some button pressing: In those two Release modes, the camera records the entire bracketed series with one push of the shutter button. To change the Release mode, press the Release Mode button (left front side of the camera) or select Release Mode from the Shooting menu. Remember, though, that you can't use flash in either Release mode. See Chapter 2 for more details about the Release mode setting.

IN THIS CHAPTER

» Understanding autofocusing options

» Choosing a specific autofocusing point

» Using continuous autofocusing to track a moving subject

» Using the touchscreen to set focus

» Taking advantage of manual-focusing aids

» Manipulating depth of field

Chapter **4**

Controlling Focus and Depth of Field

To many people, the word *focus* has just one interpretation when applied to a photograph: Either the subject is in focus or it's blurry. But an artful photographer knows that there's more to focus than simply getting a sharp image of a subject. You also need to consider *depth of field*, or the distance over which other objects in the scene appear sharply focused. This chapter explains how to manipulate both aspects of an image.

The chapter begins with details of the focusing options available for viewfinder photography; following that, you can get help with focusing during Live View photography and movie recording. Just a word of warning: The two focusing systems are quite different, and mastering them takes time and practice. So don't think that you're not up for the challenge if everything doesn't sink in right away. If you start feeling overwhelmed, take a break and simplify things by following the steps laid out at the end of Chapter 1, which show you how to take a picture using the default autofocus settings and the Auto exposure mode. Then return another day to study the advanced focusing options discussed here.

Things get much easier (and more fun) at the end of the chapter, where I explain how to control depth of field. Thankfully, the concepts related to that subject apply no matter whether you're using the viewfinder, taking advantage of Live View photography, or shooting movies.

Choosing Automatic or Manual Focusing

REMEMBER

Regardless of whether you're using the viewfinder or Live View, your first focusing task is to set the lens to automatic or manual mode. How you take this step depends on whether you're using an AF-P or AF-S lens:

>> **AF-P:** If the lens is in its retracted position, hold down the button labeled on the left in Figure 4-1 and rotate the lens barrel to extend it as shown in the figure. You can't access focusing options (or do much of anything else) while the lens is collapsed. Choose the focusing method via the Focus mode option on the control strip. (I provide details in upcoming sections.)

FIGURE 4-1:
On an AF-P lens (left), extend the lens and set the Focus mode via the control strip; on an AF-S lens (right), you can use external controls to set the lens to automatic or manual focusing.

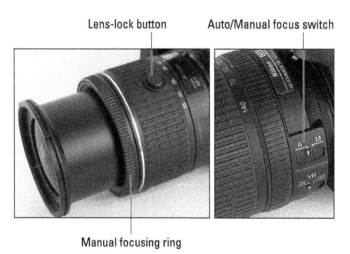

Lens-lock button   Auto/Manual focus switch

Manual focusing ring

TIP

The 18–55mm AF-P lens featured in this book offers *autofocus with manual override*. That means when the camera is set to autofocus mode, you can press the shutter button halfway to set focus initially using autofocusing and then fine-tune focus by rotating the lens focusing ring. (I labeled the focusing ring in Figure 4-1.) Here are two important points to note about manual-focus override:

● *Keep the shutter button pressed halfway while turning the manual focusing ring.* If you release the button, there's a chance that when you press it to take the picture, the camera will reset autofocus, undoing your manual adjustment.

- *You can disable manual focus override.* It's easy to inadvertently move the manual focusing ring when you don't realize it, thereby changing the focusing distance. If you prefer not to run this risk, open the Custom Setting menu, select the Autofocus submenu, and change the Manual Focus Ring in AF Mode option to Disable.

>> **AF-S:** On AF-S lenses, you usually find an external switch that sets the lens to manual or automatic focusing. For example, on the lens shown on the right in Figure 4-1, setting the switch to the A position enables autofocusing; move the switch to M for manual focusing. The switches vary depending on your lens, however. On some lenses, the switch labels are AF and MF (for autofocus and manual focus). Your lens may also offer autofocus with manual override, usually indicated by a switch labeled AF/M. The position of the manual focus ring also varies depending on the lens, so see your lens instruction guide for details.

WARNING

Note that some newer AF-S lenses are the collapsible type, so you may need to extend the lens, just as with an AF-P lens, before you can use the camera.

Whichever lens type you use, here are two important notes about autofocusing:

REMEMBER

>> **By default, the camera won't release the shutter until focus is achieved if you use autofocusing.** If you can't get the camera to lock onto your focusing target, switching to manual focusing is the easiest solution. Also be sure that you're not too close to your subject; if you exceed the minimum focusing distance of the lens, you can't focus manually, either.

For viewfinder photography, you have the option of disabling the focus-related shutter release lock during continuous autofocusing; see the upcoming section "Changing the Focus mode setting" for details.

>> **In Night Vision Effects mode, you can autofocus only in Live View mode.** If you use the viewfinder, you're limited to manual focusing. Chapter 11 covers Night Vision and other Effects modes.

Exploring Standard Focusing Options (Viewfinder Photography)

In case you're the type who doesn't read chapter introductions (I bring this up only because I'm that type), I want to reiterate that the D5600 uses different focusing technologies depending on whether you're using the viewfinder or taking advantage of Live View. This part of the chapter deals with viewfinder photography. For help with the other half of the focusing equation, skip to the section "Focusing in Live View Mode."

Mastering the D5600 focus system

The most important thing to remember about autofocusing is that how the camera sets focus is determined by two settings: Focus mode and AF-area mode. Upcoming sections offer details, but here's the short story:

>> **Focus mode:** This setting determines whether the camera uses automatic or manual focusing, as explained in the first section of this chapter. But in some exposure modes, the Focus mode setting offers a choice of autofocusing options. You can tell the camera to lock focus when you press the shutter button halfway; adjust focus continually up to the moment you depress the button fully to take the picture; or decide for you which option is best.

>> **AF-area mode:** This setting determines which focus points the camera uses to establish focus. You can tell the camera to choose a point (or multiple points) for you or to base focus on a specific point that you select.

Symbols representing both settings appear in the Information display, as shown in Figure 4-2. The symbols in the figure represent the AF-A Focus mode and the Auto-area AF-area mode. At these settings, the camera decides whether to lock focus when you press the shutter button halfway and also selects the focus point for you.

The next sections describe each Focus mode and AF-area mode setting and offer advice on which combinations work best for different subjects.

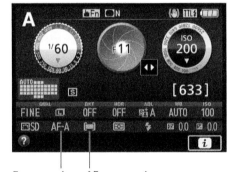

Focus mode   AF-area mode

FIGURE 4-2:
The Focus mode and AF-area mode settings appear here.

Changing the Focus mode setting

Choose the Focus mode via the Information display control strip, as illustrated in Figure 4-3. *Remember:* To activate the control strip, press the *i* button or tap the *i* symbol on the Information screen (not shown in the figure).

When the camera is in the P, S, A, or M exposure mode, you can choose from four options, which work as detailed in the following list. In other exposure modes, you can choose only AF-A and MF. The exception, again, is the Night Vision Effects mode, which limits you to manual focusing when you use the viewfinder to compose the scene.

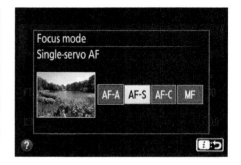

FIGURE 4-3:
You can access all Focus mode settings only in the P, S, A, and M exposure modes.

>> **AF-A (auto-servo autofocus):** This mode gives the camera control over whether focus is locked when you press the shutter button halfway or continuously adjusted until you snap the picture. The camera bases its decision on whether it detects motion in front of the lens.

WARNING

The problem with AF-A mode is that if your subject is stationary but people or objects are moving nearby, the camera may see that surrounding movement and mistakenly switch to continuous autofocus. By the same token, if the subject is moving only slightly, the camera may *not* select continuous autofocusing. So my advice is to choose one of the next two Focus modes instead, assuming you're shooting in the P, S, A, or M exposure modes.

>> **AF-S (single-servo autofocus):** Designed for shooting stationary subjects, this setting locks focus when you depress the shutter button halfway. Shutter release is disabled until focus is achieved.

>> **AF-C (continuous-servo autofocus):** Geared to photographing moving subjects, this mode initiates autofocusing when you press the shutter button halfway and then adjusts focus continuously as needed until you take the picture. (You need to keep the button pressed halfway to maintain the focus adjustment.)

TIP

By default, AF-C mode prevents you from taking a picture until focus is achieved, just like AF-S mode. But you can tell the camera to capture the shot at the instant you fully depress the shutter button regardless of whether focus is set. Make the call via the AF-C Priority Selection option, found in the Autofocus section of the Custom Setting menu and shown in Figure 4-4. Focus is the default setting; choose Release to allow shutter release before focus is set.

For the most part, I stick with Focus. Yes, I may miss a few shots waiting for the camera to focus, but if they're going to be out of focus, who cares? But when my subject is moving at a really rapid pace, I do unlock the shutter release. Although I may wind up with lots of wasted shots, I also increase the odds that I'll capture that split-second "highlight reel" moment. If the subject is slightly out of focus, I can probably retouch it enough to make it passable, especially if the picture content is truly special.

FIGURE 4-4:
This set-
ting controls
whether you
can take
a picture
before focus
is achieved in
the AF-C Focus
mode.

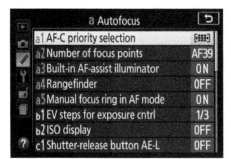

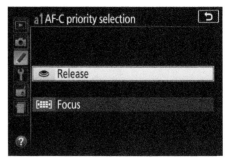

>> **MF (manual focus):** Choose this setting to shut off the autofocusing system and focus manually. On AF-P lenses, this is the only way to set the lens to manual focus.

TIP

On Nikon AF-S lenses, moving the focus switch on the lens to M (or MF) automatically sets the Focus mode to MF. However, the opposite isn't true: Setting the camera's Focus mode to MF does not free the lens focusing ring so that you can set focus manually. You must set the lens switch to the M position. For other lenses, check the lens instruction manual for focusing details.

Choosing an AF-area mode: One focus point or many?

The D5600 has 39 available autofocus points, which are located within the frame region indicated by the autofocus brackets in the viewfinder. Figure 4-5 shows you the approximate location of the individual points. (You don't actually see the points in the view-finder; when you press the shutter but-ton halfway, one or more points lights up, depending on your autofocusing settings.)

Autofocus brackets

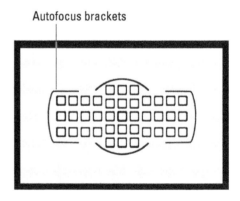

FIGURE 4-5:
The camera's 39 autofocus points are located within the portion of the frame surrounded by the AF-area brackets.

REMEMBER

The AF-area mode tells the camera which autofocus points to consider when establishing focus. You have these choices:

>> **Single-point:** This mode is designed to quickly and easily lock focus on a still subject. You select a focus point, and the camera bases focus on that point only. This option is best paired with the single-servo (AF-S) Focus mode, which

is also geared to still subjects. I explain how to select a focus point a little farther down the road.

>> **Dynamic-area:** Dynamic-area autofocusing is designed for capturing moving subjects. You select an initial focus point, but if your subject moves away from that point before you snap the picture, the camera looks to surrounding points for focusing information.

REMEMBER

To use this autofocusing option, you must first set the Focus mode to AF-C or AF-A. You then can choose from the following Dynamic-area settings, each of which analyzes a different group of autofocus points:

- *9-point Dynamic-area:* Rather than look at all 39 autofocus points, the camera takes focusing cues from the initial focusing point you select and the 8 surrounding points. If you choose the center focus point, for example, the points shown on the left in Figure 4-6 are active. This setting is ideal when you have a moment or two to compose your shot and your subject is moving in a predictable way, making it easy to reframe as needed to keep the subject within the 9-point area.

FIGURE 4-6:
The camera considers these autofocus points when you select the center focus point and use the 9-point (left) and 21-point (right) Dynamic-area modes.

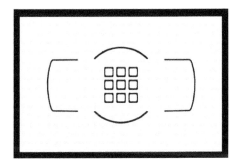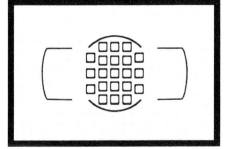

TIP

This setting provides the fastest Dynamic-area autofocusing because the camera has to analyze the fewest number of autofocusing points.

- *21-point Dynamic-area:* The camera analyzes your selected point plus the 20 surrounding points. The right screen in Figure 4-6 shows you which points are active if you select the center point.

Obviously, having 21 points active enables your subject to move a little farther afield from your selected focus point and still remain in the focusing target zone. So it works better than 9-point mode when you can't quite predict the path your subject will take.

- *39-point Dynamic-area:* The camera bases initial focusing on your selected focus point, as in the other Dynamic-area modes, but then looks to all other focus points if your subject moves from that selected point. This mode is designed for subjects that are moving so rapidly that it's hard to keep them within the framing area of the 21-point or 9-point setting — a flock of birds, for example. The drawback is focusing time: With all 39 points on deck, the camera has to do a little more work to find a focus target.

>> **3D-tracking:** This one is a variation of 39-point Dynamic-area autofocusing. As in that mode, you start by selecting a single focus point and then press the shutter button halfway to set focus. But the goal of the 3D-tracking mode is to maintain focus on your subject if you recompose the shot after you press the shutter button halfway to lock focus.

The problem with 3D-tracking is that the camera detects your subject by analyzing the colors of the object under your selected focus point. So if not much difference exists between the subject and its background, the camera can get fooled. And if your subject moves out of the frame, you must release the shutter button and reset focus by pressing it halfway again.

As with Dynamic-area mode, if you want to use 3D-tracking autofocus, you must set the Focus mode to AF-C or AF-A.

REMEMBER

You can select from the full complement of AF-area mode settings in all exposure modes *except* the Miniature and Night Vision Effects modes. Miniature mode always uses Single-point mode, and autofocusing is off-limits altogether in Night Vision mode for viewfinder photography.

You can view the current AF-area mode setting in the Information screen, in the area highlighted in Figure 4-7. The symbol in the figure represents the Auto-area mode.

Here's how to change the setting and, in modes other than Auto-area, select a focus point:

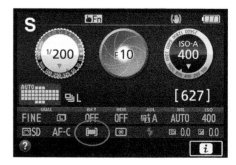

FIGURE 4-7:
This part of the Information screen shows the current AF-area mode setting (Auto-area, in the figure).

>> **Changing the setting:** Get the job done via the Information display control strip, as shown in Figure 4-8.

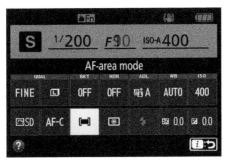

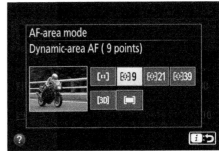

FIGURE 4-8:
Select the
AF-area mode
setting via the
Information
display control
strip.

TIP

When you return to the Information display, notice the graphic highlighted in Figure 4-9. This symbol gives you information about which focus points are active. In Auto-area mode, all the squares are solid, indicating that the camera can select any point it chooses. In the other modes, a solid gray square indicates the currently selected focus point. A fuzzy gray square indicates the point is active, meaning that if the camera can't establish focus based on the selected point, it may consider the other active points. In the figure, the symbol reflects the 9-point Dynamic-area setting with the center point selected, for example.

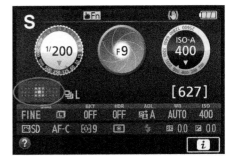

FIGURE 4-9:
This symbol gives you more information about which autofocus points are active in the current AF-area mode.

>> **Selecting a single focus point:** To choose a focus point in the Single-point, Dynamic-area, or 3D-tracking modes, exit any menus or selection screens so that the camera is in shooting mode. Then look through the viewfinder and press the shutter button halfway and release it. The currently selected point flashes red and then turns black. For example, in Figure 4-10, the point directly over the top of the clock tower is selected. Use the Multi Selector to cycle through the available focus points until the one you want to use flashes red and then turns black. You also can use the Information display Focus

Selected focus point

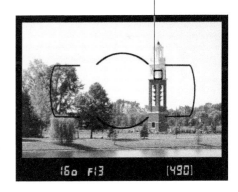

FIGURE 4-10:
Use the Multi Selector to select the focus point that's over your subject.

TIP

points symbol (see Figure 4-9) to monitor the position of the focus point; again, the selected point appears solid.

To quickly select the center focus point, press the OK button.

A few additional tips:

>> **You can reduce the number of focus points available for selection from 39 to 11.** Why would you do this? Because it enables you to choose a focus point more quickly — you don't have to keep pressing the Multi Selector zillions of times to get to the one you want to use. Make the change via the Number of Focus Points option, found in the Autofocus section of the Custom Setting menu, as shown on the left in Figure 4-11. The right half of the figure shows you which autofocus points you can select at the chosen setting.

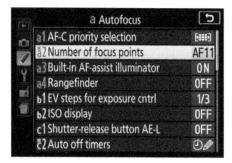
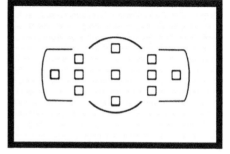

FIGURE 4-11:
You can limit the number of focus points available for selection to the 11 shown here.

If you change the setting to 11, the Information display symbol that represents the active autofocus points changes to show the reduced number of selectable points.

>> **The nine autofocus points at the center of the frame are more capable than others.** These points use *cross-type sensors,* which evaluate focus by analyzing both horizontal and vertical lines in the scene. The other points assess only horizontal lines. Cross-type sensors typically work better, especially in dim lighting, so if you're having trouble getting the camera to focus, select one of these focus points.

REMEMBER

>> **When you use spot metering, the camera bases exposure on the selected focus point.** The point you choose affects the way the camera calculates flash exposure as well. See Chapter 3 for details on spot metering; see Chapter 2 for help with flash photography.

>> **In any exposure mode except P, S, A, or M, the camera resets the AF-area mode to the default setting if you change exposure mode.** So this setting is

one that you need to check before every shoot if you aren't using the P, S, A, or M modes. Oddly, the AF-area mode isn't reset if you simply turn the camera off.

Choosing the right autofocus combo

TIP

You get the best autofocus results if you pair your chosen Focus mode with the most appropriate AF-area mode, because the two settings work in tandem. Here are the combinations I suggest:

>> **For still subjects: AF-S and Single-point.** You select a focus point, and the camera locks focus on that point when you press the shutter button halfway. (It helps to remember the *s* factor: For *still* subjects, *Single*-point and AF-*S*.)

>> **For moving subjects: AF-C and 39-point Dynamic-area.** You still begin by selecting a focus point, but the camera adjusts focus as needed if your subject moves within the frame after you press the shutter button halfway to establish focus. (Think *motion, dynamic, continuous.*) Remember to reframe as needed to keep your subject within the boundaries of the autofocus points, though. And if you want speedier autofocusing, consider switching to 21-point or 9-point Dynamic-area mode — just remember that you need to keep your subject within that smaller portion of the frame for the focus adjustment to work properly.

The next two sections spell out the steps you use to set focus with both autofocus pairings.

Autofocusing with still subjects: AF-S + Single Point

For stationary subjects, the fastest, most precise autofocus option is to pair the AF-S (single-servo) Focus mode with the Single-point AF-area mode, as shown in Figure 4-12.

After selecting these options (via the Information display control strip), follow these steps to focus:

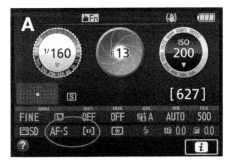

FIGURE 4-12: Select these autofocus settings for stationary subjects.

1. **Looking through the viewfinder, use the Multi Selector to position the focus point over your subject.**

   The focus point is represented by a black rectangle within the AF-area brackets. Figure 4-13 shows the point

I selected for the clock-tower scene. The point also appears solid when you view the AF-point graphic on the Information display. (Refer to Figure 4-9.)

REMEMBER

If the focus point doesn't respond, press the shutter button halfway and release it to wake up the camera. Then try again.

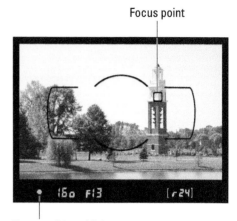

Focus point

2. **Press the shutter button halfway to set focus.**

When focus is achieved, the camera displays a green focus light in the viewfinder (refer to Figure 4-13). Unless you're using the Quiet Shutter release mode, you also hear a beep. (You can disable the sound through the Beep option on the Setup menu.)

Focus achieved light

FIGURE 4-13:
The camera won't take the picture until focus is achieved and the green focus indicator lights up.

Focus remains locked as long as you keep the shutter button pressed halfway. If you're using autoexposure (any exposure mode but M), the initial exposure settings are also chosen at the moment you press the shutter button halfway, but they're adjusted as needed up to the time you take the shot.

3. **Press the shutter button the rest of the way to take the shot.**

TIP

If needed, you can position your subject outside a focus point. Just compose the scene initially so that your subject is under a point, press the shutter button halfway to lock focus, and then reframe. However, if you're using autoexposure, you may want to lock focus and exposure together before you reframe, by pressing the AE-L/AF-L button. Otherwise, exposure is adjusted to match the new framing, which may not work well for your subject. See Chapter 3 for more details about autoexposure lock.

Focusing on moving subjects: AF-C + Dynamic Area

To autofocus on a moving subject, select AF-C for the Focus mode and choose one of the Dynamic-area options for the AF-area mode, as shown in Figure 4-14. The earlier section "Choosing an AF-area mode: One focus point or many?" provides information to help you decide whether to use the 9-, 21-, or 39-point Dynamic-area setting.

The focusing process is the same as just outlined, with the following exceptions:

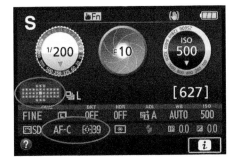

FIGURE 4-14:
These symbols indicate the AF-C and 39-point Dynamic Area settings for the Focus mode and AF-area mode.

» **When you press the shutter button halfway, the camera sets the initial focusing distance based on your selected autofocus point.** But if your subject moves from that point, the camera checks surrounding points for focus information.

» **Focus is adjusted as needed until you take the picture.** You see the green focus indicator light in the viewfinder, but it may flash on and off as focus is adjusted. The beep that you usually hear when using the AF-S Focus mode doesn't sound in AF-C mode, which is a Good Thing — otherwise, things could get pretty noisy because the beep would sound every time the camera adjusted focus.

» **Try to keep the subject under the selected focus point to increase the odds of good focus.** But as long as the subject falls within one of the other focus points (9, 21, or 39, depending on which Dynamic-area mode you selected), focus should be adjusted accordingly. Note that you don't see the focus point actually move in the viewfinder, but the focus tweak happens just the same. You can feel and sometimes even hear the focus motor doing its thing, if you pay attention.

Getting comfortable with continuous autofocusing takes some time, so it's a good idea to practice before you need to photograph an important event. After you get the hang of the AF-C/Dynamic-area system, though, I think you'll really like it.

TIP

On occasion, you may want to switch to Single-point AF-area mode when using continuous autofocusing. For example, if you're photographing a tuba player in a marching band, you want to be sure that the camera tracks focus on just that musician. With Dynamic-area, it is possible that the focus may drift to another nearby band member. The difficulty with the Single-point/Dynamic-area pairing is that you must constantly reframe to keep your subject under the single point you selected. I like to use the center point with this setup; I find it more intuitive because I just reframe as needed to keep my subject in the center of the frame. (You can always crop your image to achieve a different composition after the shot.)

PREVENTING SLOW-SHUTTER BLUR

A poorly focused photo isn't always caused by incorrect focusing. A slow shutter speed can also cause blurring if your subject or the camera itself moves during the exposure.

Chapter 3 explains shutter speed in detail, but here's the short story as it relates to focus: When you photograph moving subjects, a slow shutter speed can make them appear blurry. And when you handhold the camera, camera shake can blur the entire photo.

You can avoid camera shake by using a tripod, of course. But for times when you don't have a tripod or other way to steady the camera, some lenses offer a feature that can compensate for small amounts of camera shake. On Nikon lenses, this feature is called Vibration Reduction (VR), but other manufacturers use other names, such as Vibration Compensation or Optical Stabilization. The Nikon AF-P lens featured in this book offers this feature; enable and disable it via the Optical VR setting on the Shooting menu, shown in the left figure here. (If the option is dimmed in the menu, your AF-P lens doesn't offer Vibration Reduction.)

If you put an AF-S lens on the D5600, the Optical VR menu item disappears. Instead, if the lens offers Vibration Reduction, you enable the feature via a lens switch, usually labeled VR. Higher-end lenses sometimes offer two levels of vibration reduction, one for very normal levels of vibration and one for extreme vibration (such as when you're taking pictures while zipping across a lake in a speed boat).

Either way, when Vibration Reduction is turned on, the Information and Live View screens display the shaking hand symbol highlighted in the second figure. If you turn the feature off, the hand disappears.

For Nikon lenses, turn off Vibration Reduction when you use a tripod so that the camera doesn't try to compensate for movement that isn't occurring. If you use a third-party lens, check the user manual for details on whether the lens offers this feature and, if so, when and how to enable it.

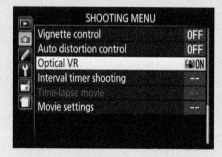
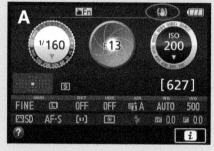

Using autofocus lock to interrupt continuous autofocusing

When you set your camera's Focus mode to AF-C (continuous-servo autofocus), focusing is continually adjusted while you hold the shutter button halfway, so the focusing distance may change if the subject moves out of the active autofocus point or you reframe the shot before you take the picture. The same is true if you use AF-A mode (auto-servo autofocus) and the camera senses movement in front of the lens, in which case it operates as I just described. Either way, the upshot is that you can't control the exact focusing distance the camera ultimately uses.

Should you want to interrupt continuous autofocusing and lock focus at the current distance, press the AE-L/AF-L button. Focus remains set as long as you hold down the button. If you release the button, continuous autofocusing begins again.

Keep in mind, though, that by default, pressing the AE-L/AF-L button also locks autoexposure. You can change this behavior, however, setting the button to lock just one or the other. Chapter 10 explains this option.

Focusing manually

Some subjects confuse even the most sophisticated autofocusing systems, causing the camera's autofocus motor to spend a long time hunting for its focus point. Animals behind fences, reflective objects, water, and low-contrast subjects are just some of the autofocus troublemakers. Autofocus systems also struggle in dim lighting, although that difficulty is often offset by the AF-assist lamp, which shoots out a beam of light to help the camera find its focusing target. (Turn the lamp on and off via the Built-in AF-assist Illuminator option, found in the Autofocus section of the Custom Setting menu.)

When you encounter situations that cause an autofocus hang-up, you can try adjusting the autofocus options discussed earlier in this chapter. But often, it's easier and faster to switch to manual focusing. For the best results, follow these manual-focusing steps:

REMEMBER

1. **Adjust the viewfinder to your eyesight.**

   If you don't adjust the viewfinder, scenes that are in focus may appear blurry and vice versa. If you haven't already taken this step, Chapter 1 provides details.

2. **Enable manual focusing.**

   Remember, with an AF-P lens, you make the switch from autofocusing to manual focusing via the Focus mode setting, accessible via the control strip.

If your lens offers an external switch to change the focusing method, move the switch to the manual position. The camera should then automatically change the Focus mode to manual (MF), but double check just to be sure.

3. **Select a focus point.**

    Use the same technique as when selecting a point during autofocusing: looking through the viewfinder, press the Multi Selector right, left, up, or down until the point you want to use flashes red.

    During autofocusing, the selected focus point tells the camera what part of the frame to use when establishing focus. And technically speaking, you don't *have* to choose a focus point for manual focusing — the camera focuses according to the position you set by turning the focusing ring. However, choosing a focus point is still a good idea, for two reasons. First, even though you're focusing manually, the camera provides feedback to let you know whether focus is correct, and that feedback is based on the selected focus point. Second, if you use spot metering, an exposure option covered in Chapter 3, exposure is based on the selected focus point.

4. **Frame the shot so that your subject is under the selected focus point.**

5. **Press and hold the shutter button halfway to initiate exposure metering.**

6. **Rotate the focusing ring on the lens to bring the subject into focus.**

    When the camera thinks focus is set on the object under the focus point, the green focus lamp in the lower-left corner of the viewfinder lights, just as it does during autofocusing.

7. **Press the shutter button the rest of the way to take the shot.**

I know that when you first start working with an SLR-style camera, focusing manually is intimidating. But if you practice a little, you'll find that it's really no big deal and saves you the time and aggravation of trying to bend the autofocus system to your will when it has "issues."

TIP

In addition to the green focus lamp, your camera offers another manual focusing aid: You can swap out the viewfinder's exposure meter with a *rangefinder*, which uses a similar, meter-like display, as shown in Figure 4-15, to indicate whether focus is set on the object in the selected focus point. If bars appear to the left of the 0, as shown in the left example in Figure 4-15, focus is set in front of the subject; if the bars are to the right, as in the middle example, focus is slightly behind the subject. The more bars you see, the greater the focusing error. As you rotate the focusing ring, the rangefinder updates to help you get focus on track. When you see a single bar on either side of the 0, you're good to go.

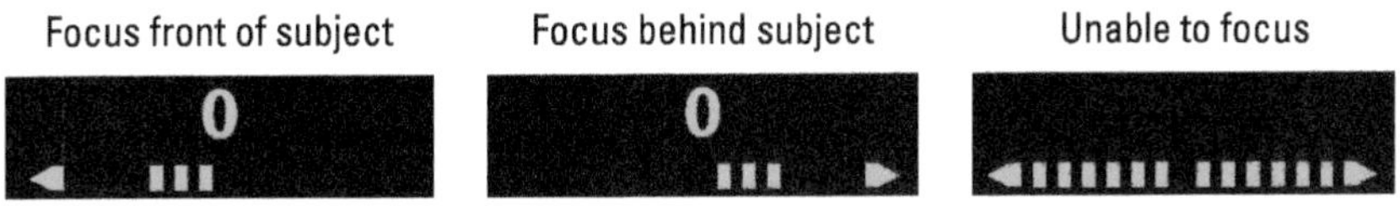

FIGURE 4-15:
The rangefinder offers manual-focusing assistance.

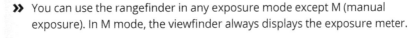

Focus front of subject   Focus behind subject   Unable to focus

Before I tell you how to activate this feature, I want to point out a couple things:

REMEMBER

>> You can use the rangefinder in any exposure mode except M (manual exposure). In M mode, the viewfinder always displays the exposure meter.

Speaking of the M exposure mode, don't confuse that manual setting with the one that controls focusing. You can use manual focusing in any exposure mode, and setting the exposure mode to M has no impact on the focusing method.

>> In exposure modes other then M, you can continue to view the exposure meter in the Information display, even with the rangefinder enabled.

>> Your lens must offer a maximum aperture of f/5.6 or lower.

>> With subjects that confuse the camera's autofocus system, the rangefinder may not work well either; it's based on the same system. If the system can't find the focusing target, the rangefinder display appears as shown on the right in Figure 4-15.

>> The rangefinder is automatically replaced by the normal exposure meter if you switch back to autofocusing, but reappears when you return to manual focus.

TIP

Personally, I leave the rangefinder off and just rely on the focus indicator light and my eyes to verify focus. I shoot in the S and A exposure modes frequently, and I find it a pain to monitor exposure in the Information display rather than in the viewfinder. But if you want to try the rangefinder, set the exposure mode to any setting but M and then head for the Autofocus submenu of the Custom Setting menu. Change the Rangefinder option from Off to On to enable the feature.

Focusing in Live View Mode

As with viewfinder photography, you can opt for autofocusing or manual focusing in Live View mode, whether you're taking still shots or recording movies. But Live View focus options and techniques differ from those you use for viewfinder photography.

The next several sections detail Live View focusing.

Using Live View autofocus

Whether you're shooting stills or movies, you control Live View autofocusing through the same two settings as for viewfinder photography: Focus mode and AF-area mode. I explain the Live View versions of these settings a few paragraphs from here; first, I need to take a quick detour to introduce your camera's tap-to-focus feature.

Using the touchscreen to set focus

Normally, you press the shutter button halfway to initiate autofocusing. But if the touchscreen is enabled, as it is by default, you have another option in Live View mode: Just tap the area of the monitor that you want the camera to use when establishing focus. (Enable the touchscreen by opening the Setup menu, selecting the Touch Controls option, and selecting Enable.)

WARNING

By default, the camera snaps the picture as soon as you lift your finger off the monitor. The feature that triggers the shutter release is called the *touch shutter*. To turn the touch shutter off and use the touchscreen for setting focus only, tap the Touch Shutter icon on the left side of the screen. I highlighted the icon in Figure 4-16. (Don't see the icon or the other data shown in the figure? Press the Info button to cycle through the Live View data display modes until the icon appears.) The word *Off* appears on the icon, as shown in the figure, when the touch shutter is disabled. Now when you tap the screen, the camera establishes focus only.

Touch Shutter symbol

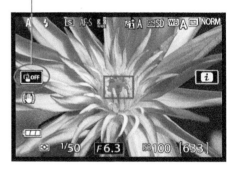

FIGURE 4-16:
Unless the Touch Shutter is disabled, as here, tapping the monitor sets focus and then immediately triggers the shutter release.

Note that not all lenses are compatible with the touch-focus feature.

Choosing a Focus mode

In Live View mode, you can choose from the following Focus mode options:

>> **AF-S (single-servo autofocus):** Set focus by pressing the shutter button halfway or by touching your subject on the monitor. Focus remains locked at the current distance as long as you keep the shutter button pressed halfway or keep your finger on the monitor.

If you lift your finger off the shutter button, the camera resets focus when you press the shutter button to take the picture. The same thing happens if you take your finger off the touchscreen unless you're using the touch shutter. In that case, the camera releases the shutter and takes the picture. For movie recording, however, you can go ahead and lift your finger off the button or touchscreen. Focus remains set at the initial focusing distance unless you press the shutter button halfway or tap the monitor to refocus.

>> **AF-F (full-time servo AF):** This option provides continuous autofocusing, similar to the AF-C mode available for viewfinder focusing. AF-F is available for all exposure modes except for these Effects modes: Color Sketch, Toy Camera, and Miniature.

As soon as you set the camera to AF-F mode, autofocusing begins automatically; you don't have to press the shutter button halfway or tap the touchscreen. Just make sure that your subject is under the Live View focus frame, which looks like a red box by default. The next section shows you how the frame appears in each of the AF-area modes and also explains how to reposition the frame if needed.

When the camera finds its target, the focus frame turns green. Focus is then adjusted as needed if your subject moves through the frame or you pan the camera. Want to interrupt continuous autofocusing and lock focus at the current distance? *That's* the time to press and hold the shutter button halfway down or put your finger on the touchscreen. As soon as you lift your finger from the button or touchscreen, continuous autofocusing begins again.

When recording movies, AF-F seems like the obvious choice if you're shooting moving subjects. But if you shoot a movie with sound recording enabled and use the internal microphone, the microphone may pick up the sound of the autofocus motor as it adjusts focus. What's the solution? Well, if you use the camera frequently for movie recording, I suggest investing in an external microphone. You then can position the mic far enough from the autofocus motor that the motor sound won't be recorded. Manual focusing is another silent option, but for moving subjects, it's fairly difficult to pull off because you have to keep turning the lens focusing ring to adjust focus as your subject moves.

>> **MF (manual focus):** Select this option to focus manually. With some lenses that have an external focus switch, moving the switch to the manual position automatically selects the MF Focus mode setting.

You can view the current Focus mode setting in the area of the Live View display highlighted on the left in Figure 4-17. To change the setting, tap the *i* icon or press the *i* button to bring up the Live View control strip. Select the Focus Mode option, as shown on the right in the figure, to access the available settings.

Focus mode setting

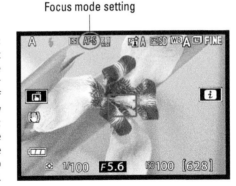 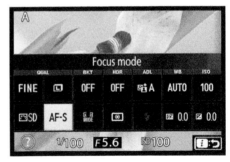

FIGURE 4-17:
The current
Focus mode
appears near
the top of
the Live View
display (left);
adjust the
setting via the
control strip
(right).

Selecting the AF-area mode

REMEMBER

Just as with viewfinder autofocusing, the AF-area mode determines what part of the frame the camera uses to set the focusing distance. But again, the available settings differ from those used for viewfinder photography. Additionally, instead of selecting one of the camera's 39 autofocus points as you do when using the viewfinder, you specify the focus target by moving a focus frame over your subject.

An icon representing the current AF-area mode appears at the top of the Live View display, as labeled in Figure 4-18. The following list provides details about all four modes, along with a look at their respective screen symbols.

>> **Wide-area:** In this mode, you see the red focus frame shown on the left in Figure 4-18. If necessary, move the frame over your subject by using the Multi Selector or, if the touchscreen is enabled, by tapping the desired focus area on the screen. When focus is achieved, the frame turns green, as shown on the right in the figure.

AF-area setting

Wide-area focus frame   Focus achieved

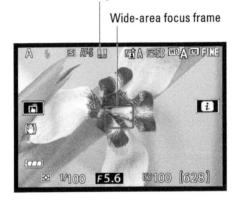 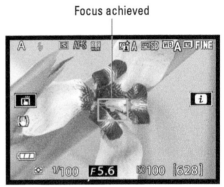

FIGURE 4-18:
In Wide-area
mode, position
the red frame
over your
subject (left);
when focus is
achieved, the
frame turns
green (right).

>> **Normal-area:** This mode works the same way as Wide-area autofocusing but uses a smaller focusing frame. The idea is to enable you to base focus on a very specific area. With such a small focusing frame, however, you can easily miss your focus target when handholding the camera. If you move the camera slightly as you're setting focus and the focusing frame shifts off your subject as a result, focus will be incorrect. For the best results, use a tripod in this mode.

>> **Face-priority:** Designed for portrait shooting, this mode attempts to hunt down and focus on faces. Each detected face is surrounded by a yellow focus frame, as shown on the left in Figure 4-19.

One frame sports interior corner brackets — in the figure, it's the frame on the right. The brackets indicate the face that the camera will use to set focus, which is typically the closest person. When your subjects are side-by-side, as here, it doesn't matter which framing box is selected as the focus point. But if you want to select a different face, use the Multi Selector to move the selected-for-focus frame over that face. You also can just tap the face if the touchscreen is enabled.

REMEMBER

Face-priority mode typically works only when your subjects are facing the camera. If the camera can't detect a face, it behaves as it does in Wide-area mode, replacing the yellow face-focus boxes with the red focus frame shown in Figure 4-18.

Face-priority symbol   Subject-tracking focus frame

Selected face   Subject-tracking symbol

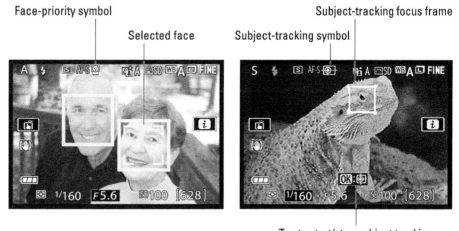

FIGURE 4-19:
Here you see the focus frames as they appear in Face-priority mode (left) and Subject-tracking mode (left).

Tap to start/stop subject tracking

>> **Subject-tracking:** This mode tracks a subject as it moves through the frame and is designed for focusing on a moving subject. When you select this mode, you see a focus frame similar to the one shown on the right in Figure 4-19.

After moving the frame over your subject, press OK or, if you enabled the touchscreen, tap the OK symbol labeled in the figure. If your subject moves, the focus frame moves with it.

If the focus frame indicates the camera has lost sight of your subject, press or tap OK to stop focus tracking. Move the frame over your subject (or reframe the shot to move the subject under the frame) and then press or tap OK again to restart tracking.

Sadly, subject tracking isn't always as successful as you might hope. For a subject that occupies only a small part of the frame — say, a butterfly flitting through a garden — autofocus may lose its way. Ditto for subjects moving at a fast pace, subjects getting larger or smaller in the frame (when moving toward you and then away from you, for example), or scenes in which not much contrast exists between the subject and the background. Oh, and scenes in which there's a great deal of contrast can create problems, too. My take on this feature is that when the conditions are right, it works well, but otherwise the Wide-area setting gives you a better chance of keeping a moving subject in focus.

REMEMBER

You can't choose the AF-area mode in the Auto or Auto Flash Off exposure modes; both modes use the Face-priority setting. Some Effects modes also restrict your choices. Miniature mode always uses Wide-area focusing, and Subject-tracking mode isn't available for the Night Vision, Toy, Color Sketch, and Selective Color modes.

In other exposure modes, adjust the setting via the control strip, as shown in Figure 4-20. Again, pressing the *i* button is the most surefire way to shift to the Live View control strip when the touchscreen is enabled, but you also can tap on the *i* icon on the right side of the screen. Be precise with where you tap, though, or the camera will think your tap is meant to set focus.

FIGURE 4-20:
Set the Live View AF-area mode through the control strip.

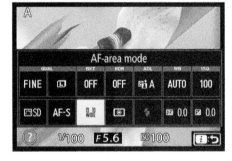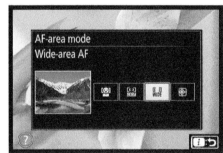

Choosing the right Live View autofocusing pairs

To recap, the way the camera sets focus during Live View still photography and movie shooting depends on your Focus mode and AF–area mode settings. Until you get fully acquainted with the various combinations of Focus mode and AF–area mode settings and can make your own decisions about which pairings you like best, I recommend the following settings (assuming, of course, that the exposure mode you're using permits them):

» **For moving subjects:** Set the Focus mode to AF-F and the AF-area mode to Wide-area. You also can try the Subject-tracking AF-area mode, but see my comments in the preceding section regarding which subjects may not be well suited to that mode.

» **For stationary subjects:** Set the Focus mode to AF-S and the AF-area mode to Wide-area. Or, if you're shooting a portrait, give the Face-priority AF-area option a try.

» **For difficult-to-focus subjects:** If the camera has trouble finding the right focusing point when you use autofocus, don't spend too much time fiddling with the different autofocus settings. Just set the camera to manual focusing and set focus yourself. Remember that every lens has a minimum focusing distance, so if you can't focus automatically or manually, you may simply be too close to your subject.

Manual focusing in Live View mode

After setting your lens to manual focusing mode, as outlined at the start of this chapter, just rotate the lens focusing ring to bring the scene into focus. But note these quirks:

» Even with manual focusing, you still see the focusing frame; its appearance depends on the current AF-area mode setting. In Face-priority mode, the frame automatically jumps into place over a face if it detects one. And if you press OK when Subject-tracking mode is enabled, the camera tries to track the subject under the frame until you press OK again. I find these two behaviors irritating, so I always set the AF-area mode to Wide-area or Normal-area for manual focusing.

» The focusing frame doesn't turn green to indicate successful focusing as it does with autofocusing.

Zooming in to check focus

Here's a cool feature available only during Live View shooting: You can magnify the display so that you can get a better view of whether your subject is in focus. This tool is available both during autofocusing and manual focusing.

 To zoom the display, press the Zoom In button. Each press gives you a closer look at the subject. A small thumbnail appears in the lower-right corner of the screen, as shown in Figure 4-21, with the yellow highlight box indicating the area that's being magnified. Press the Multi Selector to scroll the display if needed.

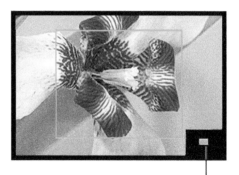

Magnified area

FIGURE 4-21:
Press the Zoom In button to magnify the display and double-check focus.

 To reduce the magnification level, press the Zoom Out button. If you're not using Subject-tracking mode, you can also press OK to quickly return to normal magnification.

Manipulating Depth of Field

Getting familiar with the concept of depth of field is one of the biggest steps you can take to becoming a better photographer. I introduce you to depth of field in Chapter 3, but here's a quick recap:

» *Depth of field* refers to the distance over which objects in a photograph appear acceptably sharp.

» With a shallow depth of field, your subject is sharply focused, but objects behind and in front of it appear blurry. How blurry those objects appear depends on three factors, which I discuss momentarily.

» With a large depth of field, the zone of sharp focus extends to include objects in front of and behind your subject.

Which arrangement works best depends on your creative vision and your subject. In portraits, for example, a classic technique is to use a short depth of field, as I did for the photo on the left in Figure 4-22. This approach increases emphasis on the subject while diminishing the impact of the background. But for the photo shown on the right, I wanted to emphasize that the foreground figures were in St. Peter's Square, so I used a large depth of field, which kept the background buildings sharply focused and gave them equal weight in the scene.

Shallow depth of field

Large depth of field

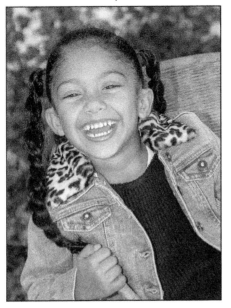 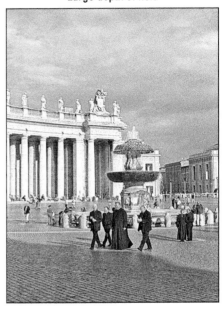

FIGURE 4-22:
A shallow depth of field blurs the background (left); a large depth of field keeps both foreground and background in focus (right).

REMEMBER

Depth of field depends on the aperture setting, lens focal length, and distance from the subject, as follows:

>> **Aperture setting (f-stop):** The aperture is one of three main exposure settings, all explained fully in Chapter 3. Depth of field increases as you stop down the aperture (by choosing a higher f-stop number). For shallow depth of field, open the aperture (by choosing a lower f-stop number). Figure 4-23 offers an example; in the f/22 version on the left, focus is sharp all the way through the frame; in the f/2.8 version on the right, focus softens as the distance from the flag increases. I snapped both images using the same focal length and camera-to-subject distance, setting focus on the flag.

Aperture, f/22; Focal length, 93mm

Aperture, f/2.8; Focal length, 93mm

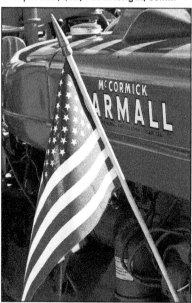
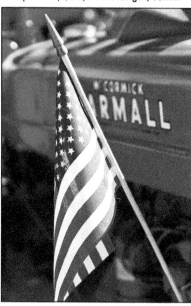

FIGURE 4-23:
A lower f-stop number (wider aperture) decreases depth of field.

>> **Lens focal length:** In lay terms, *focal length* determines what the lens "sees." As you increase focal length, measured in millimeters, the angle of view narrows, objects appear larger in the frame, and — the important point for this discussion — depth of field decreases. Additionally, the spatial relationship of objects changes as you adjust focal length. As an example, Figure 4-24 compares the same scene shot at a focal length of 127mm and 183mm. I used the same aperture and camera-to-subject distance for each shot, setting focus on the parrot.

Whether you have any focal length flexibility depends on your lens: If you have a zoom lens, you can adjust the focal length by zooming in or out. If you have a prime lens — that is, not a zoom lens — the focal length is fixed, so scratch this means of manipulating depth of field.

For more details about focal length, flip to Chapter 1 and explore the sidebar related to that topic.

>> **Camera-to-subject distance:** As you move the lens closer to your subject, depth of field decreases. This statement assumes that you don't zoom in or out to reframe the picture, thereby changing the focal length. If you do, depth of field is affected by both the camera position and focal length.

Aperture, f/5.6; focal length, 127mm

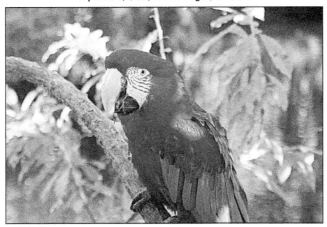

Aperture, f/5.6; focal length, 183mm

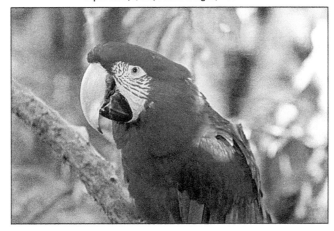

FIGURE 4-24:
Zooming to a
longer focal
length also
reduces depth
of field.

REMEMBER

Together, these three factors determine the maximum and minimum depth of field that you can achieve, as follows:

>> **To produce the shallowest depth of field:** Open the aperture as wide as possible (the lowest f-stop number), zoom in to the maximum focal length of your lens, and get as close as possible to your subject.

>> **To produce maximum depth of field:** Stop down the aperture to the highest possible f-stop number, zoom out to the shortest focal length (widest angle) your lens offers, and move farther from your subject.

A couple of final tips related to depth of field:

>> **Aperture-priority autoexposure mode (A) enables you to easily control depth of field while enjoying exposure assistance from the camera.** In this mode, you rotate the Command dial to set the f-stop, and the camera selects the appropriate shutter speed to produce a good exposure. The range of available aperture settings depends on your lens.

>> **For greater background blurring, move the subject farther from the background.** The extent to which background focus shifts as you adjust depth of field also is affected by the distance between the subject and the background. The portrait in Figure 4-22 offers an example: Notice that the wicker chair in which my model is sitting appears just slightly blurrier than she does, but the vines in the distance almost blur into a solid color.

WARNING

>> **In Live View mode, depth of field doesn't change in the preview as you change the f-stop setting.** The camera can't display the effect of aperture on depth of field properly because the aperture doesn't actually open or close until you take the photo. However, you can gauge the depth of field produced by the focal length and subject-to-camera distance in the preview.

TIP

CORRECTING LENS DISTORTION

When you shoot with a wide-angle lens, vertical structures sometimes appear to bend outward from the center of the image. This is known as *barrel distortion.* On the flip side of the coin, shooting with a telephoto lens can cause vertical structures to bow inward, which is known as *pincushion distortion.*

The Retouch menu offers a post-capture Distortion Control filter you can apply to try to correct both problems. But the D5600 also has an Auto Distortion Control feature that attempts to correct the image as you're shooting. It works with only certain types of lenses — specifically, those that Nikon classifies as type G, E, or D, excluding PC (perspective control), fisheye, and certain other lenses. To activate the option, open the Shooting menu and set the Auto Distortion Control option to On.

One caveat: Some of the area you see in the viewfinder or Live View display may not be visible in your photo because the anti-distortion manipulation requires some cropping of the scene. So frame your subject a little loosely when you enable Auto Distortion Control. Also, this feature isn't available for movie recording.

IN THIS CHAPTER

» Exploring white balance and its effect on color

» Creating custom White Balance settings

» Bracketing white balance

» Setting the Color Space (sRGB versus Adobe RGB)

» Taking a quick look at Picture Controls

Chapter **5**

Mastering Color Controls

C ompared with understanding certain aspects of digital photography — resolution, aperture, shutter speed, and so on — making sense of your camera's color options is easy-breezy. First, color problems aren't all that common, and when they are, they're usually simple to fix with a quick shift of your camera's White Balance setting. And getting a grip on color requires learning only a couple of new terms, an unusual state of affairs for an endeavor that often seems more like high-tech science than art.

This chapter explains the aforementioned White Balance control along with other features that enable you to fine-tune the way your camera renders colors, whether you're shooting photos or recording movies.

Adjusting the White Balance Setting

Every light source emits a particular color cast. The old-fashioned fluorescent lights found in most public restrooms, for example, put out a bluish-greenish light, which is why we all look sickly when we view our reflections in the mirrors in those restrooms. And if you think that your beloved looks especially attractive by candlelight, you aren't imagining it: Candlelight casts a warm, yellow-red glow that is flattering to the skin.

TECHNICAL STUFF

Science-y types measure the color of light, officially known as *color temperature,* on the Kelvin scale, which is named after its creator. You can see the Kelvin scale in Figure 5-1.

When photographers talk about "warm light" and "cool light," though, they aren't referring to the position on the Kelvin scale — or at least not in the way most people think of temperatures, with a higher number meaning hotter. Instead, the terms describe the visual appearance of the light. Warm light, produced by candles and incandescent lights, falls in the red-yellow spectrum at the bottom of the Kelvin scale; cool light, in the blue spectrum, appears in the upper part of the Kelvin scale.

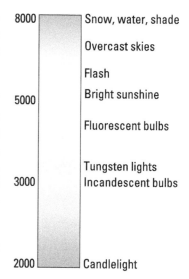

FIGURE 5-1:
Each light source emits a specific color.

At any rate, most people don't notice these fluctuating colors of light, because human eyes automatically compensate for them. Except in extreme lighting conditions, we perceive a white tablecloth as white no matter whether it's lit by candlelight, fluorescent light, or daylight. Similarly, a digital camera compensates for different colors of light through white balancing. Simply put, *white balancing* neutralizes light so that whites are always white, which in turn ensures other colors are rendered accurately. If the camera senses warm light, it shifts colors slightly to the cool side of the color spectrum; in cool light, the camera shifts colors in the opposite direction.

When the White Balance option is set to Auto, the camera takes care of this color neutralizing for you. In most cases, things work out just fine in Auto White Balance mode. But if the scene is lit by two or more light sources that cast different colors, the white balance sensor can get confused, producing an unwanted color cast like the one you see in the left image in Figure 5-2.

I shot this image in my home studio — which is a fancy name for "guest bedroom" — using tungsten photo lights, which produce light with a color temperature similar to incandescent bulbs. The problem is that windows in that room permit strong daylight to filter through. In Auto White Balance mode, the camera reacted to the daylight — which has a cooler color cast — and applied too much warming, giving my original image a yellow tint. No problem: I switched the White Balance mode from Auto to the Incandescent setting. The image on the right in Figure 5-2 shows the corrected colors.

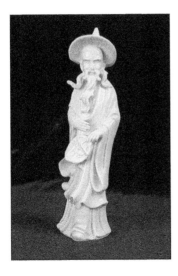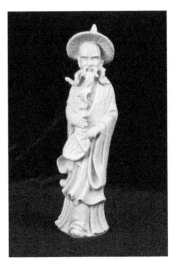

WARNING

You can control the White Balance setting only when you shoot in the advanced exposure modes: P, S, A, and M, which I introduce in Chapter 3. The next section explains how to make a simple white balance correction; following that, you can explore advanced options.

TIP

If you notice a color problem when shooting in other exposure modes and you're not comfortable using the advanced exposure modes, consider setting the Image Quality option to Raw (NEF). With Raw files, you can fine-tune colors when you process the Raw file. In fact, Raw is a better option even in the P, S, A, and M modes when you're shooting color-critical photographs because if the White Balance setting you select isn't quite right, you can tweak it when you process the file. Chapter 2 explains this Raw stuff; Chapter 9 shows you how to use the in-camera Raw converter as well as the one provided in Nikon Capture NX-D, a photo program you can download from the Nikon website.

Changing the White Balance setting

To find out which White Balance option is currently selected, check the Informa-tion and Live View displays. The setting is displayed in the areas highlighted in Figure 5-3. The icons in the figures represent the Auto setting; settings other than Auto are represented by the icons you see in Table 5-1.

TIP

In Live View mode, colors in the preview are rendered according to the current White Balance setting. If you're unsure of which setting to use, just experiment: After you adjust the setting, the preview updates to show you the effect on photo colors.

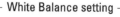

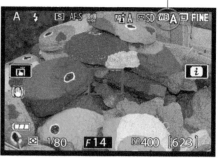

FIGURE 5-3:
A symbol
representing
the current
White Balance
setting appears
in the displays.

TABLE 5-1

Manual White Balance Settings

Symbol	Light Source
☀	Incandescent
≋	Fluorescent
☀	Direct sunlight
⚡	Flash
☁	Cloudy
⛰	Shade
PRE	Preset

You can adjust the White Balance setting in two ways:

» **Control strip:** Press the *i* button or tap the *i* icon and then select the WB
option to access the available settings, as shown in Figure 5-4.

» **Shooting menu:** Select White Balance, as shown on the left in Figure 5-5, to
reveal the selection screen shown on the right.

REMEMBER

After selecting a setting, be sure to press the OK button or tap the OK symbol,
labeled in Figure 5-5. If you instead tap the exit arrow in the upper-right
corner of the screen, the camera closes the selection screen without changing
the White Balance setting.

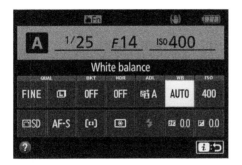

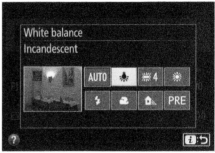

FIGURE 5-4:
Select a White
Balance setting
by using the
control strip.

Exit without making changes

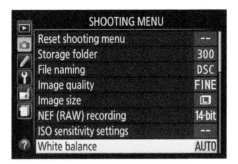

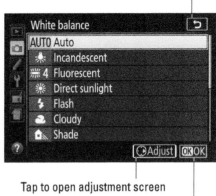

FIGURE 5-5:
To uncover
more White
Balance
options, open
the Shooting
menu.

Tap to open adjustment screen

Tap to choose highlighted setting

When you go the menu route, you can access these additional features:

>> **Fine-tune the settings.** If you choose any setting but Fluorescent, pressing the Multi Selector right or tapping the Adjust icon labeled in Figure 5-5 takes you to a screen where you can fine-tune the setting, a process I explain in the next section.

>> **Select a specific type of fluorescent bulb.** When you choose Fluorescent from the menu, as shown on the left in Figure 5-6, you can select a specific type of bulb. The selection screen, shown on the right in the figure, appears automatically when you tap Fluorescent in the initial menu; you can also display the screen by pressing the Multi Selector right. Either way, select the option that most closely matches your bulbs and then press or tap OK. Or, to go to the fine-tuning screen, press the Multi Selector right or tap the Adjust icon.

>> **Create a custom white balance preset.** Selecting the PRE option as the White Balance setting enables you to create and store a precise, customized White Balance setting, as explained in the upcoming section "Creating white

balance presets." This feature provides the fastest way to achieve accurate colors when the scene is lit by multiple light sources that have differing color temperatures. Scroll to the second page of the menu to reach the PRE setting (not shown in Figures 5-5 and 5-6).

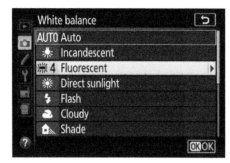
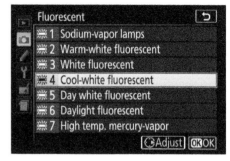

The selected White Balance setting remains in force until you change it. Get in the habit of checking the setting before every shoot or change in lighting conditions to make sure you don't need to modify it.

WARNING

Fine-tuning White Balance settings

You can fine-tune any White Balance setting except a custom preset that you create by using the PRE option. Here are the steps for making the adjustment:

1. **Display the Shooting menu and select the White Balance option.**

2. **Use the Multi Selector to highlight the White Balance setting you want to adjust.**

   Don't simply tap the setting; if you do, the camera just selects that setting and closes the menu screen.

3. **Press the Multi Selector right or tap the Adjust symbol at the bottom of the display to get to the screen shown in Figure 5-7.**

   If you select Fluorescent, you first go to a screen where you select a specific type of bulb. After highlighting a bulb type, press the Multi Selector right or tap Adjust to get to the fine-tuning screen.

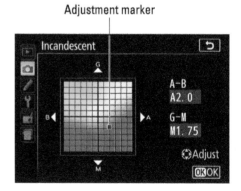

Adjustment marker

FIGURE 5-7:
Move the black square around the color grid to fine-tune the selected White Balance setting.

REMEMBER

4. **Fine-tune the setting by moving the adjustment marker in the color grid.**

   I labeled the marker in Figure 5-7. The grid is set up around two color pairs: Green and Magenta, represented by G and M; and Blue and Amber, represented by B and A. To adjust the White Balance setting, move the marker in the direction you want to shift colors. You can either tap inside the grid, tap the arrows on the sides of the grid, or press the Multi Selector to reposition the marker.

TIP

   As you move the marker, the A–B and G–M boxes on the right side of the screen show you the current amount of color shift. A value of 0 indicates the default amount of color compensation applied by the selected White Balance setting. In Figure 5-7, for example, I moved the marker two levels toward amber and two levels toward magenta to specify that I wanted colors to be a tad warmer.

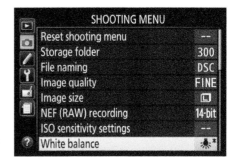

5. **Tap OK or press the OK button to complete the adjustment.**

After you fine-tune a White Balance setting, an asterisk appears next to the icon representing the setting on the Shooting menu, as shown in Figure 5-8. You see an asterisk next to the White Balance setting in the Information and Live View displays as well.

FIGURE 5-8:
The asterisk next to the White Balance setting symbol indicates you applied a fine-tuning adjustment.

Creating white balance presets

If none of the standard White Balance settings does the trick and you don't want to fool with fine-tuning them, take advantage of the PRE (Preset Manual) feature. This option enables you to do two things:

>> Base white balance on a direct measurement of the actual lighting conditions.

>> Match white balance to an existing photo.

REMEMBER

Although you can create a preset using either method, you can store only one preset at a time. For example, if you create a preset based on lighting conditions on Monday and then decide on Tuesday to create a different one based on a photo, the light-based preset goes kaput.

The next sections provide instructions for creating both types of presets.

Setting white balance with direct measurement

To use this technique, you need a piece of card stock that's either neutral gray or absolute white — not eggshell white, sand white, or any other close-but-not-perfect white. (You can buy reference cards, made just for this purpose, in many camera stores for less than $20.)

Position the reference card so that it receives the same lighting you'll use for the photo. Then take these steps:

1. **Set the camera to the P, S, A, or M exposure mode.**

   If the exposure meter reports that the image will be under- or overexposed at the current exposure settings, make the necessary adjustments now. (Chapter 3 tells you how.) Otherwise, the camera can't create your preset.

2. **Frame your shot so that the reference card fills the viewfinder.**

   You must use the viewfinder to take the reference shot; you can't create a preset in Live View mode.

WARNING

3. **From the Shooting menu, select White Balance and then select PRE Preset Manual, as shown on the left in Figure 5-9.**

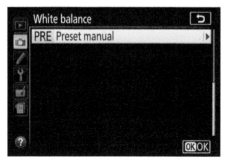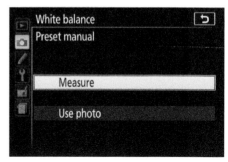

FIGURE 5-9:
Select these options to set white balance by measuring a white or gray card.

4. **Press the Multi Selector right or tap the PRE menu option again to display the screen shown on the right in Figure 5-9.**

5. **Select Measure.**

   The camera asks whether you want to overwrite existing data.

6. **Select Yes.**

   Now you see a message telling you to take your picture. You have about 6 seconds to do so. (The letters *PRE* flash in the viewfinder and Information display to let you know the camera is ready to record your white balance reference image.)

7. **Take the reference shot.**

If the camera is successful at recording the white balance data, the letters *Gd* flash in the viewfinder, and the message "Data Acquired" appears in the Information display. If the camera can't set the custom white balance, you instead see the message *No Gd* in the viewfinder, and a message in the Information display urges you to try again. Try adjusting the lighting before doing so.

TIP

You also can create a direct-measurement preset via the Information display. First, set the White Balance option to PRE. After you exit the menu or control strip and return to the Information display, press the OK button for a couple seconds until the letters *PRE* start to flash in the display. Then take your reference shot. (This technique doesn't work for Live View shooting.)

After you complete the process, the camera sets the White Balance option to PRE so that you can begin using your preset. Whenever you want to use the preset again, just choose PRE as the White Balance setting.

Matching white balance to an existing photo

Suppose that you're the marketing manager for a small business and one of your jobs is to shoot portraits of the company bigwigs for the annual report. You build a small studio just for that purpose, complete with a couple of photography lights and a nice, conservative beige backdrop. Of course, the bigwigs can't all show up to get their pictures taken in the same month, let alone on the same day. But you have to make sure the colors in that beige backdrop remain consistent for each shot, no matter how much time passes between photo sessions. This scenario is one possible use for a feature that enables you to create a White Balance preset based on an existing photo.

WARNING

Two words of caution:

» Basing white balance on an existing photo works well only in strictly controlled lighting situations, where the color temperature of the lights is consistent from day to day.

» Your new preset wipes out the current preset, including one created by using the direct measurement option described in the preceding section.

To select a photo as your reference image, it must be stored on the installed memory card. If the image isn't already on the card, use a card reader to copy the photo to the card. You must put the image in a folder created by the camera, so if using a new card, format it by using the Format Card option on the Setup menu. When viewing the card contents on your computer, you should see a main folder named

DCIM; open that folder to view the camera-created folders. By default, the first folder created by the camera carries the label 100D5600.

With that chore out of the way, install the memory card in the camera and open the Shooting menu and select White Balance. Then select PRE Preset Manual and press the Multi Selector right to display the same screen you see on the right in Figure 5-9. Instead of choosing Measure, however, select Use Photo. You're then presented with a screen that shows either the previously selected reference photo or any empty white thumbnail — indicating you haven't taken advantage of the Use Photo option before.

To select a new reference photo, choose Select Image and then work your way through the next few screens, on which you choose the folder that holds your image and then the image itself. The camera then displays the screen containing the reference photo thumbnail, which now shows your selected photo. Choose This Image to wrap things up. The camera sets the White Balance setting to PRE, and any time you use that setting, the camera uses your reference image as the basis for rendering colors.

Bracketing white balance

Chapter 3 introduces you to automatic exposure bracketing, which records the same image at different exposure settings or Active D-Lighting settings. You also can bracket white balance, creating a series of three images.

Colors in the first image are rendered according to the current White Balance setting. The second image is shifted toward amber, creating warmer colors; the third image, toward blue, resulting cooler colors.

REMEMBER

Note the following details about this feature:

>> **Bracketing is available only in the P, S, A, and M exposure modes.** Chapter 3 tells you how to use these exposure modes, if you haven't yet discovered them.

>> **You must set the Image Quality option to one of the JPEG options (Fine, Normal, or Basic).** Why is the Raw (NEF) setting off-limits? Because with Raw, white balance and other color settings aren't established until you process your images. The camera does use the selected White Balance setting to create the image that's displayed on the camera during playback mode and on your computer after you download the file. But you can change the White Balance setting or otherwise adjust colors when you process the Raw file, a step I discuss in Chapter 9. Long story short, there's no reason to waste time bracketing white balance when you shoot in the Raw format.

» **A single press of the shutter button creates all three images.** The camera captures the first photo at the selected White Balance setting and then creates two copies, one shifted toward amber and one toward blue.

» **You can shift colors from one to three steps between frames.** As an example of the maximum color shift you can achieve, check out Figure 5-10, which I created using a three-step shift. As you can see, even at that "max" setting, the differences between the shots are subtle.

Neutral	Amber +3	Blue +3

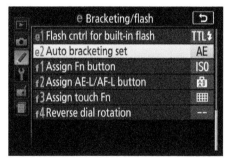

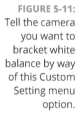

FIGURE 5-10: I created three color variations by using white balance bracketing.

To use white balance bracketing, take these steps:

1. **Open the Custom Setting menu and scroll to the Auto Bracketing Set option, as shown on the left in Figure 5-11.**

2. **Select the WB setting, as shown on the right in the figure.**

FIGURE 5-11: Tell the camera you want to bracket white balance by way of this Custom Setting menu option.

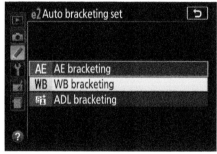

3. **Press the shutter button halfway and release it to return to shooting mode.**

4. **Press the *i* button or tap the onscreen *i* symbol to access the control strip.**

5. **Select the BKT option, as shown on the left in Figure 5-12, and then set the bracketing amount on the next screen, shown on the right in the figure.**

The figures shown the Information screen version of the control strip, but things work the same way in Live View mode.

FIGURE 5-12:
Enable
bracketing and
set the amount
of color shift
from the
control strip.

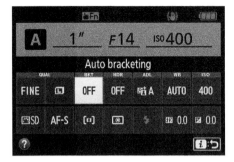
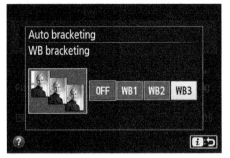

After you enable bracketing, the Information display shows bracketing indicators, as shown in Figure 5-13, reminding you that white balance bracketing is in force. The same indicator appears in the lower-right corner of the Live View display.

6. **To record the bracketed series, press the shutter button once.**

The camera captures the first image at the current White Balance setting and then spends a few seconds creating two bracketed copies.

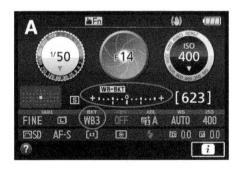

7. **When you finish taking your bracketed shots, return to the control strip and turn off bracketing.**

WARNING

FIGURE 5-13:
These markings remind you that white balance bracketing is enabled.

This step is important because the bracketing setting remains in effect even after you shut off the camera, and it's all too easy to overlook the fact that the feature is enabled when you head out for your next shoot.

If you view your photos in a playback mode that displays color data, the White Balance readout indicates which shots were shifted along the color axis. For the amber version, you see the letter *A*; for the blue version, *B*. Next to the letter, the value 1, 2, or 3 indicates the increment of color shift. For the neutral shot, the readout displays 0, 0. Chapter 8 shows you how to view this type of data during playback.

CHOOSING A COLOR SPACE: sRGB VERSUS ADOBE RGB

By default, your camera captures images using the *sRGB color space,* which refers to an industry-standard spectrum of colors. (The *s* is for *standard,* and the *RGB* is for *red, green, blue,* which are the primary colors in the digital color world.) This color space was created to help ensure color consistency as an image moves from camera (or scanner) to monitor and printer; the idea was to create a spectrum of colors that all devices can reproduce.

Because sRGB excludes some colors that *can* be reproduced in print and onscreen, at least by some devices, your camera also enables you to shoot in the Adobe RGB color space, which contains a larger spectrum of colors. You tell the camera which color space you prefer via the Color Space option on the Shooting menu.

Although using a larger color spectrum sounds like a no-brainer, choosing Adobe RGB isn't necessarily the right choice. Consider these factors when making your decision:

- Some colors in the Adobe RGB spectrum can't be reproduced in print; the printer substitutes the closest printable color, if necessary.

- If you print and share photos without making adjustments in your photo editor, sRGB is a better choice because most printers and web browsers are designed around sRGB.

- To retain the original Adobe RGB colors when you work with your photos, your editing software must support that color space — not all programs do. You also must be willing to study the topic of digital color a little because you need to use specific software and printing settings to avoid mucking up the color works.

One final tip: The picture filename indicates which color space you used. Filenames of Adobe RGB images start with an underscore, as in _DSC0627.jpg. For pictures captured in sRGB, the underscore appears in the middle of the filename, as in DSC_0627.jpg.

Taking a Quick Look at Picture Controls

When you capture photos using the JPEG Image Quality settings (Fine, Normal, or Basic), colors are also affected by the Picture Control setting. This option affects other picture characteristics that the camera tweaks when you shoot in the JPEG format, including contrast and sharpening.

Sharpening is a software process that boosts contrast in a special way to create the illusion of slightly sharper focus. I emphasize, "slightly sharper focus." Sharpening produces a subtle *tweak*; it's not a fix for poor focus.

The symbols highlighted in Figure 5-14 indicate the current Picture Control setting. The following list describes each Picture Control and shows the two-letter code used to represent it in the displays:

Picture Control setting

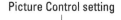

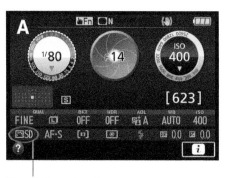

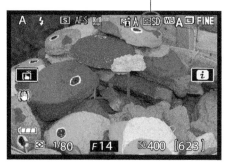

FIGURE 5-14: This two-letter code represents the Standard Picture Control setting.

Picture Control setting

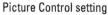

>> **Standard (SD):** The default setting, this option captures the image "normally" — that is, using the characteristics that Nikon offers up as suitable for the majority of subjects.

>> **Neutral (NL):** At this setting, the camera doesn't enhance color, contrast, and sharpening as much as in the other modes. The setting is designed for people who want to precisely manipulate these picture characteristics in a photo editor. By not overworking colors, sharpening, and so on when producing your original file, the camera delivers an original that gives you more latitude in the digital darkroom.

>> **Vivid (VI):** In this mode, the camera amps up color saturation, contrast, and sharpening.

>> **Monochrome (MC):** This setting produces black-and-white photos.

TIP

I'm not keen on creating black-and-white images this way. I prefer to shoot in full color and then convert the picture to black and white in my photo editor. That technique just gives you more control over the look of your black-and-white photos. Assuming you work with a decent photo editor, you can control what original tones are emphasized in your black-and-white version, for example. Additionally, keep in mind that you can always convert a color image to black and white, but you can't go in the other direction. You also can create a black-and-white copy of your color image directly in the camera by using the Monochrome tool on the Retouch menu. That tool produces the same result that you get if you capture the image using the Monochrome Picture Control setting. Chapter 11 covers the Retouch menu.

>> **Portrait (PT):** This mode tweaks colors and sharpening in a way that is designed to produce nice skin texture and pleasing skin tones.

>> **Landscape (LS):** This mode emphasizes blues and greens and increases contrast and sharpness.

>> **Flat (FL):** A close cousin to the Neutral setting, the Flat setting produces images with little contrast or sharpness and with reduced color saturation. Like Neutral, this one is meant for photos that you plan to edit extensively to alter color, contrast, and sharpening. It's also especially useful to videographers who do a lot of post-processing to their footage. Nikon claims that this mode holds onto the widest possible tonal range that the camera can capture in the JPEG format. (*Tonal range* refers to the range of brightness values in an image.)

The extent to which Picture Controls affect an image depends on the subject, but Figure 5-15 gives you a general idea of what to expect from the color options. As you can see, Standard, Vivid, and Landscape produce pretty similar results, as do Portrait and Neutral. As for Flat — well, to my eye, that rendition *needs* editing to bring it to life.

TIP

In all exposure modes except P, S, A, and M, the camera selects the Picture Control setting. But even in the modes that give you control over the option, I recommend sticking with Standard, which is the default for the P, S, A, and M modes. Standard captures most subjects well, and you have lots of other, more important settings to remember. Also keep in mind that if you shoot in the Raw format and then process the Raw file using Nikon Capture NX–D, which I discuss in Chapter 9, you can choose a Picture Control at the time you process the file. The camera uses the currently selected setting just to create the image preview you see on the monitor and in whatever photo browser you use to view images on your computer.

Standard

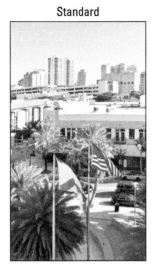

Neutral

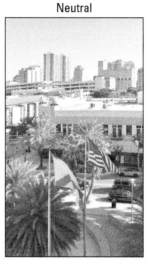

Vivid

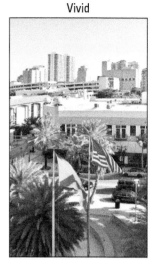

Portrait

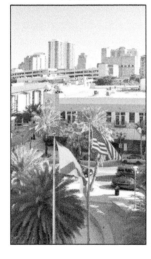

Landscape

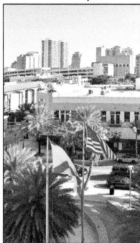

Flat

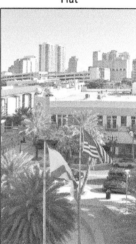

FIGURE 5-15:
Picture
controls
apply preset
adjustments
to color,
sharpening,
and contrast
to images
you shoot in
the JPEG file
format.

 If you do want to change the Picture Control setting, you can access it via the control strip, as shown in Figure 5-16, or the Shooting menu, as shown in Figure 5-17. In Live View mode, the display updates to show the effect of the new Picture Control. The preview isn't completely accurate, but it gives you a general idea of how your picture will be captured at the current setting.

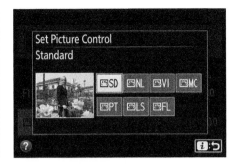

FIGURE 5-16:
The fastest
way to select a
Picture Control
is by using the
control strip.

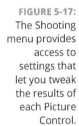

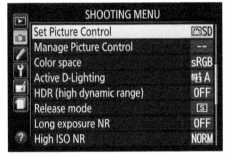

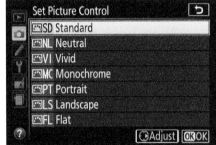

FIGURE 5-17:
The Shooting
menu provides
access to
settings that
let you tweak
the results of
each Picture
Control.

I should also alert you to a feature that may make Picture Controls a little more useful to some people: You can modify any Picture Control to more closely render a scene the way you envision it. For example, if you like the bold colors of Vivid mode but don't think that the effect goes far enough, you can adjust the setting to amp up colors even more.

To reserve page space in this book for functions that will be the most useful to the most readers, I opted not to provide full details about customizing Picture Controls. But the following steps provide a quick overview of the process so that if you encounter the menu screens that contain the related options, you'll have some idea of what you're seeing:

1. **Set the Mode dial to P, S, A, or M.**

2. **Choose Set Picture Control from the Shooting Menu.**

3. **Highlight the Picture Control you want to modify.**

   For example, I highlighted the Vivid setting on the left in Figure 5-18.

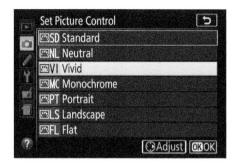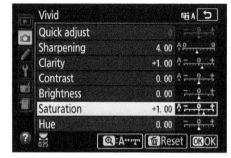

FIGURE 5-18:
After select-
ing a Picture
Control, press
right to display
options for
adjusting its
effect on your
pictures.

4. **Press the Multi Selector right.**

   You see the screen shown on the right in Figure 5-18, containing sliders that you use to modify the Picture Control. Which options you can adjust depend on the Picture Control.

5. **Highlight a picture characteristic and then press the Multi Selector right or left to adjust the setting.**

   TIP

   A few pointers:

   - Pressing the Multi Selector adjusts the setting value in increments of 1. To make a smaller adjustment, rotate the Command dial, which nudges the value in increments of 0.25.

   - A white triangle under each adjustment scale indicates the current setting for the option. If you adjust the value, that triangle turns gray, and a second, yellow marker appears to represent the new setting. A numerical value for the adjustment also appears to the left of the scale.

   - The letter A at the left end of a slider bar indicates that you can enable an Auto adjustment instead of inputting a specific value. At the Auto setting, the camera tweaks the specified characteristic depending on the type of scene it thinks you're capturing. To try this feature, tap the A symbol at the bottom of the screen or press the Zoom In button. To go back to manual adjustment, tap or press Zoom In again.

   - Instead of varying individual characteristics of a Picture Control, you can choose the top option on the list, Quick Adjust. Through this setting, you can easily increase or decrease the overall effect of the Picture Control. Note that the Quick Adjust setting becomes disabled, as shown on the right in Figure 5-18, as soon as you adjust any of the other slider values.

   - Reset all options to their defaults by pressing the Delete button or by tapping the Reset icon at the bottom of the screen.

6. **Tap the OK symbol or press the OK button.**

    To remind you that you adjusted the Picture Control, an asterisk appears next to the Picture Control name on the menu and by the Picture Control symbol in the Information and Live View displays.

Again, these steps are intended only as a starting point for playing with Picture Controls. You can find more details in the electronic version of the camera manual, which is available for download from the Nikon support pages for your camera.

Chapter **6**

Putting It All Together

E arlier chapters of this book break down each and every picture-taking feature on your camera, describing in detail how the various controls affect exposure, picture quality, focus, color, and the like. This chapter pulls together all that information to help you set up your camera for specific types of photography.

Keep in mind, though, that there are no hard-and-fast rules for the "right way" to shoot a portrait, a landscape, or whatever. So feel free to wander off on your own, tweaking this exposure setting or adjusting that focus control, to discover your own creative vision. Experimentation is part of the fun of photography, after all — and thanks to your camera monitor and the Delete button, it's an easy, completely free proposition.

Recapping Basic Picture Settings

Your subject, creative goals, and lighting conditions determine which settings you should use for certain picture-taking options, such as aperture and shutter speed. I offer my take on those options throughout this chapter. But for many basic options, I recommend the same settings for almost every shooting scenario. Table 6-1 shows you those recommendations and also lists the chapter where you can find details about each setting.

TABLE 6-1   **All-Purpose Picture-Taking Settings**

Option	Recommended Setting	See This Chapter
Active D-Lighting	Off	3
AF-area mode	Still subjects, Single-point; moving subjects, 9-, 21-, or 39-point Dynamic-area	4
Exposure mode	P, S, A, or M	3
Focus mode	For autofocusing on still subjects, AF-S; moving subjects, AF-C	4
Image Quality	JPEG Fine or Raw (NEF)	2
Image Size	Large or medium	2
ISO Sensitivity	100	3
Metering	Matrix	3
Release mode	Action photos: Continuous Low or High; all others: Single Frame	2
White Balance	Auto	5

REMEMBER

One key point: The instructions in this chapter assume you set the exposure mode to P, S, A, or M, as indicated in the table. These modes, detailed in Chapter 3, are the only ones that give you access to the entire cadre of camera features. In most cases, I recommend using S (shutter-priority autoexposure) when controlling motion blur is important, and A (aperture-priority autoexposure) when controlling depth of field is important. These two modes let you concentrate on one side of the exposure equation and let the camera handle the other. Of course, if you're comfortable making both the aperture and shutter speed decisions, you may prefer to work in M (manual) exposure mode instead. P (programmed autoexposure) is my last choice because it makes choosing a specific aperture or shutter speed more cumbersome.

Additionally, this chapter discusses choices for viewfinder photography. Although most picture settings work the same way during Live View photography as they do for viewfinder photography, the focusing process is quite different. For help with Live View focusing, visit Chapter 4.

Shooting Still Portraits

By *still portrait*, I mean that your subject isn't moving. For subjects who aren't keen on sitting still, skip to the next section and use the techniques given for action photography instead. Assuming you do have a subject willing to pose, the classic portraiture approach is to keep the subject sharply focused while throwing the background into soft focus. This artistic choice emphasizes the subject and helps diminish the impact of any distracting background objects.

The following steps show you how to achieve this look:

1. **Set the Mode dial to A (aperture-priority autoexposure) and select a low f-stop value.**

    A low f-stop setting opens the aperture, which not only allows more light to enter the camera but also shortens depth of field (the distance over which focus appears acceptably sharp). However, for a group portrait, don't go too low or else the depth of field may not be enough to keep everyone in the sharp-focus zone. Take test shots and inspect your results at different f-stops to find the right setting.

    REMEMBER

    To adjust f-stop in A mode, rotate the Command dial or use the touchscreen controls (start by tapping the arrow box under the f-stop readout on the display). As soon as you set the f-stop, the camera selects the shutter speed for you, but you need to make sure the selected speed isn't so slow that movement of the subject or camera will blur the image. You can monitor the f-stop and shutter speed in the Information display and viewfinder, as shown in Figure 6-1.

Shutter speed   Aperture (f-stop)

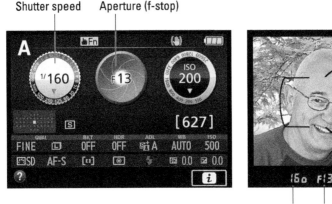

FIGURE 6-1:
You can
monitor
aperture
(f-stop) and
shutter speed
settings in the
displays.

Shutter speed   Aperture (f-stop)

2. **To further soften the background, zoom in, get closer, and put more distance between the subject and background.**

   Zooming in to a longer focal length also reduces depth of field, as does moving closer to your subject. And the greater the distance between the subject and background, the more the background blurs.

WARNING

   Avoid using a lens with extremely short or long focal lengths (wide angle and super-telephoto lenses), which can distort the face and other features. A lens with a focal length of 85mm to 120mm is ideal for a classic head-and-shoulders portrait.

3. **Check composition.**

   Two pointers on this topic:

   - *Consider the background.* Scan the entire frame, looking for background objects that may distract the eye from the subject. If necessary, reposition the subject against a more flattering backdrop.

   - *Frame the subject loosely to allow cropping to a variety of frame sizes.* Your camera produces images that have an aspect ratio of 3:2. That means your portrait perfectly fits a 4 x 6 print size but will require cropping to print at any other proportion, such as 5 x 7 or 8 x 10.

4. **For indoor portraits, shoot flash-free, if possible.**

   Shooting by available light rather than by flash produces softer illumination and avoids the problem of red-eye. To get enough light to go flash-free, turn on room lights or, during daylight, pose your subject next to a sunny window, as I did for the image in Figure 6-2.

REMEMBER

In the A exposure mode, simply keeping the built-in flash unit closed disables the flash. If flash is unavoidable, see my flash tips at the end of this step list to get better results.

5. **For outdoor portraits, use a flash if possible.**

Even in daylight, a flash usually adds a beneficial pop of light to subjects' faces, as illustrated in Figure 6-3. A flash is especially important when the background is brighter than the subjects, as in this example.

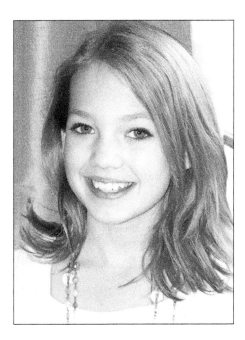

FIGURE 6-2:
For more pleasing indoor portraits, shoot by available light instead of using flash.

In the A exposure mode, press the Flash button on the side of the camera to raise the built-in flash. For daytime portraits, set the Flash mode to Fill Flash. (That's the regular, basic Flash mode.) For nighttime images, try red-eye reduction or slow-sync flash; again, see the flash tips at the end of these steps to use either mode most effectively.

WARNING

The fastest shutter speed possible for flash photography on the D5600 is 1/200 second, so in bright light, you may need to stop down the aperture to avoid overexposing the photo, as I did for the bottom image in Figure 6-3. Doing so, of course, brings the background into sharper focus, so if that creates an issue, move the subject into a shaded area instead.

6. **Press and hold the shutter button halfway to initiate exposure metering and autofocusing.**

Or, if you're focusing manually, set focus by rotating the focusing ring on the lens.

7. **Press the shutter button the rest of the way.**

No flash

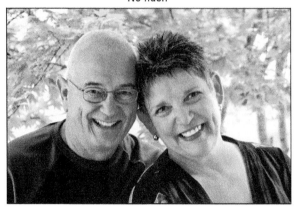

Fill flash

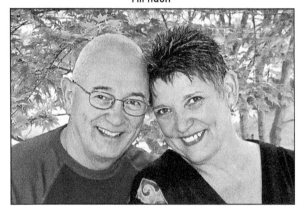

FIGURE 6-3:
To properly
illuminate the
face in outdoor
portraits, use
flash.

TIP

When flash is unavoidable, try these tricks for better results:

>> **Indoors, turn on as many room lights as possible.** With more ambient light, you reduce the flash power that's needed to expose the picture. Adding light also causes the pupils to constrict, further reducing the chances of red-eye. As an added benefit, the smaller pupil allows more of the subject's iris to be visible in the portrait, so you see more eye color.

>> **Pay attention to white balance if your subject is lit by both flash and ambient light.** If you set the White Balance setting to Auto, as I recommend in Table 6-1, enabling flash tells the camera to warm colors to compensate for the cool light of a flash. If your subject is also lit by other light sources, such as sunlight, the result may be colors that are slightly warmer or cooler (more blue) than neutral. A warming effect typically looks nice in portraits, giving the skin a subtle glow. If you aren't happy with the result, see Chapter 5 to find out how to fine-tune white balance.

>> **Try using a Flash mode that enables red-eye reduction or slow-sync flash.** If you choose the first option, warn your subject to expect both a preliminary light from the AF-assist lamp, which constricts pupils, and the flash. And remember that slow-sync flash uses a slower-than-normal shutter speed, which produces softer lighting and brighter backgrounds than normal flash. (Chapter 2 explains the various Flash modes.)

Figure 6-4 offers an example of how using slow-sync flash can improve an indoor portrait. When I used regular flash, the shutter speed was 1/60 second. At that speed, the camera has little time to soak up any ambient light. As a result, the scene is lit primarily by the flash. That caused two problems: The strong flash created glare on the subject's skin, and the window frame is more prominent because of the contrast between it and the darker bushes outside the window. Although it was daylight when I took the picture, the skies were overcast, so at 1/60 second, the exterior appears dark.

Regular fill flash, 1/60 second

Slow-sync flash, 1/4 second

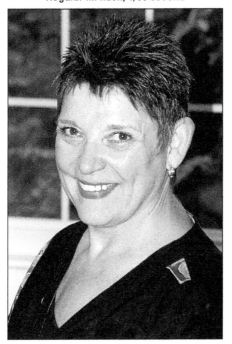 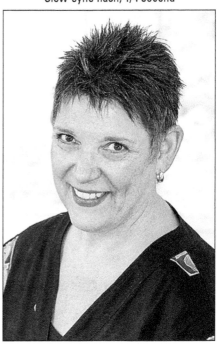

FIGURE 6-4: Slow-sync flash produces softer, more even lighting and brighter backgrounds.

In the slow-sync example, shot at 1/4 second, the exposure time was long enough to permit the ambient light to brighten the exteriors to the point that the window frame almost blends into the background. And because much less flash power was needed to expose the subject, the lighting is much more flattering. In this case, the bright background also helps to set the subject apart because of her dark hair and shirt. If the subject had been a pale blonde, this setup wouldn't have worked as well. Again, note the warming effect that can occur when you use Auto White Balance and shoot in a combination of flash and daylight and help eliminate shadows even more.

WARNING

Using a slower-than-normal shutter speed increases the risk of blur due to camera shake, so use a tripod or otherwise steady the camera. Remind your subjects to stay absolutely still, too, because they'll appear blurry if they move during the exposure. I was fortunate to have both a tripod and a cooperative subject for my examples, but I probably wouldn't opt for slow-sync for portraits of young children or pets.

» **For professional results, use an external flash with a rotating flash head.** Aim the flash head upward so that the flash light bounces off the ceiling and falls softly down onto the subject. External flashes can be pricey, but the results make the purchase worthwhile if you shoot lots of portraits. Compare the two portraits in Figure 6-5 for an illustration. In the first example, using the built-in flash resulted in strong shadowing behind the subject and harsh, concentrated light. To produce the better result on the right, I used a Nikon Speedlight external flash and bounced the light off the ceiling. I also moved the subject a few feet farther in front of the background to create more background blur.

Direct flash

Bounce flash

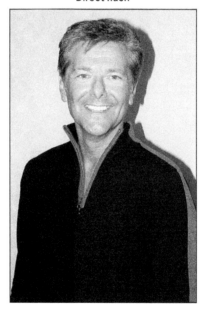 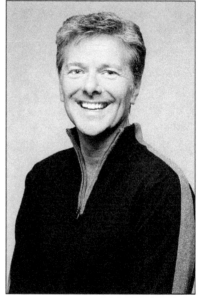

FIGURE 6-5:
To eliminate harsh lighting and strong shadows (left), use bounce flash and move the subject farther from the background (right).

Make sure that the surface you use to bounce the light is white; otherwise, the flash light will pick up the color of the surface and influence the color of your subject.

>> **Invest in a flash diffuser to further soften the light.** A *diffuser* is simply a piece of translucent plastic or fabric that you place over the flash to soften and spread the light — much like how sheer curtains diffuse window light. Diffusers come in lots of different designs, including models that fit over the built-in flash.

Capturing Action

Using a fast shutter speed is the key to capturing a blur-free shot of any moving subject, whether it's a flower in the breeze, a spinning Ferris wheel, or, as in the case of Figure 6-6, a racing cyclist.

Along with the basic capture settings outlined earlier, in Table 6-1, try the techniques in the following steps to photograph a subject in motion:

1. **Set the Mode dial to S (shutter-priority autoexposure).**

   In this mode, you control the shutter speed, and the camera takes care of choosing an aperture setting that will produce a good exposure.

2. **Select the shutter speed.**

   Refer to Figure 6-1 to locate shutter speed in the Information display and viewfinder. In S mode, you adjust shutter speed by rotating the Command dial or by using the touchscreen control found under the shutter-speed display in the Information screen.

   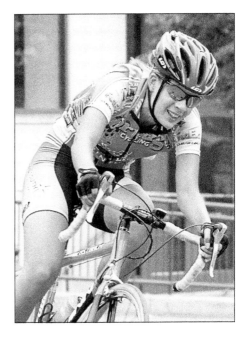

   FIGURE 6-6:
   Use a high shutter speed to freeze motion.

   What shutter speed should you choose? It depends on the speed of your subject, so you need to experiment. But generally speaking, 1/320 second should be plenty for all but the fastest subjects (race cars, boats, and so on).

For slow subjects, you can even go as low as 1/250 or 1/125 second. My subject in Figure 7-6 zipped along at a pretty fast pace, so I set the shutter speed to 1/640 second. Remember, though, that when you increase shutter speed, the camera opens the aperture to maintain the same exposure. At low f-stop numbers, depth of field becomes shorter, so you have to be more careful to keep your subject within the sharp-focus zone as you compose and focus the shot.

TIP

You also can take an entirely different approach to capturing action: Rather than choose a fast shutter speed, select a speed slow enough to blur the moving objects, which can create a heightened sense of motion and, in scenes that feature very colorful subjects, cool abstract images. I took this approach when shooting the carnival ride featured in Figure 6-7. For the left image, I set the shutter speed to 1/30 second; for the right version, I slowed things down to 1/5 second. In both cases, I used a tripod, but because nearly everything in the frame was moving, the entirety of both photos is blurry — the 1/5 second version is simply more blurry because of the slower shutter.

1/30 second | 1/5 second

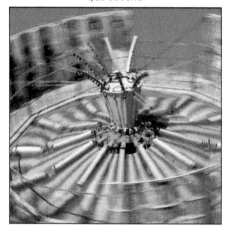 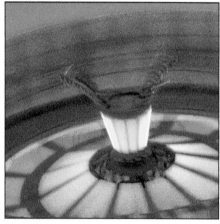

FIGURE 6-7:
Using a shutter speed slow enough to blur moving objects can be a fun creative choice, too.

3. **In dim lighting, raise the ISO setting, if necessary, to allow a fast shutter speed.**

Unless you're shooting in bright daylight, you may not be able to use a fast shutter speed at a low ISO, even if the camera opens the aperture as far as possible. If auto ISO override is in force, ISO may go up automatically when you increase the shutter speed — Chapter 3 has details on that feature. Raising the ISO does increase the possibility of noise, so you have to decide whether a noisy shot is better than a blurry shot.

Why not add flash to brighten the scene? Well, adding flash is tricky for action shots, unfortunately. First, the flash needs time to recycle between shots, which slows the capture rate. Second, the built-in flash has limited range, so don't waste your time if your subject isn't close by. And third, remember that the fastest shutter speed you can use with flash is 1/200 second by default, which may not be high enough to capture a quickly moving subject without blur.

4. **For rapid-fire shooting, set the Release mode to Continuous Low or Continuous High.**

   In both modes, you can capture multiple images with a single press of the shutter button. Continuous Low captures up to 3 frames per second (fps), and Continuous High bumps the frame rate up to about 5 fps. As long as you hold down the button, the camera continues to record images. Here again, though, you need to go flash-free; otherwise, you get one shot per press of the shutter button, just as in Single Frame release mode.

   The fastest way to access the Release mode setting is to press the Release mode button on the left front side of the camera.

5. **Select speed-oriented focusing options.**

   For fastest shooting, try manual focusing: It eliminates the time the camera needs to lock focus when you use autofocusing. If you use autofocus, select these two autofocus settings for best performance:

   - *Focus mode:* AF-C (continuous-servo autofocus).

   - *AF-area mode:* Choose one of the Dynamic-area settings. Chapter 4 has information to help you decide whether the 9-point, 21-point, or 39-point setting is best for your subject.

   At these settings, the camera sets focus initially on your selected focus point, but then looks to the surrounding points for focusing information if your subject moves away from the selected point. Focus is adjusted continuously until you take the shot.

   You can adjust both focus settings via the control strip; press the *i* button or tap the onscreen *i* icon to activate the strip. The focus settings are found adjacent to each other on the second row of the strip.

6. **Compose the subject to allow for movement across the frame.**

   Frame your shot a little wider than you normally might so that you lessen the risk your subject will move out of the frame before you record the image. You can always crop to a tighter composition later. (I used this approach for my cyclist image — the original shot includes a lot of background that I later cropped away.) It's also a good idea to leave more room in front of the subject than behind it. This makes it obvious that your subject is going somewhere.

TIP

Action-shooting strategies also are helpful for shooting candid portraits of kids and pets. Even if your subjects aren't currently running, leaping, or otherwise cavorting, snapping a shot before they do move is often tough. So if an interaction catches your eye, set your camera into action mode and fire off a series of shots as fast as you can.

Capturing Scenic Vistas

Providing specific capture settings for landscape photography is tricky because there's no single best approach to capturing a beautiful stretch of countryside, a city skyline, or another vast subject. Most people prefer using a wide-angle lens, for example, to incorporate a large area of the landscape into the scene, but if you're far away from your subject, you may like the results you get from a telephoto or medium-angle lens. When shooting the scene in Figure 6-8, for example, I had to position myself across the street from the buildings, so I captured the shot using a focal length of 82mm.

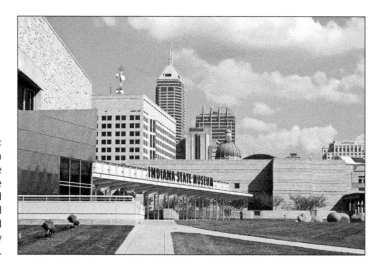

FIGURE 6-8:
Use a high f-stop value to keep the foreground and background sharply focused.

And consider depth of field: One person's idea of a super cityscape might be to keep all buildings in the scene sharply focused, but another photographer might prefer to shoot the same scene so that a foreground building is sharply focused while the others are less so, thus drawing the eye to that first building.

I can, however, offer a few tips to help you photograph a landscape the way *you* see it:

>> **Shoot in aperture-priority autoexposure mode (A) so you can control depth of field.** If you want extreme depth of field so that both near and distant objects are sharply focused (refer to Figure 6-8), select a high f-stop value. I used an aperture of f/18 for this shot. For short depth of field, use a low value.

>> **If the exposure requires a slow shutter speed, use a tripod to avoid blurring.** The downside to a high f-stop is that you may need a slower shutter speed to produce a good exposure. If the shutter speed drops below what you can comfortably handhold, use a tripod to avoid picture-blurring camera shake.

If you don't have a tripod handy and can't find any other way to stabilize the camera, turn on Vibration Reduction, if your lens offers that feature. This option helps to compensate for slight camera movement, increasing chances of a sharp handheld shot.

With a Nikon AF-P lens, you enable the feature via the Optical VR setting on the Shooting menu. AF-S lenses that offer Vibration Reduction typically have a lens switch, marked VR, that you use to turn the feature on and off.

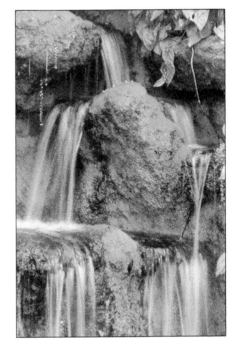

>> **For dramatic waterfall shots, consider using a slow shutter to create that "misty" look.** The slow shutter blurs the water, giving it a soft, romantic appearance, as shown in Figure 6-9. Again, use a tripod to ensure that the rest of the scene doesn't also blur due to camera shake. Shutter speed for the image in Figure 6-9 was 1/5 second.

TIP

In very bright light, you may overexpose the image at a very slow shutter, even if you stop the aperture all the way down and select the camera's lowest ISO setting. As a solution, consider investing in a *neutral density filter* for your lens. This type of filter works something like sunglasses for your camera: It simply reduces the amount of light that passes through the lens, without

FIGURE 6-9:
For misty waterfalls, use a slow shutter speed and a tripod.

affecting image colors, so that you can use a slower shutter than would otherwise be possible.

» **At sunrise or sunset, base exposure on the sky.** The foreground will be dark, but you can usually brighten it in a photo editor, if needed. If you base exposure on the foreground, on the other hand, the sky will become so bright that all the color will be washed out — a problem you usually can't fix after the fact. You can also invest in a *graduated neutral-density filter,* which transitions from dark to clear. You orient the filter so the dark half falls over the sky and the clear part falls over the dimly lit portion of the scene. This setup enables you to better expose the foreground without blowing out the sky colors.

Also experiment with the Active D-Lighting and HDR features that I cover in Chapter 3; both are designed to create images that contain a greater range of brightness values than is normally possible.

» **For cool nighttime city pics, experiment with slow shutter speeds.** Assuming that cars or other vehicles with their lights on are moving through the scene, the result is neon trails of light like those you see in the foreground of the image in Figure 6-10. Shutter speed for this image was about 10 seconds.

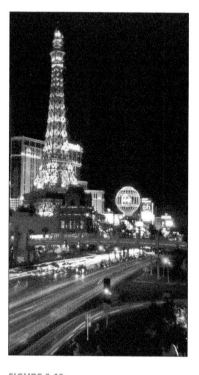

FIGURE 6-10:
Using a slow shutter speed creates neon light trails in nighttime city street scenes.

TIP

Rather than change the shutter speed manually between each shot, try *Bulb* mode. Available only in M (manual) exposure mode, this option records an image for as long as you hold down the shutter button. So just take a series of images, holding down the button for different lengths of time for each shot. In Bulb mode, you also can exceed the standard maximum exposure time of 30 seconds.

As is the case for other slow-shutter photos, using a tripod is a must for this type of shot; any camera shake will blur the stationary objects in the scene. And note that enabling Vibration Reduction isn't sufficient for the very slow shutter speeds used to capture either my waterfall picture in Figure 6-9 or the city scene in Figure 6-10.

>> **For the best lighting, shoot during the *magic hours*.** That's the term photographers use for early morning and late afternoon, when the light cast by the sun is soft and warm, giving everything that beautiful, gently warmed look.

TIP

Can't wait for the perfect light? Tweak your camera's White Balance setting, using the instructions laid out in Chapter 5, to simulate the color of magic-hour light.

>> **In tricky light, bracket exposures.** *Bracketing* simply means to take the same picture at several different exposure settings to increase the odds that at least one of them will capture the scene the way you envision. Bracketing is especially a good idea in difficult lighting situations, such as sunrise and sunset. Chapter 3 shows you how to make bracketing easier by using automatic exposure bracketing.

If depth of field is important to your shot, set the camera to the M or A exposure modes. That way, the camera adjusts shutter speed between shots, leaving your selected f-stop intact so that depth of field — which is in part determined by the f-stop — remains consistent throughout all your shots.

>> **For wide-angle landscape shots, try including a person or other object in the foreground.** By comparing the size of the person or object with the surrounding landscape, the viewer gets a better idea of the vastness of the setting.

Capturing Dynamic Close-Ups

For great close-up shots, try these techniques:

>> **Check your lens manual to find out its minimum close-focusing distance.** How "up close and personal" you can get to your subject depends on your lens, not on the camera body.

>> **Take control over depth of field by setting the camera mode to A (aperture-priority autoexposure) mode.** Whether you want a shallow, medium, or extreme depth of field depends on the point of your photo. In classic nature photography, for example, the artistic tradition is a very shallow depth of field, as shown in Figure 6-11, and requires an open aperture (low f-stop value). If you want the viewer to be able to clearly see all details throughout the frame — for example, you're shooting a product shot for a sales catalog — you need to go in the other direction, stopping down the aperture as far as possible.

>> **Remember that depth of field decreases when you zoom in or move closer to your subject.** Go back to that product shot: If you need depth of field beyond what you can achieve with the aperture setting, you may need to back away, zoom out, or both. (You can always crop your image to show just the parts of the subject that you want to feature.)

>> **When shooting flowers and other nature scenes outdoors, pay attention to shutter speed, too.** Even a slight breeze may cause your subject to move, causing blurring at slow shutter speeds.

>> **Experiment with using flash for better outdoor lighting.** Just as with portraits, a tiny bit of flash can sometimes improve close-ups when the sun is the primary light source. Again, though, keep in mind that the maximum shutter

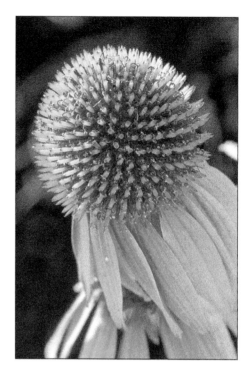

FIGURE 6-11:
Shallow depth of field is a classic technique for close-up floral images.

speed possible when you use the built-in flash is 1/200 second. So in very bright light, you may need to use a high f-stop setting to avoid overexposing the picture. You can also adjust the flash output via the Flash Compensation control. Chapter 2 offers details.

>> **When shooting indoors, avoid using the built-in flash as your primary light source when you're positioned very near the subject.** At close range, the light from your flash may be too harsh even if you reduce flash power by using the Flash Compensation feature. If flash is inevitable, turn on as many room lights as possible to reduce the flash power that's needed. (If you have multiple light sources, though, you may need to tweak the White Balance setting.)

>> **To get really close to your subject, invest in a macro lens or a set of diopters.** A true macro lens, which enables you to set focus really, really close to your subjects, is an expensive proposition; prices range from a few

hundred to a couple thousand dollars. If you enjoy capturing the tiny details in life, though, it's worth the investment.

Nikon has a great guide to its macro lenses — officially titled *Micro-Nikkor Lenses* — at its www.nikonusa.com website, if you're ready to start shopping.

For a less-expensive way to go, you can spend about $40 for a set of *diopters,* which are like reading glasses that you screw onto your lens. Diopters come in several strengths — +1, +2, +4, and so on — with a higher number indicating a greater magnifying power. I took this approach to capture the extreme close-up in Figure 6-12, attaching a +2 diopter to my lens. The downside of using a diopter, sadly, is that it typically produces images that are very soft around the edges, a problem that doesn't occur with a good macro lens.

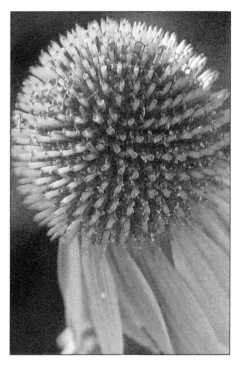

FIGURE 6-12:
To extend your lens's close-focus capability, you can add magnifying diopters.

Coping with Special Situations

A few subjects and shooting situations pose some additional challenges not already covered in earlier sections. To close this chapter, here's a quick list of ideas for tackling a variety of common tough–shot photos:

» **Shooting fireworks:** First off, use a tripod; fireworks require a long exposure, and trying to handhold your camera simply won't work. If you're using a zoom lens, zoom out to the shortest focal length (widest angle). Switch to manual focusing and set focus at infinity (the farthest focus point possible on your lens). Set the exposure mode to manual, choose a relatively high f-stop setting — say, f/16 or so — and start at a shutter speed of 1 to 5 seconds. From there, it's simply a matter of experimenting with different shutter speeds. Also play with the timing of the shutter release, starting some exposures at the moment the fireworks are shot up, some at the moment they burst open, and so on.

For the example featured in Figure 6-13, I used a shutter speed of about 5 seconds and began the exposure as the rocket was going up — that's what creates the "corkscrew" of light that rises up through the frame.

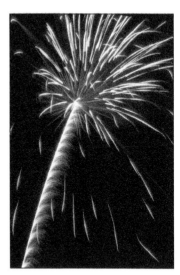

Be especially gentle when you press the shutter button — with a very slow shutter, you can easily create enough camera movement to blur the image. To avoid that issue, use a remote control to trigger the shutter release. (See Chapter 2 for help with remote-control shooting.)

FIGURE 6-13:
A shutter speed of 5 seconds captured this fireworks shot.

» **Shooting through glass:** To capture subjects that are behind glass, such as animals at a zoo, you can try a couple of tricks. First, set your camera to manual focusing — the glass barrier can give the autofocus mechanism fits. Disable the flash to avoid creating any unwanted reflections, too. Then, if you can get close enough, your best odds are to put the lens right up to the glass. (Be careful not to scratch your lens.) If you must stand farther away, try to position your lens at a 90-degree angle to the glass.

» **Shooting out a car window:** Set the camera to shutter-priority autoexposure or manual mode and dial in a fast shutter speed to compensate for the movement of the car. Also turn on Vibration Reduction, if your lens offers it. Oh, and keep a tight grip on your camera.

» **Shooting in strong backlighting:** When the light behind your subject is very strong, the result is often an underexposed subject. You can try using flash to better expose the subject, assuming you're shooting in an exposure mode that permits flash. The Active D-Lighting feature covered in Chapter 3 can also help brighten your subject without blowing out highlights. And don't forget that your camera has a built-in HDR (high dynamic range) mode, which blends two exposures to include more shadows and highlights in the scene. (Chapter 3 has examples.)

For another creative choice, you can purposely underexpose the subject to create a silhouette effect, as shown in Figure 6-14. Base the exposure on the brightest areas of the background so that the darker areas of the frame remain dark.

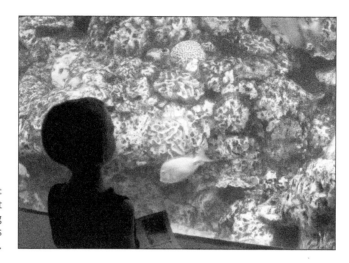

FIGURE 6-14:
Experiment with shooting backlit subjects in silhouette.

IN THIS CHAPTER

» Recording your first movie using the default settings

» Understanding the frame rate, frame size, and movie quality options

» Adjusting audio-recording options

» Controlling exposure during movie recording

» Playing and trimming movies

» Taking a still photo during recording

Chapter **7**

Shooting, Viewing, and Trimming Movies

n addition to being a stellar still-photography camera, your D5600 enables you to record HD (high-definition) movies. This chapter tells you everything you need to know to take advantage of the movie-recording options.

REMEMBER

Check that: This chapter tells you *almost* everything about movie recording. What's missing here is detailed information about focusing, which works the same way for movie shooting as it does when you use Live View to shoot a still photo. Rather than cover the subject twice, I detail your focusing options in Chapter 4 and provide just a recap in these pages.

Also visit the end of Chapter 1, which lists precautions to take while Live View is engaged, whether you're shooting stills or movies. (To answer your question: No, you can't use the viewfinder for movie recording; Live View is your only option.)

Shooting Movies Using Default Settings

Video enthusiasts will appreciate the fact that the D5600 enables you to tweak a variety of recording settings. But if you're not up to sorting through those options, just use the default settings. (You can restore the critical defaults by opening the Shooting menu and choosing Reset Shooting Menu.)

The following steps show you how to record a movie using the default settings:

1. **Set the Mode dial on top of the camera to Auto.**

   In this mode, the camera takes care of most movie settings for you, including ones that affect exposure and color.

2. **Engage Live View by rotating the LV, shown in Figure 7-1, toward the back of the camera.**

   The viewfinder goes dark, and your subject appears on the monitor.

3. **Press the Info button until the display is set to Show Movie Indicators view, shown in Figure 7-2.**

   Later sections decode all the symbols you see; for now, pay attention to these bits of information:

   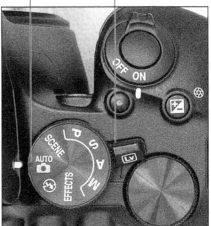

   Live View on/off switch

   Exposure mode setting

   FIGURE 7-1:
   Rotate the Live View switch to toggle between Live View and viewfinder photography.

   • The shaded bars at the top and bottom of the screen represent the vertical boundaries of the movie frame. All movies are captured at the normal HD aspect ratio of 16:9.

   • The available recording time appears in the area labeled in Figure 7-2. At the default recording settings, your movie can be 20 minutes long, assuming your memory card has enough free space to hold the entire movie. You need at least 4GB (gigabytes) of space.

   • If the letters REC with a slash through them appear near the recording time readout, recording isn't possible. You see this symbol if no memory card is inserted or the card is full, for example.

- Note the status of the touch shutter, labeled in Figure 7-2. The icon shown in the figure indicates the touch shutter is turned off, which is the setting I recommend for movie recording. (Tap the icon to enable and disable the feature.) With the touch shutter off, you can tap the touchscreen to set focus only. When the touch shutter is on, the camera takes a still picture as soon as you lift your finger off the monitor.

Touch shutter symbol

Available recording time

Focus mode

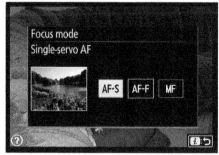

FIGURE 7-2:
Press the Info button to cycle through the Live View display modes until you see these movie-recording symbols.

4. **Choose a Focus mode (AF-S, AF-F, or MF).**

   AF-S and AF-F are autofocus modes; MF sets the camera to manual focusing mode. (If your lens has an exterior auto/manual focusing switch, also move that switch to the auto or manual focus position.)

You can see the current Focus mode setting at the top of the monitor, as shown in Figure 7-2. To change the setting, use the control strip, as shown in Figure 7-3. *Remember:* Press the *i* button or tap the onscreen *i* symbol (shown in Figure 7-2) to bring up the control strip.

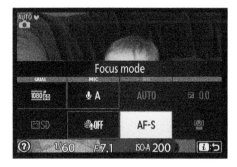

FIGURE 7-3:
Set the Focus mode via the control strip.

Here's a refresher on the two autofocus modes, detailed in Chapter 4:

- *AF-S:* Choose this option if you expect your subject to remain the same distance from the camera throughout the movie — for example, if you're recording a piano performance. (Think AF-*S,* for *stationary subject.*)

- *AF-F:* This setting produces full-time, continuous autofocusing, with the camera adjusting focus as your subject moves or you pan the camera to follow the action.

Although AF-F autofocusing is best for tracking moving subjects, the built-in microphone sometimes picks up the sound of the focusing motor. To avoid this issue, you can attach an external microphone and place it far enough from the camera that it can't hear the focus motor. Or you can disable audio recording on the camera and use a separate device to capture sound. Of course, you then have to merge the soundtrack and the video in a video editing program. (See the section "Controlling Audio," later in this chapter, for more details on sound recording.)

5. **Compose your initial shot.**

The shaded areas at the top and bottom of the monitor indicate the boundaries of the default frame size, 1920 x 1080 pixels, which produces a 16:9 aspect ratio.

6. **If necessary, move the focusing frame over your subject.**

By default, the camera uses the Face-Priority AF-area mode, which means that if the camera detects a face in the scene, a yellow focus frame over the face, as shown in Figure 7-4. When the scene contains more than one face, you see multiple frames; the one with the interior corner markings indicates the face chosen as the focus point. You can use the Multi Selector or tap the screen to move the frame over a different face.

Time remaining   Recording symbol

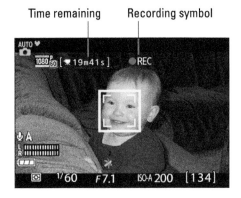

FIGURE 7-4:
The red Rec symbol appears while recording is in progress.

If the camera doesn't detect a face, it instead uses the Wide-area AF-area mode, and the focus frame appears as a red rectangle. Again, use the touchscreen or Multi Selector to move the frame over your subject.

7. **Focus the shot.**

The process varies depending on the Focus mode you selected in Step 4, as follows:

- *AF-F autofocusing:* As soon as you set the Focus mode to AF-F, autofocusing begins. You don't need to take any action except wait for the focusing frame to turn green, indicating that initial focus is set.

To interrupt continuous autofocusing and lock in the current focusing distance, press and hold the shutter button halfway down. You also can use the touchscreen, putting your finger on the desired focus point. When you lift your finger off the button or screen, continuous autofocusing begins again.

- *AF-S:* Press the shutter button halfway or tap the focus frame on the touchscreen. Again, the focus frame turns green when focus is achieved. Focus is locked at that distance and you can then take your finger off the shutter button or touchscreen if you want.

8. **To begin recording, press the red movie-record button on top of the camera (refer to Figure 7-1).**

Most shooting data disappears from the screen, and a red Rec symbol appears, as shown in Figure 7-4. As recording progresses, the area labeled *Time remaining* in the figure shows you how many more minutes of video you can record.

During recording, you can set a new focus point by pressing the shutter button halfway or tapping the touchscreen. After the camera finds the new focus target, release the button or lift your finger off the touchscreen. In AF-S mode, focus is locked at the new distance; in AF-F mode, continuous autofocusing resumes. Keep in mind that the video footage may include some blurry frames during the time when the camera is finding the new focus point.

9. **To stop recording, press the movie-record button again.**

Wait for the memory card access light to turn off before powering down the camera; while the light is on, data is still being written to the memory card. Look for the light on the back of the camera, just below the Delete (trash can) button.

TECHNICAL STUFF

Movies are created in the MOV format, which means you can play them on your computer using most video-playback programs. You also can view movies in Nikon ViewNX-i, the free software Nikon makes available on the support pages of its website. To view your movies on an HDTV screen, see the end of Chapter 8 to find out how to connect your camera to your set.

Two quick tips to add to these recording basics:

TIP

» **Declutter the display by pressing the Info button.** The display changes to the Hide Indicators display mode. In that mode, you see only the focus frame(s). In addition, four white horizontal marks appear, indicating the 16:9 movie-framing area. After you begin recording, the indicators disappear, and black bars appear at the top and bottom of the screen to indicate the available framing area. You also can press Info again to display a grid over the scene, which is helpful for keeping the horizon level in the frame.

Here's an important caveat, though: In these display modes, pressing the *i* button brings up the control strip for still photography. To view the movie version, you must use the Show Movie Indicators display.

>> **Optical Vibration Reduction does not work during movie recording.** Even though you see the "shaking hand" symbol on the left side of the display (refer to Figure 7-2), indicating the feature is enabled, no stabilization occurs after you begin recording. (See Chapter 4 for more information about this feature, which can result in sharper photographs when you handhold the camera.)

>> **You can stop recording and capture a still image in one fell swoop.** Just press and hold the shutter button until you hear the shutter release. The number found within the brackets in the lower-right corner of the screen indicates how many still photos you can fit in the empty card space if you stop recording. As each second of recording ticks by and card space is depleted, the value that indicates the number of remaining still shots drops. For another option, you can save a single frame of your movie as a still photo. The last section of this chapter tells you how.

Adjusting Video Settings

REMEMBER

If you're interested in taking more control over your recordings, start by exploring the Frame Size/Frame Rate and Movie Quality settings. Together, these settings determine the look of your video and its file size, which in turn determines the length of the movie you can record.

Using the Live View control strip, you can adjust both settings at once — more about that option later. But unless you're an experienced videographer, it's helpful to look at them separately first so that you understand what each option adds to the mix.

Start by scrolling to the second page of the Shooting menu, shown on the left in Figure 7-5. Choose Movie Settings to display the screen shown on the right, where the Frame Size/Frame Rate and Movie Quality options head the list of the recording settings.

FIGURE 7-5:
Select Movie
Settings from
the Shooting
menu and then
select Frame
Size/Frame
Rate.

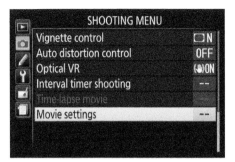
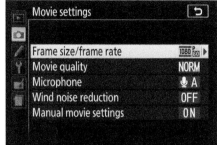

If you're a video novice, here's what you need to know to choose the best settings for your movie:

>> **Frame Size/Frame Rate:** Choose Frame Size/Frame Rate, as shown on the right in Figure 7-5, to display the screen shown in Figure 7-6. For now, concentrate on the numbers that follow the symbol to the left of each setting. The first pair of numbers indicates frame size, or movie *resolution* (number of pixels). In the world of HDTV, 1920 x 1080 pixels is considered *Full HD,* whereas 1280 x 720 is known as *Standard HD,* which produces slightly lesser quality than Full HD (although I suspect few people can determine the difference).

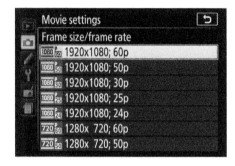

FIGURE 7-6:
You get a choice of two frame sizes and frame rates ranging from 60 to 24 frames per second.

The second value represents the frame rate, measured in frames per second (fps). Available frame rates range from 60 to 24 frames per second, with each delivering a slightly different video quality, as follows:

● *24 fps is the standard for motion pictures.* It gives your videos a softer, more movielike look.

● *25 fps gives your videos a slightly sharper, more "realistic" look.* This frame rate is the standard for television broadcast in countries that follow the PAL video-signal standard, such as some European countries.

- *30 fps produces an even crisper picture than 25 fps.* This frame rate is the broadcast video standard for the United States and other countries that use the NTSC signal standard.

- *50 and 60 fps are often used for recording high-speed action and creating slow-motion footage.* With more frames per second, fast movements are rendered more smoothly, especially if you slow down the movie playback for a slo-mo review of the action.

  How about 50 versus 60? You're back to the PAL versus NTSC question: 50 fps is a PAL standard, and 60 is an NTSC standard.

  As for the letter *p* following the frames-per-second value, it indicates that footage is recorded using the *progressive* video format, which is the most current dSLR video-recording technology. The D5600 uses only this format; the older *interlaced (i)* format isn't provided.

  Now back to the symbol at the left side of each option: It simply puts into graphic form the selected setting. However, only the horizontal frame size is presented (1080 or 720). So the graphic on line one of Figure 7-6, for example, indicates that the Frame Size is set to 1920 x 1080 and the Frame Rate is set to 60p.

» **Movie Quality:** This option determines how much compression is applied to the video file. The compression level affects the *bit rate,* or how much data is used to represent 1 second of video, measured in Mbps (megabits per second). You get two choices: High and Normal. The High setting results in a higher bit rate, which means better quality and larger files. Normal produces a lower bit rate and smaller files.

  To adjust the Movie Quality setting, select Movie Settings from the Shooting menu, as shown on the left in Figure 7-7. On the next screen, select Movie Quality, as shown on the right side of the figure, to access the screen where you change the setting.

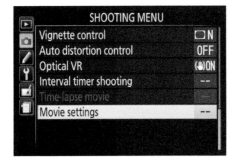
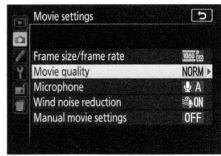

FIGURE 7-7: To set the Movie Quality, follow this menu path.

If you take a magnifying glass to the Live View display, you also can view the current Frame Size/Frame Rate and Movie Quality settings near the upper-left corner of the screen, as shown in Figure 7-8. The Frame Size/Frame Rate symbols are the same ones you see on the menu selection screen; the Movie Quality is indicated by a star or lack thereof. If you see a star, as shown in the figure, the Movie Quality is set to High. No star means the option is set to Normal (which is the default).

Frame size/frame rate

Quality set to High

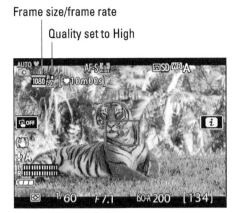

FIGURE 7-8:
In the default Movie display mode, the Frame Size/Frame Rate and Movie Quality settings appear here.

After you're comfortable with both settings, you can save time by adjusting them as a combo pack via the control strip, shown in Figure 7-9. Just to add a little confusion to an already baffling situation, the option name on the control strip is Qual; it's highlighted in the left screen shown in the figure. On the settings screen (the right side of the figure), you see boxes representing each of the possible combinations of frame size, frame rate, and movie quality. As you scroll through the settings, a label at the top of the screen tells you what Frame Size/Frame Rate and Movie Quality the current option delivers. For example, the chosen setting in the figure results in a 1920 x 1080 Frame Size, 60 fps Frame Rate, and High Movie Quality.

Maximum recording time

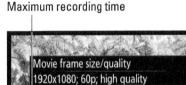

FIGURE 7-9:
For fast access to video settings, press the *i* button to bring up the movie-recording version of the control strip.

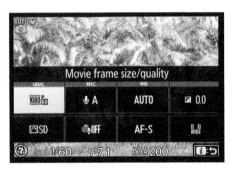

MAXIMUM RECORDING TIMES

The maximum recording time of a single video clip depends on the Frame Size/Frame Rate and Movie Quality options, as outlined here. Your memory card also must have enough free space to hold the entire movie; the maximum file size for a movie at any setting is 4GB. Recording stops automatically when you reach the maximum file size for recording time or run out of memory card space.

Frame Size	FPS	Quality	Maximum Movie Length
1920 x 1080	60, 50	High	10 minutes
		Normal	20 minutes
1920 x 1080	30, 25, 24	High	20 minutes
		Normal	29 minutes, 59 seconds
1280 x 720	60, 50	High	20 minutes
		Normal	29 minutes, 59 seconds

TIP

As you cycle through the settings, the box on the left side of the screen tells you the maximum length of movie you can create at the current pairing of Frame Size/Frame Rate and Movie Quality. When you max things out for both options (top frame size, top frame rate, and high quality), the maximum recording time is 10 minutes, as shown on the right in Figure 7-9. The "Maximum recording times" sidebar lists how many minutes of video you can capture in a single recording at each setting.

Controlling Audio

You can record sound using the camera's built-in microphone, labeled on the left in Figure 7-10, or attach an external microphone such as the Nikon ME-1 to the jack labeled on the right in the figure. During on-camera playback, sound comes from the speaker, labeled on the left in the figure.

If you use the built-in mic, you can adjust two audio settings, Microphone and Wind Noise Reduction, explained in the next two sections. For an external mic, only the Microphone setting applies.

Speakers   Built-in stereo microphone   External microphone jack

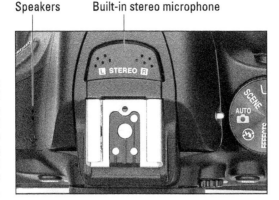 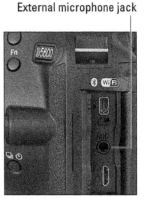

FIGURE 7-10:
You can record audio with the internal microphone (left) or plug in an external microphone (right).

Setting microphone sensitivity

WARNING

The most critical audio-recording control is the Microphone setting, which affects the sensitivity of the microphone. You can set the mic to record even the faintest of sounds, capture just the loudest, or something in between. However, you must choose the setting *before* you start the recording; you can't change it while the recording is in progress.

You can choose from the following settings:

>> **Auto Sensitivity:** The camera automatically adjusts the volume according to the level of the ambient noise. This setting is the default.

>> **Manual Sensitivity:** You specify the volume level, with settings ranging from 1 to 20.

>> **Microphone Off:** Choose this setting to record video with no sound.

Symbols representing the current setting appear in the display, as shown in Figure 7-11. (If you don't see similar data on your screen, press the Info button to change the display style.) The microphone symbol indicates that audio recording is enabled; the letter *A* indicates the Auto Sensitivity option. If you set the camera to Manual Sensitivity, your selected volume level appears instead. Turn audio recording off, and you see a microphone with a slash through it.

Microphone setting and volume meter

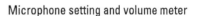

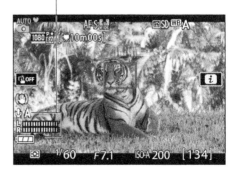

FIGURE 7-11:
These symbols indicate the current Microphone setting and volume level.

Beneath those symbols, you see two horizontal bars that indicate sound volume. When you're recording stereo sound, the top bar shows the sound level of the left audio channel; the bottom bar, the right channel.

TECHNICAL STUFF

Audio levels are measured in decibels (dB), and levels on the volume meter range from –40 (very, very soft) to 0 (as loud as can be measured digitally). Ideally, sound should peak consistently in the –12 range. The indicators on the meter turn yellow in this range. If the sound level is too high, the bar at the top of the meter turns red — a warning that audio may be distorted.

To adjust the Microphone setting, you can go two routes:

>> **Shooting menu:** Choose Movie Settings from the Shooting menu to display the screen shown on the left in Figure 7-12. Select Microphone to display the screen shown on the right, which lists the three settings plus a volume meter. After highlighting your choice, press or tap OK.

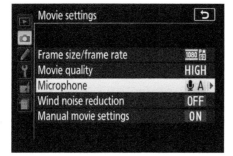
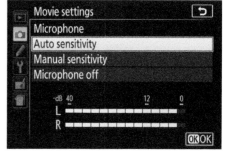

FIGURE 7-12: You can access the Microphone settings via the Movie Settings option on the Shooting menu.

If you choose Manual Sensitivity, you see the screen shown in Figure 7-13, and you can set a specific volume level from 1 to 20. Press the Multi Selector up and down or tap the up/down arrows in the middle of the screen to change the setting. Again, the volume meters are guide you as you adjust the level.

Don't forget to press the OK button or tap the OK symbol to make your change official.

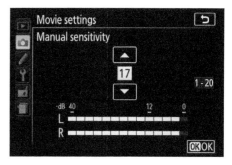

FIGURE 7-13: The Manual microphone option enables you to set a specific volume level.

>> **Control strip:** Press the *i* button or tap the *i* symbol on the display to display the control strip. Select the Microphone setting, as shown on the left in Figure 7-14, to display the second screen in the figure. Again, you see the volume meters plus symbols representing the Auto, Manual, and Off settings, as labeled in the figure. If you choose Manual, options appear to enable you to set the volume level. Press the OK button or tap the OK icon onscreen to lock in the setting. Then press the *i* button or tap the *i* icon to exit the settings screen.

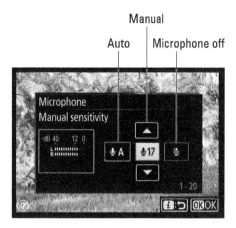

FIGURE 7-14:
You can
adjust the
Microphone
setting from
the control
strip.

Reducing wind noise

Ever seen a newscaster out in the field, carrying a microphone that looks like it's covered with a big piece of foam? That foam thing is a wind filter. It's designed to lessen the sounds the wind makes when it hits the microphone.

You can enable a digital version of the same thing via the Wind Noise Reduction option. Essentially, the filter works by reducing the volume of noises that are similar to those made by wind. The problem is that some noises *not* made by wind can also be muffled when the filter is enabled. So when you're indoors or shooting on a still day, keep this option set to Off, as it is by default. Also note that when you use an external microphone, the Wind Filter feature has no effect.

To turn Wind Noise Reduction on or off, use the control strip, as shown in Figure 7-15. Or visit the Shooting menu, open the Movie Settings screen, and choose Wind Noise Reduction.

When the feature is enabled, the symbol labeled on the right in Figure 7-15 appears with the other microphone settings. The symbol disappears with Wind Noise Reduction turned off.

REMEMBER

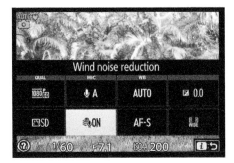
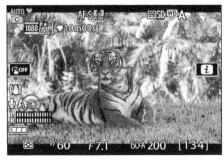

FIGURE 7-15:
Access the
Wind Noise
Reduction
setting via the
control strip, as
shown here, or
via the Movie
Settings option
on the Shoot-
ing menu.

Exploring Other Recording Options

In addition to settings reviewed in the preceding sections, you can control a few other aspects of your cinematic effort. The following list runs through these options; Figure 7-16 labels the symbols that represent these settings in the display.

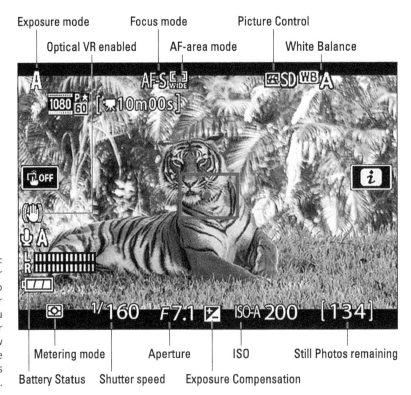

FIGURE 7-16:
Here's your
road map to
other major
settings you
can monitor
in the Show
Movie
Indicators
display mode.

>> **Exposure mode:** You can record movies in any exposure mode (Auto, Scene modes, Effects modes, P, M, and so on). As with still photography, your choice determines which camera settings you can access. (The Movie Settings menu options are available in all modes, however.)

>> **Exposure settings:** The aperture (f-stop), shutter speed, ISO, Metering mode, and Exposure Compensation settings, all labeled in Figure 7-16, determine movie exposure. In the P, S, A, and M modes, as well as in Night Vision Effects mode, you have some control over all these options except Metering mode; the camera always uses Matrix metering for movie recording. See the next section for details on adjusting exposure. For all other exposure modes, the camera handles exposure automatically.

>> **Focus options:** Your options are the same as for Live View still photography, detailed in Chapter 4. As a quick recap, you adjust autofocusing behavior through Focus mode and AF-area mode; look for the current settings in the spots labeled in Figure 7-16.

   * *Focus mode:* Choose AF-S to lock focus when you press the shutter button halfway or tap your subject on the touchscreen; choose AF-F for continuous autofocusing. See the first section of this chapter for details about how each option works for movie recording. For manual focusing, choose MF.

   * *AF-area mode:* You can choose from Face-priority, Wide-area, Normal-area, or Subject-tracking. The default setting is Face- priority; if the camera doesn't detect a face in the frame, it automatically uses Wide-area focusing instead. With any of these modes, you start by moving the focusing frame over your subject. How things work from there depends on the specific mode; again, Chapter 4 provides step-by-step instructions.

Adjust both settings via the control strip; press the *i* button or tap the screen *i* symbol to bring up the strip.

>> **White Balance and Picture Control:** The colors in your movie are rendered according to the current White Balance and Picture Control settings, both detailed in Chapter 5. However, you have control over these options only when the Mode dial is set to P, S, A, or M. The current settings appear in the areas labeled in Figure 7-16; you can adjust both options either via the Shooting menu or the control strip.

TIP

Want to record a black-and-white movie? Select Monochrome as the Picture Control. Instant *film noir.*

Manipulating Movie Exposure

Normally, the camera automatically adjusts exposure during movie recording. Exposure is calculated using Matrix (whole frame) metering, regardless of which Metering mode setting is selected. But in a few exposure modes, you can adjust exposure by changing the following settings:

>> **Shutter speed and ISO:** Both options are set by the camera by default. But if you enable the Manual Movie Settings option on the Movie Settings menu, as shown in Figure 7-17, you can control both settings. (Look for the current settings in the areas labeled in Figure 7-16.) This path is one for experienced videographers, however. If you fit that category, here are a few things you need to know:

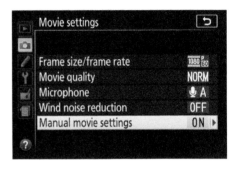

FIGURE 7-17:
Enable this option to take control over movie exposure.

- *Exposure mode:* You must set the Mode dial to M (manual) exposure to take advantage of this option.

- *Shutter speed:* You can select shutter speeds as high as 1/4000 second. The slowest shutter speed depends on your chosen frame rate. For 24p, 25p, and 30p, you can drop as low as 1/30 second; for 50p, 1/50 second; and for 60p, 1/60 second. To set the shutter speed in M mode, rotate the Command dial.

WARNING

If you choose a shutter speed outside the stated ranges, the camera chooses the closest in-range setting after you begin recording.

- *ISO:* You can set the ISO value as low as 100 or as high as 25600. Note that Auto ISO Sensitivity control doesn't work when the Manual Movie Settings option is enabled; the camera sticks with your selected setting regardless of whether you enable Auto ISO — and, more importantly, regardless of whether your selected setting produces an under- or overexposed movie.

To adjust ISO quickly, press the Fn button while rotating the Command dial. You can also select the ISO value via the ISO Sensitivity settings option on the Shooting menu. (The setting doesn't appear on the control strip when you use the Show Movie Indicators version of the Live View display.)

>> **Aperture (f-stop):** You can adjust the f-stop *before* (but not during) recording if you set the Mode dial to A (aperture-priority autoexposure) or M (manual exposure). This option enables you to control depth of field in your movies; Chapter 3 explains the aperture setting's role in depth of field.

In A mode, rotate the Command dial or use the touchscreen to change the f-stop (tap the f-stop value at the bottom of the display to access the setting). In M mode, press and hold the Exposure Compensation button while rotating the Command dial.

One quirk to note: If Manual Movie Settings is enabled, as explained in the preceding bullet point, and the Mode dial is set to M (manual exposure), you must exit Live View mode before you can change the aperture setting. Rotate the LV switch to disable Live View and then adjust the aperture by using the touchscreen or by pressing the Exposure Compensation button while rotating the Command dial. Rotate the LV switch again to return to Live View mode.

>> **Exposure Compensation:** Exposure Compensation, detailed in Chapter 3, enables you to override the camera's autoexposure decisions, asking for a brighter or darker picture. You can apply this adjustment for movies when you use the following exposure modes: P, S, A, or M; any Scene mode; or the Night Vision Effects mode. Note that the display shows the +/– symbol you see in Figure 7-18 only when Exposure Compensation is in force.

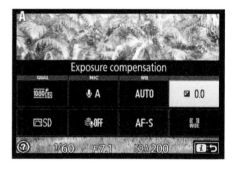

FIGURE 7-18:
You can apply Exposure Compensation for movie shooting when you use certain exposure modes.

You can access the Exposure Compensation setting via the control strip, as shown in Figure 7-18. In any exposure mode except M, you also can press and hold the Exposure Compensation button while rotating the Command dial. (That button/dial combo adjusts the aperture when you use the M exposure mode.)

In Live View mode, the monitor preview updates to show you the results of the Exposure Compensation adjustment. However, the preview can provide this feedback only up to settings of +3.0 to –3.0, even though you can set the value as high as +/– EV 5.0.

REMEMBER

Just to head off any possible confusion: For viewfinder photography, Exposure Compensation isn't needed in M exposure mode; if you want a brighter or darker exposure, you just change the aperture, shutter speed, or ISO Sensitivity settings. But because the camera doesn't give you control over shutter speed or ISO during movie recording — *unless you enable Manual Movie Settings* — you need some way to tell the camera that you want a brighter or darker picture in M mode, and Exposure Compensation is it.

>> **Autoexposure lock:** In any exposure mode except Auto or Auto Flash Off, you can lock exposure at the current settings by pressing and holding the AE-L/AF-L button. Chapter 3 also tells you more about autoexposure lock.

Screening Your Movies

To play your movie, press the Playback button. In single-image playback mode, you can spot a movie file by looking for the little movie camera icon in the upper-left corner of the screen, as shown in Figure 7-19. A honking big "play" arrow also appears in the middle of the screen in the default playback display mode and in some other display modes. (Press the Multi Selector up/down to change the display mode.)

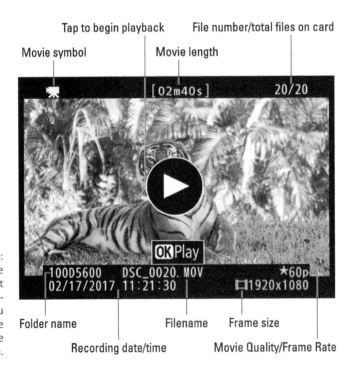

FIGURE 7-19: When you use the default playback display mode, you see this movie data on the screen.

The default display mode also shows other movie-related data, including the Frame Size, Frame Rate, and Movie Quality setting, as labeled in Figure 7-19. (Remember: A star next to the Frame Rate value means that you set the Movie Quality option to High.)

To start playback, tap the play arrow or tap the OK/Play box located below the arrow. If the touchscreen is disabled, press the OK button instead.

In the Thumbnail and Calendar playback modes, both described in Chapter 8, you see little dots along the edges of image thumbnails to represent movie files. Tap the thumbnail or press OK to shift to single-image view and then start playback as I just described.

After playback begins, you see the data labeled in Figure 7-20. The progress bar and Time Elapsed value show you how much of the movie has played so far; you can also see the total movie length.

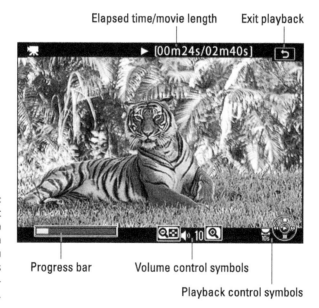

FIGURE 7-20: The icons at the bottom of the screen remind you which buttons to use to control playback.

You can control playback as follows:

>> **Exit playback:** Press the Multi Selector up, tap the return arrow in the upper-right corner of the screen, or press the Playback button again.

>> **Pause/resume playback:** If the touchscreen is enabled, tap the display once to pause; tap again to resume playback. You also can press the Multi Selector

down to pause playback and press OK to resume playback. (That white circle labeled *Playback control symbols* in the figure is designed to remind you of the Multi Selector's movie-playback role.)

>> **Fast-forward/rewind:** Press the Multi Selector right or left to fast-forward or rewind the movie, respectively. Press again to double the fast-forward or rewind speed; keep pressing to increase the speed. Hold down the button to fast-forward or rewind all the way to the end or beginning of the movie.

You also can tap on the progress bar to advance or rewind the movie to the spot you tap. (Well, theoretically, anyway: If you suffer from fat-finger syndrome like me, finding the exact spot to tap on the progress bar isn't easy.)

>> **Forward/rewind 10 seconds:** Rotate the Command dial to the right to jump 10 seconds forward through the movie; rotate to the left to jump back 10 seconds. Again, note the little wheel symbol in the lower-left corner of the frame; that's your reminder to use the Command dial to perform 10-second jumps through the movie. The camera pauses playback after every jump; tap the screen or press OK to resume playback.

>> **Advance frame by frame:** First press the Multi Selector down or tap the screen to pause playback. Then press the Multi Selector right to advance one frame; press left to go back one frame.

>> **Adjust playback volume:** See the markings labeled *Volume control symbols* in Figure 7-20? They remind you that you can press the Zoom In button to increase volume and press the Zoom Out button to lower it. The number value tells you the current volume level (10, in the figure). You also can tap the symbols to adjust volume, but I find it difficult to tap just the right spot. And if you miss the tap target, the camera pauses the movie.

Trimming Movies

You can do some limited movie editing in camera. I emphasize: *limited* editing. You can trim frames from the start of a movie and clip off frames from the end, and that's it.

To eliminate frames from the start of a movie, take these steps:

1. **Display your movie in single-image view.**

2. **Tap the playback icon or press OK to begin playback.**

3. **When you reach the first frame you want to keep, pause the movie by tapping the screen or pressing the Multi Selector down.**

The onscreen display updates to show you the controls that appear on the left in Figure 7-21.

FIGURE 7-21: With the movie paused, press the *i* button or tap the *i* symbol to access the movie-editing screens.

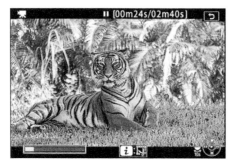

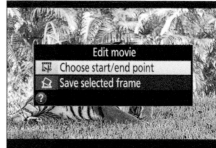

4. **Press the *i* button or tap the *i* symbol at the bottom of the screen.**

You see the menu options shown on the right in Figure 7-21.

5. **Select Choose Start/End Point.**

6. **Select Start Point.**

You're returned to the playback screen, which now appears as shown in Figure 7-22. Two markers appear above the progress bar, indicating the current start point and end point set for your edited movie. The yellow marker represents the active point (the start point, on the left side of the progress bar, in this case). In addition, the AE-L/AF-L symbol appears; more about the point of that feature momentarily.

7. **Press the Multi Selector up or tap the scissors symbol (lower-right corner of the frame) to lop off all frames that came before the current frame.**

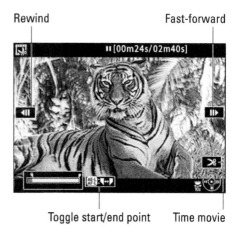

Rewind   Fast-forward

Toggle start/end point   Time movie

FIGURE 7-22: The markers above the progress bar indicate the currently selected start and end points of your edited movie.

Now you see a screen offering options that enable you to preview the movie, save the movie as a new file, overwrite the original file, or cancel the operation altogether. To preview the movie, select Preview and press OK. After the preview plays, you're returned to the menu screen.

8. **To preserve your original movie and save the trimmed one as a new file, choose Save as New File.**

    Alternatively, you can opt to overwrite the existing file, but you can't get the original file back if you do.

To instead trim footage from the end of a film, follow the same steps, but this time pause playback on the last frame you want to keep in Step 3. Then, in Step 6, select Choose End Point instead of Choose Start Point.

TIP

If you prefer, you can tackle both editing tasks in one pass: After you follow Step 6, press the AE/L-AF-L button or tap the corresponding icon at the bottom of the screen. The marker at the right end of the progress bar, which represents the end point of the trimmed movie, turns yellow. You can now rewind the movie until you reach the frame that you want to use as the end of the video. Keep tapping or pressing the AE-L/AF-L control to toggle between the start/end point controls on the progress bar. To finalize the edit, press the Multi Selector up or tap the scissors symbol.

During playback, edited files are indicated by a little scissors icon that looks like the one at the bottom of the edit screen in Figure 7-22.

Saving a Movie Frame As a Still Image

TIP

To save a frame of the movie as a still photo, begin playing the movie and pause playback when you reach the frame you want to save. (Tap the screen or press the Multi Selector down to pause the movie.)

Next, press the *i* button or tap the *i* symbol to bring up the Edit Movie screen. Choose Save Selected Frame and then press the Multi Selector up or tap the scissors symbol in the lower-right corner of the screen. On the confirmation screen that appears, select Yes.

Your frame is saved as a JPEG photo; the resolution of the picture matches the movie frame size. When you view the photo during playback, it's marked with a little scissors icon in the upper-left corner. You can't apply editing features from the Retouch menu to the file, nor can you view all the shooting data that's normally associated with a JPEG picture.

TIP

Before you begin movie playback, you also can press the *i* button to display a mini-menu that contains the Edit Movie option. Select that option to access the Edit Movie screen (the one shown on the right in Figure 7-21). After choosing the editing function you want to use, start playback and proceed as outlined in the steps here and in the preceding section.

3

After the Shot

IN THIS PART . . .

Get the details on picture playback, including how to customize playback screens.

Delete files you don't want, assign ratings to pictures and movies, and protect your best work from being accidentally deleted.

Transfer files from the camera to the computer.

Convert Raw images using the built-in conversion tool or the one available in Nikon Capture NX-D.

Prepare photos for online sharing.

IN THIS CHAPTER

» Exploring picture playback functions

» Magnifying photos to check small details

» Taking advantage of Calendar view

» Changing the playback display style

» Viewing your photos and movies on an HDTV screen

Chapter **8**

Playback Mode: Viewing Your Photos

Without question, my favorite thing about digital photography is being able to view my pictures the instant after I shoot them. No more guessing whether I captured the image or need to try again, as in the film days; no more wasting money on developing pictures that stink.

Seeing your pictures is just the start of the things you can do when you switch your camera to playback mode, though. You also can review the settings you used to take the picture, display graphics that alert you to exposure problems, and magnify a photo to check details. This chapter introduces you to these playback features and more.

Note: Some information applies only to photos; if a feature also works for movie, I spell that out. For details on movie playback, see Chapter 7.

Picture Playback 101

Unless the D5600 is your first digital camera, you're probably familiar with the basics of picture playback, which are similar on every digital camera. If you turn on the camera's touchscreen, you can even use the same touchscreen gestures that you use when inspecting photos on a smartphone or tablet. (Turn the touchscreen on via the Touch Controls option on the Setup menu; you can enable touch features for playback only or for both playback and shooting.)

Later sections detail special playback functions on your camera. But first, the following steps provide the basics:

1. **Press the Playback button to put the camera in playback mode.**

   Figure 8-1 shows you where to find the button. By default, you see a single photo along with some picture information, as shown in the figure. If you instead see a screen that has a movie-camera icon in the upper-left camera, you're looking at a movie file; again, Chapter 7 details movie playback.

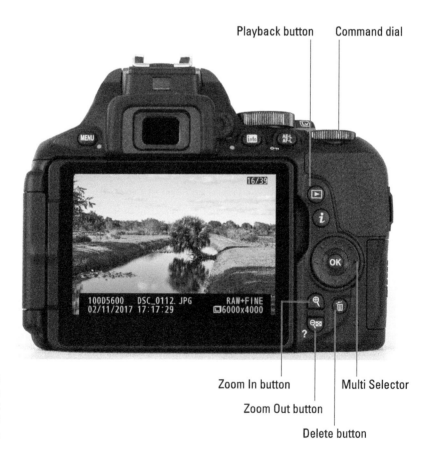

FIGURE 8-1:
These buttons play the largest roles in picture playback.

Playback button   Command dial

Zoom In button

Zoom Out button

Multi Selector

Delete button

If you see multiple thumbnails after you press the Playback button, press the OK button to switch to single-photo view. If you instead see a calendar display, press OK twice. (Upcoming sections explain how to use these alternative displays.)

2. **To scroll through your picture and movie files, swipe a finger across the touchscreen, rotate the Command dial, or press the Multi Selector right or left.**

I labeled the Command dial and Multi Selector in the figure. To view the next picture using the touchscreen, swipe your finger from right to left across the screen. Swipe from the left to go back one picture.

In single-frame playback view, you can magnify or reduce the display size by pressing the Zoom In and Zoom Out buttons, respectively. If the touchscreen is enabled, you also can pinch outward to magnify the display and pinch inward to reduce the display size, just as you do on a smartphone or tablet. The upcoming section "Zooming in for a closer view" talks more about the magnification feature. Note that the playback magnification feature doesn't work for movies.

3. **To erase an embarrassing photo or movie before anyone can see it, press the Delete button, labeled in Figure 8-1.**

A confirmation screen appears; press Delete again to give the go-ahead to erase the photo. (Chapter 9 offers additional ways to erase.)

4. **To return to picture-taking mode, press the Playback button again or press the shutter button halfway and then release it.**

Choosing Which Images to View

Your camera organizes picture and movie files into folders that are assigned generic names: 100D5600, 101D5600, and so on. You also can create custom-named folders by following the steps I outline in Chapter 10.

Which folders' photos and movies appear during playback depends on the Playback Folder option on the Playback menu, shown in Figure 8-2. You can choose from three settings:

>> **D5600:** Displays all pictures taken with the D5600, regardless of which folder they call home.

>> **All:** Displays all pictures taken with the D5600 as well as any shot with another camera. The only requirement is that the files be in an image format the camera recognizes. (You can usually view JPEG files and Nikon Raw files, but not Raw files from another brand of camera.)

>> **Current:** Displays only images in the folder that the camera is currently using to store new images. You can see the name of that folder by looking at the Storage Folder option on the Shooting menu. (The default folder name appears on the menu as simply *100.*)

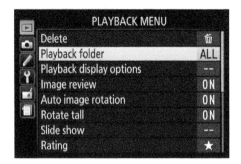

FIGURE 8-2:
If your memory card contains multiple image folders, use this menu option to specify which ones you want to view.

Adjusting Playback Timing

By default, your camera displays a picture for a brief period immediately after you capture the image — you don't have to switch to playback mode. When you do shift to playback mode, the monitor is set by default to turn off after 5 minutes of inactivity. (The automatic shutoff helps conserve battery power because the monitor is one of the biggest drains on the battery.)

You can alter these features as follows:

>> **Adjust the display time for Playback mode.** Open the Custom Setting menu, choose Timers/AE Lock, and then choose Auto Off Timers. The screen shown on the left in Figure 8-3 appears.

FIGURE 8-3:
You can control how long pictures are displayed in Playback mode before automatic monitor shutdown occurs.

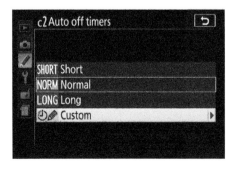
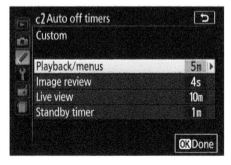

Ignore the first three options for now; they control the shutoff timing for a variety of camera operations in addition to playback shutoff. Instead, choose Custom, to display the screen shown on the right in the figure. Select Playback/Menus to display another screen where you can choose playback shutoff settings ranging from 8 seconds to 10 minutes. After you select a setting, press the OK button to lock in your choice. Then, tap OK Done (lower-right corner of the right screen in Figure 8-3) or press the OK button to exit that screen.

REMEMBER

As the setting name implies, the Playback/Menus option also controls the length of time camera menus are displayed before automatic shutdown occurs. For details on Auto Off Timers, check out Chapter 10.

>> **Alter the Image Review settings.** You also can adjust whether each photo you take is displayed automatically after the camera finishes writing the image to the memory card and, if so, how long the picture appears before the camera shifts back to shooting mode.

By default, the Image Review period is 4 seconds. Along with your photo, the screen shows a bit of shooting data, including the exposure mode, number of shots remaining, battery status, and Image Size and Quality. In the upper-right corner of the screen, you also see a pair of numbers indicating how many files are on the memory card and the number of the frame you just captured. For example, 4/15 means that you're looking at the 4th of 15 files on the card.

TIP

You can change the length of the Image Review display through the same Custom Settings menu option that controls regular playback shutoff (Auto Off Timers). After choosing Custom, as shown on the left in Figure 8-3, choose Image Review and select a display time. Choices range from 4 seconds to 10 minutes.

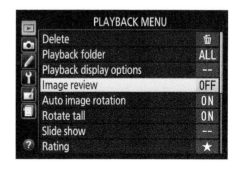

FIGURE 8-4:
To save battery power, you may want to disable Image Review.

To disable Image Review altogether, open the Playback menu and set that option to Off, as shown in Figure 8-4. You can still view your pictures at any time by pressing the Playback button.

Enabling Automatic Picture Rotation

When you take a picture, the camera can record the image *orientation* — whether you held the camera normally, creating a horizontally oriented image, or turned the camera on its side to shoot a vertically oriented photo. During playback, the camera can then read the orientation data and automatically rotate the image so that it appears in the upright position, as shown on the left in Figure 8-5. If you disable rotation, vertically oriented pictures appear sideways, as shown on the right in Figure 8-5. Regardless of these settings, your pictures aren't rotated during the Image Review display period, however. Nor are movie files rotated.

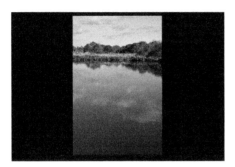 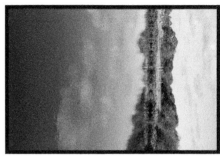

FIGURE 8-5: You can display vertically oriented pictures in their upright position (left) or sideways (right).

TECHNICAL STUFF

Photographers use the term *portrait orientation* to refer to vertically oriented pictures and *landscape orientation* to refer to horizontally oriented pictures. The terms stem from the traditional way that people and places are captured in paintings and photographs — portraits, vertically; landscapes, horizontally.

To set up your photo rotation preferences, use the following Playback menu options, both shown in Figure 8-6:

>> **Auto Image Rotation:** This option (highlighted in the figure) determines whether the orientation data is included in the picture file. The default setting is On.

>> **Rotate Tall:** This option controls whether the camera pays attention to the orientation data. If you disable the Rotate Tall option, even photos that were taken with Auto Image Rotation turned on aren't rotated on the camera monitor. However, the images may be rotated when viewed in a computer program or app that can read the orientation data.

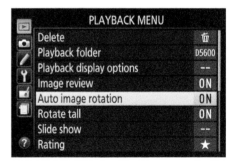

FIGURE 8-6: Visit the Playback menu to enable or disable image rotation.

By default, a certain amount of data, including the filename and shooting date, appears with your picture. To find out how to hide the data so that you see only the image, as shown in Figure 8-5, visit the section "Viewing Picture Data," later in this chapter.

Shifting to Thumbnails Display

Instead of viewing images one at a time, you can display 4 or 12 thumbnails, as shown in Figure 8-7, or even a whopping 80 thumbnails.

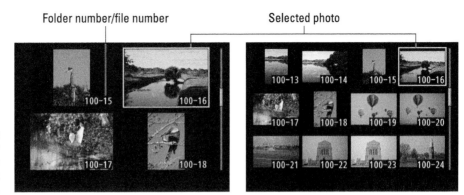

FIGURE 8-7: You can view multiple image thumbnails at a time.

Use these techniques to change to thumbnails view and navigate your photos:

>> **Display thumbnails.** If the touchscreen is enabled, pinch in: That is, put your thumb and a finger on opposite corners of the monitor and drag both toward the center of the screen. You also can press the Zoom Out button. Either way, your first pinch or press of the Zoom Out button cycles from single-picture view to 4-thumbnail view. Keep pinching or pressing to shift to 12-picture view and then to 80 thumbnail view. One more pinch or press takes you to Calendar view, a nifty feature explained in the next section.

>> **Display fewer thumbnails.** For touchscreen operation, pinch out: Place your thumb and forefinger in the center of the screen and drag both toward the edge of the monitor. If you prefer, press the Zoom In button instead. Each pinch or press shifts you one step closer to full-frame view.

>> **Scroll to the next screen of thumbnails:** Drag your finger up or down the screen or press the Multi Selector up and down.

>> **Select an image.** To perform certain playback functions while in Thumbnail view, you first need to select an image. A yellow box surrounds the selected image (refer to Figure 8-7). To select a different image, just tap its thumbnail. Or rotate the Command dial or use the Multi Selector to move the highlight box over the image. (This process works differently in Calendar view; again, see the next section for help.)

TIP

>> **Toggle between thumbnails display and full-frame view.** To quickly shift from any thumbnails view to singe-image view, select the image you want to inspect. Then press OK or tap the selected thumbnail.

If a photo is displayed in single-image view, you can return to the previous thumbnails display by pressing the OK button. (There's no touchscreen equivalent for this operation.) If a movie is displayed, pressing OK begins movie playback. So instead, press the Zoom Out button to go back to Thumbnail view.

The four- and nine-thumbnail displays include the name of the folder that holds the images as well as the frame number of each file, as shown in Figure 8-7. The frame number isn't the same thing as the filename; it just tells you which file you're viewing in a series of files. In 72-thumbnail view, the folder number and frame number of the currently selected image both appear at the bottom of the screen.

Displaying Photos in Calendar View

In Calendar view, you see a little calendar on the screen, as shown on the left in Figure 8-8. By selecting a date on the calendar, you can quickly navigate to all the pictures you shot on that day. A thumbnail-free date indicates that your memory card doesn't contain any photos from that day. Note that the calendar is based on the information you specified for the Time Zone and Date setting on the Setup menu, so if you haven't yet entered that data, now's a good time to take that step.

To take advantage of Calendar view, follow these steps:

1. **Pinch in (on the touchscreen) or press the Zoom Out button as needed to cycle through the Thumbnail display modes until you reach Calendar view.**

   If you're viewing images in full-frame view, for example, you need to pinch or press four times to get to Calendar view.

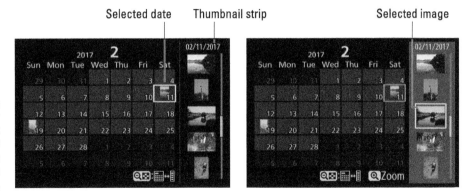

Selected date Thumbnail strip

Selected image

FIGURE 8-8:
Calendar
view makes it
easy to view
all photos
shot on a
particular day.

2. **Select the date on which you shot the images you want to see.**

A yellow box highlights the currently selected date. In Figure 8-8, for example, February 11 is selected. To select a different date, tap it in the calendar display or move the highlight box over it by using the Multi Selector or rotating the Command dial. After you select a date, the right side of the screen displays thumbnails of pictures taken on that date.

TIP

The number of the month appears at the top of the screen. If the memory card contains more than one month's worth of pictures, left and right scroll arrows appear at the top of the display (not shown in Figure 8-8). You can tap those arrows or use the Command dial or Multi Selector to display a different month.

?

3. **To access the images on the selected date, tap the Zoom Out icon at the bottom of the screen, or press the Zoom Out button, or press OK.**

The thumbnail strip becomes active (refer to the right side Figure 8-8), and you can scroll through the thumbnails by using the touchscreen, Command dial, or Multi Selector. The currently selected image is highlighted by a yellow box.

4. **To temporarily display a larger view of the selected thumbnail, hold down the Zoom In button.**

In the zoomed view, the image filename appears under the larger preview, as shown in Figure 8-9. When you release the Zoom In button, the large preview disappears, and the calendar display shown on the right in Figure 8-8 comes back into view.

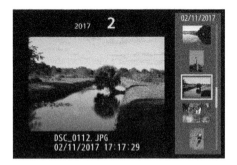

FIGURE 8-9:
Highlight a photo in the thumbnail strip and press the Zoom In button to temporarily display it at a larger size.

5. **To jump from the thumbnail strip back to the calendar so you can select a different date, tap the Zoom Out icon or press the Zoom Out button again.**

You can keep pressing the button or tapping the icon to jump between the calendar and the thumbnail strip as much as you want.

6. **To exit the thumbnail strip and view the selected image in single-image view, tap the thumbnail or press OK.**

If the calendar page is currently active instead of the thumbnail strip, press OK twice (the first press takes you to the thumbnail strip).

TIP

After Step 6, you can return immediately to Calendar view by pressing the OK button, but only if you don't scroll to the next or previous picture first. Otherwise, you have to cycle through all the thumbnail views to get to Calendar view.

Zooming in for a closer view

When you display a photo in single-frame view, as shown on the left in Figure 8-10, you can magnify it to get a close-up look at important details, as shown on the right. Here's the scoop:

FIGURE 8-10: When viewing images in single-frame view (left), pinch out on the touchscreen or press the Zoom In button to magnify the picture (right).

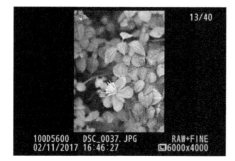
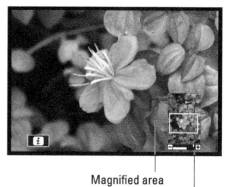

Magnified area

Zoom level bar

» **Zoom in:** Pinch out on the touchscreen or press the Zoom In button. You can magnify the image to a maximum of 13 to 33 times its original display size, depending on the picture resolution (Image Size). Just keep pressing the button or pinching out until you reach the magnification you want.

» **Zoom out:** To zoom out to a reduced magnification, pinch in or press the Zoom Out button.

>> **View another part of the magnified picture:** When an image is magnified, a thumbnail showing the entire image appears briefly in the lower-right corner of the monitor (refer to the right side of Figure 8-10). The yellow outline in the thumbnail indicates the area that's consuming the rest of the monitor space. To scroll the display and view a different portion of the image, you can use the Multi Selector or just drag your finger across the screen.

The bar at the bottom of the navigation window gives you an indication of the magnification level; the closer the white bar gets to the right end of the bar, the greater the magnification level. The bar turns green when you reach 100 percent magnification. You can increase the magnification a bit beyond that level.

After a few seconds, the navigation thumbnail disappears; just tap the screen or press the Multi Selector in any direction to redisplay it.

>> **View more images at the same magnification:** Here's another neat trick: While the display is zoomed, rotate the Command dial to display the same area of the next photo at the same magnification. So if you shot the same subject several times, you can easily check to see how a particular detail appears in each one.

>> **Return to full-frame view:** You can switch from any magnification level to full-screen view by pressing OK.

While the image is magnified, you also can press the *i* button or tap the onscreen *i* symbol to access two additional functions:

>> **Inspect each face in a group portrait.** When you magnify a photo that contains two or more faces, the picture-in-picture thumbnail displays a white border around each face that the camera can detect. If you press the *i* button or tap the *i* symbol that appears when you first magnify the image, a mini-menu appears, offering two options: Face Zoom and Trim. Select Face Zoom and then press the Multi Selector right or left to jump from face to face for a closer look. Press the *i* button or tap the *i* symbol again to exit Face Zoom mode. (Again, after the symbol disappears, you can redisplay it and other onscreen symbols by tapping the screen or pressing the Multi Selector.)

When it works correctly, this is a nice tool for checking for closed eyes, red-eye, and, of course, spinach in the teeth. Unfortunately, the camera sometimes fails to detect faces, especially if the subject isn't looking directly at the camera. And when the photo contains only a few faces, you may find it easier to simply move the magnification box around the screen yourself, without bothering with Face Zoom.

>> **Crop the photo to the currently displayed area:** This feature creates a new image that contains just the area currently visible in the magnified view. (Your original photo is left intact.) After pressing the *i* button or tapping the *i* icon,

choose Trim from the aforementioned mini-menu. (If the photo doesn't contain any faces that the camera can detect, Trim is the only available option.) On the next screen, choose Done to create the cropped copy.

For other cropping options, check out the Trim function on the Retouch menu, which I detail in Chapter 11.

Viewing Picture Data

In single-picture view, you can choose from the six display modes shown in Figure 8-11. By default, however, only the first mode shown in the figure, File Information, is available.

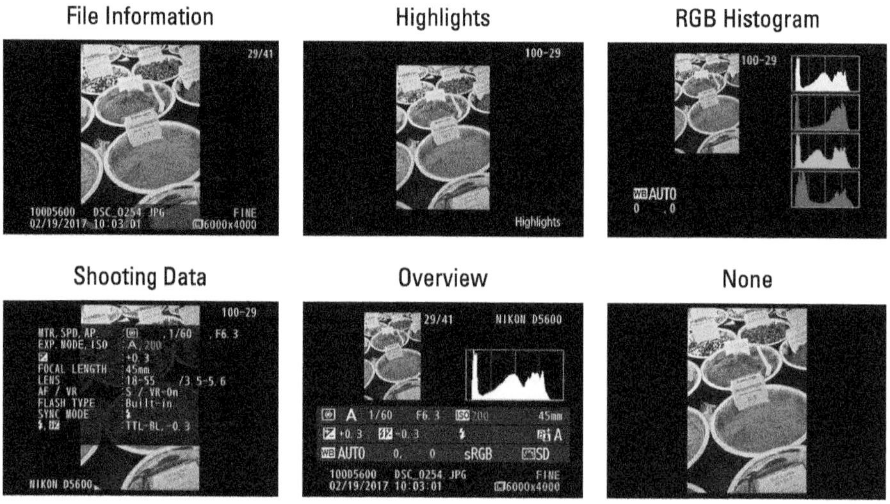

File Information	Highlights	RGB Histogram

Shooting Data	Overview	None

FIGURE 8-11:
You can set the camera to offer these displays; during playback, press the Multi Selector up or down to cycle from one display to the next.

To use the other display options, you must enable them from the Playback menu by following these steps:

1. **Open the Playback menu and choose Playback Display Options, as shown on the left in Figure 8-12.**

    A menu listing all hidden display modes appears, as shown on the right in the figure. A check mark in the box next to a display mode means the mode is enabled. In the figure, I selected all the display modes.

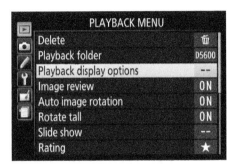

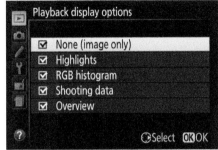

FIGURE 8-12:
Only File Information mode
is available by
default; enable
the others via
the Playback
menu.

2. **To toggle a display mode on or off, tap it.**

   You also can highlight the mode and then press the Multi Selector right or tap the Select box at the bottom of the screen. Notice that the File Information option is missing from the menu — you can't disable this display mode.

3. **After turning on the options you want to use, tap or press OK.**

REMEMBER

After enabling the additional display modes and returning to playback mode, press the Multi Selector up or down to cycle from one display to the next.

The next several sections explain exactly what details you can glean from each display mode, save for None (image-only). I present them here in the order they appear if you cycle through the modes starting with File Information mode and pressing the Multi Selector down. You can spin through the modes in the other direction by pressing the Multi Selector up.

File Information mode

In the File Information mode, the monitor displays the data shown in Figure 8-13. Here's the key to what information appears, starting at the top of the screen and working down:

» **Frame number/Number frames:** The first value indicates the number of the currently displayed photo; the second tells you the total number of files in the same

Frame number/Number frames

Folder   Filename   Image Quality

Data and time   Image Size

FIGURE 8-13:
In File Information mode, you can view these bits of data.

folder. (Note that movie files are also included in the total frame number count.)

» **Folder name:** The camera names folders automatically unless you create custom folders, a trick you can explore in Chapter 10. The first camera-created folder is 100D5600. Each folder can contain up to 9,999 images. When you exceed that limit, the camera creates a new folder and assigns the next folder number: 101D5600, 102D5600, and so on.

» **Filename:** The camera also automatically names your files. Filenames end with a 3-letter code that represents the file format, which is either JPG (for JPEG) or NEF (for Raw) for still photos. (Chapter 2 discusses these formats.) If you record a movie, the file extension is MOV. If you create a dust-off reference image file, a feature designed for use with Nikon Capture NX-D, the camera uses the extension NDF. I explain more about Capture NX-D in the next chapter.

TECHNICAL STUFF

The first four characters of filenames also can vary as follows:

- *DSC_:* You captured the photo in the default Color Space, sRGB. This setting is the best choice for most people, for reasons you can explore in Chapter 5.

- *_DSC:* If you change the Color Space setting to Adobe RGB, the underscore character comes first.

REMEMBER

Each image is also assigned a 4-digit file number, starting with 0001. When you reach image 9999, the file numbering restarts at 0001, and the new images go into a new folder to prevent any possibility of overwriting the existing image files. For more information about file numbering, see the Chapter 1 section that discusses the File Number Sequence option, found on the Custom Setting menu. (I recommend keeping this option turned on.)

» **Date and Time:** Just below the folder and filename info, you see the date and time you took the picture.

» **Image Quality:** Here you can see which Image Quality setting you used when taking the picture. Again, Chapter 2 has details, but the short story is this: Fine, Normal, and Basic are the three JPEG recording options, with Fine representing the highest JPEG quality. Raw refers to the Nikon Raw format, NEF (for Nikon Electronic Format). If you captured the picture in both formats, you see Raw+Fine (or Normal or Basic) but only one. . . . Only one thumbnail appears to represent each file.

» **Image Size:** This value tells you the image resolution, or pixel count. See Chapter 2 to find out about resolution.

Figure 8-14 shows you some additional symbols that appear when you use certain after-the-shot features, as follows:

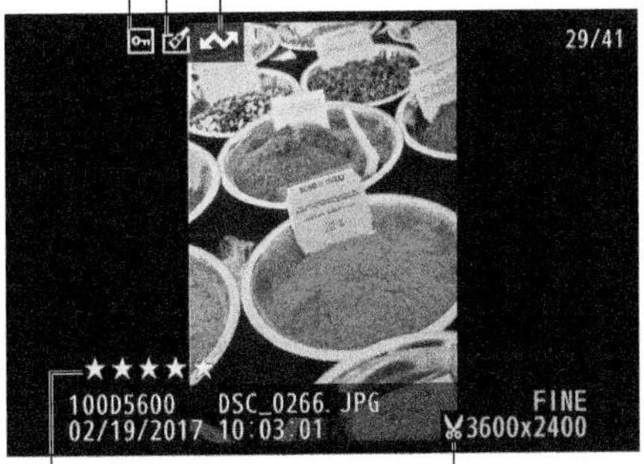

>> **Rating symbol:** Chapter 9 explains how you can rate a picture or movie, assigning it one to five stars or, if you're totally disgusted with the file, labeling it with a trash can so that you can easily locate it to delete it. The rating shown in Figure 8-14 indicates a five-star photo, for example. (I grade on a curve.) If you don't assign any rating, this area of the playback screen appears empty.

>> **Protected symbol:** The key icon indicates you used the file-protection feature to prevent the image or movie from being erased when you use the camera's Delete function. See the next chapter to find out more. (***Note:*** Formatting your memory card, a topic discussed in Chapter 1, *does* erase even protected pictures.) Again, this area appears empty if you didn't apply protection.

>> **Retouch symbol:** This icon appears on images that you created by applying one of the Retouch menu features to a picture. For some Retouch operations, the Image Size/Image Quality area of the display also changes. For example, if you use the Trim function to crop an image, you see a pair of scissors next to the Image Size value, as shown in the figure. Chapter 11 explains this feature and other Retouch menu options.

>> **Send to Smart Device symbol:** After you tag a photo for transfer to a smartphone or tablet, this symbol appears. See this book's appendix for details about wireless transfer.

Protected symbol
Retouched symbol
Send to Smart Device symbol
Rating symbol
Trimmed symbol

FIGURE 8-14:
These symbols appear only if you use the related playback and retouching features.

Highlights (blinkies) mode

One of the most difficult problems to correct in a photo-editing program is known as *blown highlights* in some circles and *clipped highlights* in others. In plain English, both terms mean that *highlights* — the brightest areas of the image — are so overexposed that areas that should include a variety of light shades are instead totally white. For example, in a cloud image, pixels that should be light to very light gray become white due to overexposure, resulting in a loss of detail in those clouds.

REMEMBER

Highlights display mode alerts you to clipped highlights by blinking the affected pixels on and off. But just because you see the flashing alerts doesn't mean you should adjust exposure — the decision depends on where the alerts occur and how the rest of the image is exposed. If your subject appears fine and the blinkies are in the background, don't worry about it. If you adjust exposure to get rid of the blown highlights, your subject will then be underexposed. In other words, sometimes you simply can't avoid a few clipped highlights when the scene includes a broad range of brightness values.

REMEMBER

Like all playback display modes (except File Information), Highlights mode is disabled by default. Follow the instructions in the "Viewing Picture Data" section, earlier in this chapter, to enable it. You can get a look at the Highlights display in Figure 8-11; there's not much to it except the label Highlights at the bottom of the screen and the number of files/total number of files at the top. The rating, retouch, protected, and send-to-smart device markings also appear if you used those features. (Refer to Figure 8-14.)

RGB Histogram mode

Press the Multi Selector down to shift from Highlights mode to RGB Histogram mode, which displays your image as shown in Figure 8-15. Again, you can view your picture in this mode only if you enable it via the Display Mode option on the Playback menu. (See "Viewing Picture Data," earlier in this chapter, for help.)

Underneath the image thumbnail, you see just a few pieces of data. In the lower-left corner, you see the White Balance settings used for the shot. In the figure, the data shows that the picture was captured using the Auto White

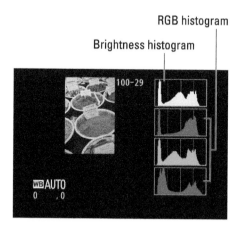

FIGURE 8-15:
RGB Histogram mode presents exposure and color information in chart-like fashion.

Balance with zero adjustment along the blue-to-amber axis and zero adjustment along the green-to-magenta axis. (Chapter 5 details White Balance options.) At the top of the display, you see the Frame number/Total frames data, also part of the standard File Information display data. If you used the rating, protect, retouch, or send-to-smart device functions, symbols representing those features also appear (refer to Figure 8-14).

The keys to RGB Histogram mode, though, are those chart-like thingies called *histograms.* You get two types of histograms: The top one is a Brightness histogram; the three others are known collectively as an RGB (red, green, blue) histogram.

The next two sections explain what information you can discern from the histograms. But first, here's a cool trick to remember: If you press the Zoom In button in this display mode, you can zoom the thumbnail to a magnified view. The histograms then update to reflect only the magnified area of the photo. Use the Multi Selector or drag in the image thumbnail to scroll the display to see other areas of the picture. To return to the regular view and once again see the whole-image histogram, press OK.

Reading a Brightness histogram

You can get an idea of image exposure by viewing your photo on the camera monitor and by looking at the blinkies in Highlight mode. But the Brightness histogram provides a way to gauge exposure that's a little more detailed.

REMEMBER

A Brightness histogram indicates the distribution of shadows, highlights, and *midtones* (areas of medium brightness) in an image. Figure 8-16 shows you the histogram for the spice photo featured in Figure 8-15.

The horizontal axis of the histogram represents the possible picture brightness values — the maximum *tonal range,* in photography-speak — from the darkest shadows on the left to the brightest highlights on the right. And the vertical axis shows how many pixels fall at a particular brightness value. A spike indicates a heavy concentration of pixels at that brightness value.

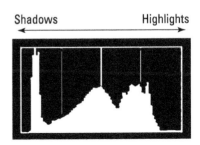

FIGURE 8-16:
The Brightness histogram indicates tonal range, from shadows on the left to highlights on the right.

Keep in mind that there is no "perfect" histogram that you should try to achieve. Instead, interpret the histogram with respect to the distribution of shadows, highlights, and midtones that comprise your subject. You wouldn't expect to see lots of shadows, for example, in a photo of a polar bear walking on a snowy landscape. Pay attention, however, if you see a very high concentration of pixels at the far right or left end of the histogram, which can indicate a seriously overexposed or underexposed image, respectively.

TIP

When shooting subjects that contain a significant amount of white, I usually underexpose the photo just a hair. That way, I make sure that I don't blow out highlights. In such cases, the histogram may show no or few pixels at the right end of the scale. Again, though, you have to read the histogram with an eye toward getting the exposure of the main subject correct. Had I increased exposure enough to grow the highlight population for my spice photo, I could have created blown highlights in the silver edges of the spice bowls.

Understanding RGB histograms

When you view your images in RGB Histogram display mode, you see two histograms: the Brightness histogram, covered in the preceding section, and an RGB histogram. Figure 8-17 shows you the RGB histogram for the spice photo.

TECHNICAL STUFF

To make sense of an RGB histogram, you first need to know that digital images are known as *RGB images* because they're created from three primary colors of light: red, green, and blue. Whereas the Brightness histogram reflects the brightness of all three color channels rolled into one, RGB histograms let you view the values for each channel.

When you look at the brightness data for a single channel, though, you glean information about color saturation rather than image brightness. (*Saturation* refers to the purity of a color; a fully saturated color contains no black or white.) I don't have space

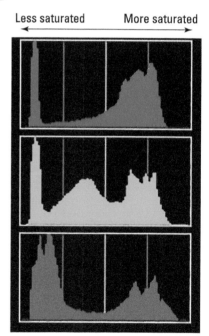

Less saturated ◄————— ————► More saturated

FIGURE 8-17:
The RGB histogram can indicate problems with color saturation.

in this book to provide a full lesson in RGB color theory, but the short story is that when you mix red, green, and blue light, and each component is at maximum brightness, you create white. Zero brightness in all three channels creates black. If you have maximum red and no blue or green, though, you have fully saturated red. If you mix two channels at maximum brightness, you also create full saturation. For example, maximum red and blue produce fully saturated magenta. And, wherever colors are fully saturated, you can lose picture detail. For example, a rose petal that should have a range of tones from medium to dark red may instead be a flat blob of pure red.

The upshot is that if all the pixels for one or two channels are slammed to the right end of the histogram, you may be losing picture detail because of overly saturated colors. If all three channels show a heavy pixel population at the right end of the histogram, you may have blown highlights — again, because the maximum levels of red, green, and blue create white. Either way, you may want to adjust the exposure settings and try again.

A savvy RGB histogram reader can also spot color balance issues by looking at the pixel values. But frankly, color balance problems are fairly easy to notice just by looking at the image on the camera monitor. See Chapter 5 to find out how to correct any color problems that you spot during picture playback.

Shooting Data display mode

In Shooting Data mode, you can view multiple screens of information, which you scroll through by pressing the Multi Selector up and down. Figure 8-18 shows just the first screen of data.

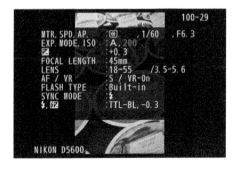

Most of the data you see won't make sense until you explore Chapters 3 through 6, which explain the exposure, color, and focusing settings available on your camera. But I want to call your attention to a few facts now:

FIGURE 8-18:
Here you see the first Shooting Data screen.

>> The current folder and frame number appear in the upper-right corner of the display (100-29 in Figure 8-18).

>> If the ISO value on Shooting Data Page 1 appears in red, as in Figure 8-18, the camera overrode the ISO Sensitivity setting that you selected in order to produce a good exposure. This shift occurs only if you enable automatic ISO adjustment in the P, S, A, and M exposure modes; see Chapter 3 for details.

» The upper-left corner of the monitor shows the Protected, Retouch, and Send to Smart Device icons, if you used these features. If you use the Rating feature, the rating you assigned appears in the lower-left corner of the screen. Figure 8-14 offers a look at the icons; they don't appear in Figure 8-18 because the related features weren't enabled for the photo.

» The Comment item, which is the final item on the third Shooting Data screen, contains a value if you used the Image Comment feature on the Setup menu. I cover this option in Chapter 10.

» The fourth screen appears only if you included copyright data with your picture, a feature you can explore in Chapter 10.

» By using the Nikon SnapBridge app and a compatible smartphone or tablet, as detailed in the appendix of this book, you can tag pictures with location data. The data is acquired from your smart device. If you take advantage of this option, the information appears on a separate Shooting Data display screen. (Technically, Nikon calls this screen Location Data mode, but for all practical purposes, it's part of the Shooting Data display mode. It's enabled automatically when you turn on the Shooting Data mode.)

Before you can access Shooting Data mode, you must enable it via the Playback Display Options setting on the Playback menu. See the earlier section "Viewing Picture Data" for details. After turning on the option, press the Multi Selector down to shift from RGB Histogram mode to Shooting Data mode.

Overview mode

In this mode, the playback screen contains a small image thumbnail along with scads of shooting data — although not quite as much as Shooting Data mode — plus a Brightness histogram. Figure 8-19 offers a look.

The earlier section "Reading a Brightness histogram" tells you what to make of that part of the screen. Just above the histogram, you see the Protected, Retouch, and Send to Smart Device symbols (if you used those features), and the Frame number/Total

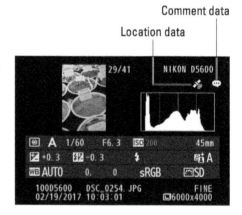

Comment data

Location data

FIGURE 8-19:
In Overview mode, you can view your picture along with the major camera settings you used to take the picture.

frames data appears at the upper-right corner of the image thumbnail. If you used the Rating feature, the rating appears under the thumbnail. (Again, refer to Figure 8-14 to see these symbols.)

TIP

Two more tiny symbols to notice: The speech bubble just above the histogram indicates you enabled the Image Comment feature (see Chapter 10). I labeled the symbol in Figure 8-19. To actually read the comment, you need to go to the third data screen of Shooting Data display mode. The Location Data symbol, also labeled in the figure, appears if you used your smart device and the Nikon SnapBridge app to tag a photo with information about where you were when you shot the photo. The appendix details this and other SnapBridge features.

To sort out the maze of other information, the following list breaks down the five rows that appear under the thumbnail and histogram. In the accompanying figures as well as in Figure 8-19, I include all possible data simply for the purpose of illustration. If any of the items don't appear on your screen, it simply means that the relevant feature wasn't enabled when you captured the shot.

Here's a rundown of the rows:

>> **Row 1:** This row shows the exposure settings labeled in Figure 8-20, along with the focal length of the lens you used to take the shot. As in Shooting Data mode, the ISO value appears red (as in the figure) if you enabled auto ISO override in the P, S, A, or M exposure modes and the camera adjusted the ISO for you.

FIGURE 8-20:
Here you can inspect major exposure settings along with the lens focal length.

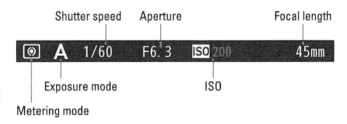

Shutter speed · Aperture · Focal length · Exposure mode · ISO · Metering mode

>> **Row 2:** This row contains a few additional exposure settings, labeled in Figure 8-21. See Chapter 3 for explanations of all these settings except Flash Compensation and Flash Mode, which I cover at the end of Chapter 2.

FIGURE 8-21:
This row con-
tains additional
exposure
information.

Exposure Compensation   Flash mode

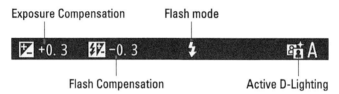

Flash Compensation   Active D-Lighting

>> **Row 3:** Items on this row, shown in Figure 8-22, pertain to color options you can explore in Chapter 5.

FIGURE 8-22:
Look at this
row for details
about color
settings.

White Balance   Color Space

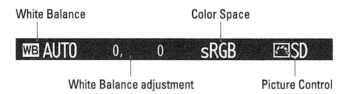

White Balance adjustment   Picture Control

>> **Rows 4 and 5:** The final two rows of data (refer to Figure 8-19) show the same information you get in File Information mode, explained earlier in this chapter.

Viewing Your Photos on a Television

If your television offers HDMI input, you can connect your camera to it so that you can view your pictures and movies on the TV screen. You need a Type C mini-pin HDMI cable to connect the devices; prices start at about $20.

Before making the connection, open the Setup menu, choose HDMI, and check the status of the two HDMI settings, as illustrated in Figure 8-23. By default, the camera decides the proper video resolution to send to the TV, but you can choose a specific resolution via the Output Resolution option. If you enable the Device Control option, you can use the buttons on the TV's remote control to perform the functions of the OK button and Multi Selector during full-frame picture playback and slide shows. This feature works only if your television offers a technology called HDMI CEC. (If your TV remote control doesn't offer HDMI CEC capability, control playback by using the camera buttons, just as you do when viewing pictures on the camera monitor.)

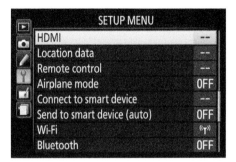

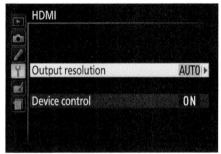

FIGURE 8-23:
Select options
for HD play-
back here.

After choosing the HDMI options, turn the camera off. Plug the end of the HDMI cable that has
the smaller connector into the camera's HDMI
port, found on the right side of the camera
and shown in Figure 8-24. The other end of
the cable goes into the HDMI port on your TV.
(Check your TV instruction manual to find the
location of the proper port and for information
about enabling playback from an auxiliary input
device.) Turn on your camera to send the signal
to the TV.

HDMI port

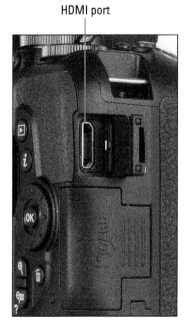

FIGURE 8-24:
The HDMI-out port is under the
door on the side of the camera.

IN THIS CHAPTER

» **Rating photos and movies**

» **Deleting unwanted files**

» **Protecting files from accidental erasure**

» **Downloading files to your computer**

» **Processing Raw files**

» **Shrinking files for online use**

Chapter **9**

Working with Picture and Movie Files

E very creative pursuit involves its share of cleanup and organizational tasks. Painters have to wash brushes, embroiderers have to separate strands of floss, and woodcrafters have to haul out the wet/dry vac to suck up sawdust. Digital photography is no different: At some point, you have to stop shooting so that you can download and process your files.

This chapter explains these after-the-shot tasks. First up is a review of several in-camera file-management operations: rating files, deleting unwanted files, and protecting your best work from accidental erasure.

Following that, you can get help with transferring files to your computer, processing files that you shot in the Raw (NEF) format, and creating low-resolution copies of photos for online sharing. Along the way, I introduce you to Nikon ViewNX-i and Capture NX-D, two free computer programs that you can use to handle some of these tasks.

Note: If you own a smartphone, tablet, or other device that can run Nikon's Snap-Bridge app, check out the appendix. It offers information about connecting your camera to the smart device so you can transfer photos wirelessly to that device and, from there, upload images to your favorite social media site or Nikon Image Space, a free online photo-storage and -sharing site.

Rating Photos and Movies

Using your camera's Rating feature, you can assign a rating to a picture or movie file: five stars for your best shots, one star for those you wish you could reshoot, and so on. You can even assign a Discard rating to flag files that you think you want to delete.

Rating pictures has several benefits. First, when you create a slide show (as outlined in Chapter 11), you can tell the camera to display only photos or movies that have a certain rating. Second, assigning the Discard tag makes it easy to spot the rotten apples amid all your great work when you take the step of erasing files. (Merely assigning the tag doesn't actually erase the file.) Finally, some photo programs can read the rating and then sort files according to rating. That feature makes it easier to cull your photo and movie collection and gather your best work for printing and sharing.

Before showing you how to rate files, I need to share one rule of the road: If you previously protected a file by using the Protect feature described in the next section, you can't assign a rating to it. To remove protection, display the file and press the AE-L/AF-L button.

Assuming that the file isn't protected, you can assign a rating in two ways:

>> **Assign a rating in Playback mode:** Press the Playback button to shift to playback mode, if you're not already there. Then scroll to the photo or movie you want to rate or, if you're viewing pictures in Thumbnail or Calendar view, select the photo (the yellow highlight box indicates the selected file). Next, press the *i* button or tap the onscreen *i* symbol to display the *i*-button menu shown on the left in Figure 9-1. Select Rating to display the second screen in the figure. Tap the rating you want to assign or use the Multi Selector to highlight it and then press the OK button. Choose Not Rated to remove an existing rating.

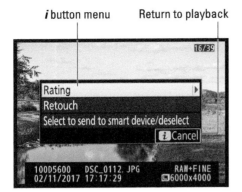

i button menu   Return to playback

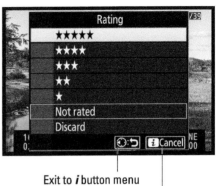

Exit to i button menu

Return to playback

FIGURE 9-1:
During playback, press the *i* button and select Rating to access the ratings screen.

The two touchscreen symbols labeled on the right screen in Figure 9-1 enable you to exit to the *i*-button menu or to exit all menus and return to playback, respectively. You can exit the *i*-button menu by tapping the Cancel button labeled on the left in the figure or by just pressing the Playback button.

» **Rate photos via the Playback menu.** Choose Rating from the menu, as shown on the left in Figure 9-2, to display the thumbnails screen shown on the right side of the figure. Select the photo or movie you want to rate by tapping it or by pressing the Multi Selector right or left to move the yellow highlight box over the image. Rotate the Command dial or swipe your finger up or down to scroll the screen vertically.

Five-star rating   Discard rating

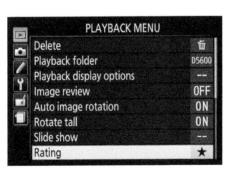

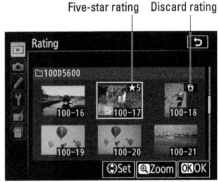

FIGURE 9-2:
You also can rate photos choosing Rating from the Playback menu.

The best way to assign a rating is to simply press the Multi Selector up or down. As you do, the current rating appears with the thumbnail, as labeled in the figure. You also can use the touchscreen to assign a rating: Tap the thumbnail or the Set symbol at the bottom of the screen according to how many stars you want to assign. Tap once for one star, twice for two stars, and so on.

The problem with the touchscreen method is that there's no way to lower the rating or remove it after you tap. You also can't get to the Discard rating via touchscreen. So I stick with using the Multi Selector to handle the rating chores. Just remember that when you're selecting a photo or movie to rate, you can press the Multi Selector only left or right; pressing up/down assigns a rating.

Remember these additional points about rating photos through the Playback menu:

- If you need a closer look at an image than the Thumbnail view provides, select the image and then press the Zoom In button or tap the Zoom icon at the bottom of the screen. The image then appears in Full-Frame view. After inspecting the photo, release the button or tap the return arrow in the upper-right corner of the monitor to return to the Rating screen.

- You can rate as many files as you want while the rating screen is open. Unfortunately, you still have to select and rate each file individually; there's no way to select a batch of files and assign a particular rating.

- When you finish rating files, press the OK button or tap the OK symbol to exit the Rating screen and return to the Playback menu. Don't forget this step: If you do, the rating doesn't stick.

However you assign a rating, it appears with the image in any playback display mode except None (in that mode, no data appears with your image). Figure 9-3 shows you where to find the rating in the default display mode (File Information mode). For more about playback display modes, see Chapter 8.

Rating symbol

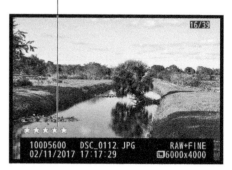

FIGURE 9-3:
The rating appears here in File Information playback mode.

Protecting Files

You can safeguard files from being accidentally erased or altered by using the camera's Protect feature. After you protect a file, the camera doesn't allow you to delete the file or apply any of the editing tools found on the Retouch menu. In fact, you can't even assign a rating to a protected file.

WARNING

However, the protection feature only prevents you from erasing the file by using the camera's Delete functions, explained in the next section. Formatting your memory card *does* erase protected pictures, along with any other data on the card. So before you format the card, make sure to transfer all files to your computer or other storage device. See the Chapter 1 section related to working with memory cards for more about card formatting.

To protect a file, put the camera into playback mode. In Full-Frame view, scroll to the photo you want to protect. In Thumbnail or Calendar view, select the image as explained in Chapter 8. Then just press the AE-L/AF-L button. A key symbol appears with the image, as shown in Figure 9-4, to indicate that the photo is locked. (The same key symbol appears directly below the AE-L/AF-L button to remind you which button to press to lock a file.) To remove protection from the current file, press the AE-L/AF-L button again.

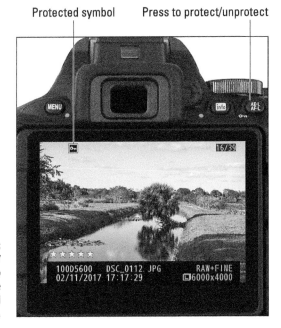

FIGURE 9-4: Press the AE-L/AF-L button to give an image protected status.

When you protect a picture, it may show up as a read-only file when you transfer it to your computer, depending on whether the software you use can read the protection tag. Files that have the read-only status can't be altered until you unlock them. To take that step in Nikon ViewNX-i, open the File menu, choose Protect Files, and then select Unprotect.

Deleting Files

You have three options for erasing files from a memory card when it's in your camera. The next few sections give you the lowdown.

REMEMBER

One reminder: None of the Delete features erase files that you protect via the option that I outline in the preceding section. To remove file protection, display the file in playback mode and press the AE-L/AF-L button.

Deleting files one at a time

During playback, you can use the Delete button to erase photos and movie files. But the process varies depending on the current playback mode:

>> In Full-Frame view, press the Delete button.

>> In Thumbnail view, select the picture you want to erase and then press Delete. (You can either tap the thumbnail or use the Multi Selector or Command dial to move the yellow selection box over the thumbnail.)

>> In Calendar view, select the date on the calendar that contains the file. Then press the Zoom Out button or tap the Zoom Out symbol onscreen to activate the thumbnail list. Use the Multi Selector to highlight the file's thumbnail and then press the Delete button.

After you press Delete, you see a message asking whether you really want to erase the picture. If you do, press the Delete button again or tap the Yes symbol on the screen. To cancel the process, press the Playback button or tap the Cancel symbol.

TIP

By default, the camera displays your photo briefly after the shot is recorded. (You enable or disable this feature via the Image Review option on the Playback menu.) During the Image Review period, you can press the Delete button to trash the file immediately. But you have to be quick, or else the camera returns to shooting mode.

Deleting all files

Open the Playback menu, select Delete, and then select All, as illustrated in Figure 9-5. When the camera asks you to verify that you want to delete all your pictures and movies, choose Yes and then press the OK button.

FIGURE 9-5:
To delete all
files except
those that you
protected,
select these
Playback menu
options.

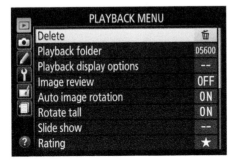
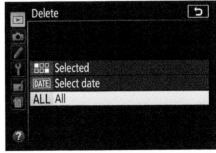

REMEMBER

If your memory card contains multiple folders, choosing All deletes only pictures in the folder that is currently selected via the Playback Folder option on the Playback menu. For information, see the Chapter 8 section related to choosing which images to view. (Set the Playback Folder to All if you truly want to dump photos from all folders.)

Deleting a batch of selected files

To get rid of more than a few files — but not all pictures and movies on the card — don't waste time erasing each file, one at a time. Instead, you can tag multiple files for deletion and then take them all out to the trash at one time.

To start, select Delete from the Playback menu. You then see the screen shown on the left in Figure 9-6, which offers two options for selecting specific files to erase:

?

>> **Selected:** Use this option if the files you want to delete weren't all taken on the same day. Choose Selected to display a screen of thumbnails, as shown on the right in the figure. Select the first photo you want to delete by tapping it or by using the Multi Selector or Command dial to move the yellow box over it. Then tap Set or press the Zoom Out button. A trash can appears in the upper-right corner of the thumbnail. In the figure, the photo in the top-right corner of the screen is tagged for erasure.

If you change your mind, tap Set or press the Zoom Out button again to remove the Delete tag. To undo deletion for all selected photos, press the Playback button or tap the return arrow in the upper-right corner of the screen.

Delete symbol

Discard rating symbol

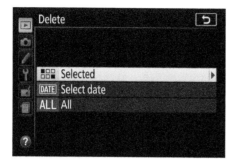

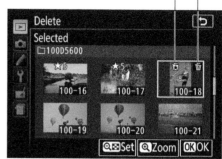

FIGURE 9-6:
This Delete menu option offers a quick way to delete a batch of photos.

For a closer look at the selected image, tap the Zoom symbol onscreen or press and hold the Zoom In button. To exit the magnified view, release the button or tap the return arrow.

REMEMBER

Images that you tag with the Discard rating, as explained in the first section of this chapter, are *not* officially marked for the trash heap. The right screen in Figure 9-6 shows you the symbols representing both the Discard rating and the Delete tag. Notice that the Discard symbol includes a star, which you see with all rating symbols. The Delete tag, on the other hand, looks exactly like the symbol on the Delete button. At any rate, it's the Delete symbol that triggers the camera to dump the file. The Discard tag is just there to help you find images that you earlier decided you might want to erase.

» **Select Date:** Use this option, highlighted on the left in Figure 9-7, to quickly delete any record of that day you'd rather not remember. After choosing Select Date, you see a list of dates, as shown on the right in the figure. To trash all files from that date, put a check mark in the box to the left of the date. The easiest option is to just tap the box. But you also can press the Multi Selector up or down to highlight the date and then press right to toggle the check mark on and off.

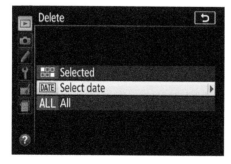

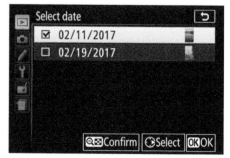

FIGURE 9-7:
With the Select Date option, you can quickly erase all photos taken on a specific date.

Can't remember which photos are associated with the selected date? Try these tricks:

- To display thumbnails of all files recorded on the selected date, tap the Confirm box at the bottom of the screen or press the Zoom Out button.

- While thumbnails are displayed, tap Zoom or press the Zoom In button to magnify the selected thumbnail.

- To return from Thumbnail view to the date list, tap the Back button (bottom of the screen, marked with the Zoom Out button symbol) or press the Zoom Out button again.

After tagging files for deletion or specifying a date to delete, tap OK or press the OK button. Select Yes when the camera asks for confirmation that you want to erase the files.

TIP

You have one alternative way to quickly erase all files shot on a specific date: In Calendar display mode, highlight the date and then press the Delete button. You see the standard confirmation screen; press Delete again to wrap up. Visit Chapter 8 for the scoop on Calendar display mode.

I also use the Protect feature when I want to keep a handful of pictures on the card but delete the rest. Rather than use the options I just described to select all the pictures I want to trash, I protect the handful I want to preserve. Then I choose the All option from the Delete menu to dump the rest. The protected pictures remain intact.

Taking a Look at Nikon's Photo Software

To move pictures and movies to your computer, you need some type of software to download, view, and manage the files. If you don't have a favorite photo program for handling these tasks, Nikon offers the following free solutions:

» **Nikon ViewNX-i:** Shown in Figure 9-8, this program offers basic photo-organizing and -editing tools. In addition, a tool built into the program, Nikon Transfer, simplifies the job of sending pictures from a memory card or your camera to your computer. I explain the process in the next section.

Click to hide/display File & Camera Information panel

Display/hide focus point   Open image in Capture NX-D

Focus point

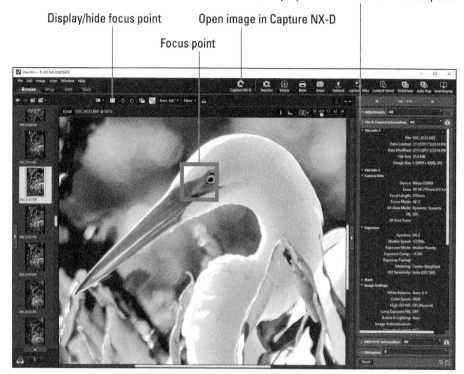

FIGURE 9-8:
You can see
the selected
focus point and
other camera
settings
when you
view photos
in Nikon
ViewNX-i.

Your program may not initially look like the one in the figure because I customized the screen layout to suit my needs. You can do the same via the options on the View and Window menus after opening the program.

Here are two features I especially like about ViewNX-i:

TIP

- *Viewing picture settings (metadata):* You can display a panel that shows the settings you used when shooting the picture, as shown in Figure 9-8. The settings are stored as *metadata* (extra data) in each picture's file. Although other photo programs can display some metadata, they often can't show all the detailed information that you can see in ViewNX-i.

  Don't see the panel? Open the Window menu and choose Adjustments/ Metadata. You may then need to click the triangle labeled *Click to hide/ display File & Camera Information panel* to expand the panel. Drag the scroll bar on the right side of the panel to view any hidden information.

- *Displaying focus points:* Click the Focus Point button, also labeled in Figure 9-8, to display one or more red rectangles on the photo, as shown in the figure. The rectangles indicate which focus point (or points) the camera used to establish focus, which can be helpful for troubleshooting focus problems.

If the focus point is over your subject, but the subject is blurry, the cause is likely not due to focusing at all, but to subject or camera movement during a too-long exposure (slow shutter speed). You won't see the focus point if you used manual focusing, and it also may not appear if you used continuous autofocusing.

The program also contains some limited photo-editing tools. To access, click the Edit tab near the top-left corner of the program window. If you can't accomplish what you want to do using the ViewNX-i tools, click the icon labeled *Open image in Capture NX-D* to access a more robust set of editing features.

>> **Nikon Capture NX-D:** Shown in Figure 9-9, this program offers pro-level photo-editing tools, including a good Raw processing tool, which I show you how to use later in this chapter. You also can view camera metadata in this program, as shown in the figure. Click the tabs labeled in the figure to toggle the panel display between the Information tab, which displays metadata, and the Edit tab, which contains editing tools.

Click to view Information tab

Click to view Edit tab

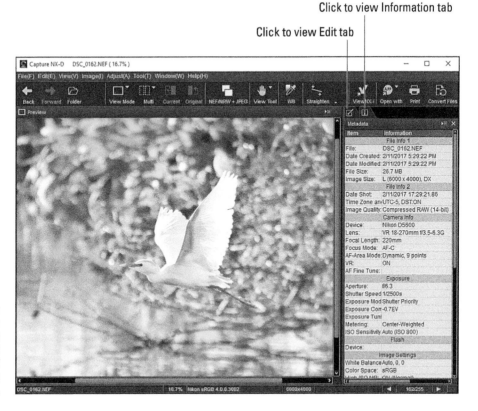

FIGURE 9-9:
Capture NX-D offers a more advanced assortment of photo editing tools.

TIP

GETTING HELP WITH THE NIKON SOFTWARE

For years, you could access a built-in user manual via the Help menu found in Nikon's photo programs. But things work differently now: You can go online and download a copy of the user manual or simply check the online help pages for answers. (I suggest downloading a copy of the manual so you don't need an active Internet connection to get help.)

To take advantage of these options the first time, you do need to be online, however. When your Internet browser is up and running, launch the Nikon program whose Help system you want to access. In that program, open the Help menu (top of the program window) and then choose the Help item from menu. Your browser then displays a window that offers two options. Click the Go to Help Site link to jump to the program's pages at the Nikon website, and then click Get PDF Manual to download the instruction manual.

The manual is provided in the PDF format (Portable Document Format), so you can read it in Adobe Acrobat (available free from the Adobe website, www.adobe.com) or any program that can display PDF documents.

You can download both programs from the Nikon website (in the United States, www.nikonusa.com). Head for the Support section of the website, where you'll find a link to camera software. Be sure to download the latest versions. At the time I write this chapter, ViewNX-i is Version 1.2.4; NX-D is Version 1.4.3. Older versions of the software lack support for D5600 files. Also make sure that your computer meets the software operating-system requirements. (The program is available for both Windows-based and Mac computers.)

Downloading Pictures to the Computer

You can copy picture and movie files from a memory card to your computer in two ways:

>> **Use a memory card reader.** A card reader, if you're unfamiliar, is a small device that attaches to your computer (or, in some cases, is built into the computer). When you put a camera memory card into the reader, your computer recognizes the card as another drive on the system, and you can then access the files on the card.

>> **Connect the camera to the computer via a USB cable.** This option requires purchase of a specific Nikon cable, part UC-E20. You may be able to order it from Nikon directly (about $12) or from an online camera superstore. Local camera stores don't usually carry the cable because it's not a commonly requested item.

TIP

I recommend using a card reader because sending pictures directly from the camera requires that the camera be turned on during the download process, wasting battery power. Additionally, unlike the cable, which is specific to this camera (and a handful of Nikon point-and-shoot cameras) a card reader can do universal duty, handling cards from any devices that use SD cards for storage. For example, I have a tablet that stores data on a mini-SD card, which is a tiny version of a standard SD card. The mini-cards usually come with an adapter that enables them to be read as a regular SD card, so I can use my card reader to transfer files from my tablet as well as my camera.

If your computer doesn't have a card reader, you can buy a standalone one at any electronics or camera store. Make sure the reader meets two specifications: First, it uses the type of connection compatible with your computer (USB connection is the most common). Second, check that the reader accepts the type of card your camera uses (SD) as well as the capacity of the cards you use. Currently, the highest capacity SD cards are labeled SDXC (Secure Digital Expanded Capacity). Some older card readers still being sold can't read the high-capacity cards.

Also, the faster the transfer speed of the card reader, the faster your image files can be sent to the computer. For USB connections, a USB 3 reader or higher moves files more quickly than a USB 2 reader. If your computer only has USB 2 ports, don't worry; you won't enjoy the fastest speeds, but the reader will still work if it's backward-compatible with USB 2.

What about wireless transfer, you ask? Well, there is one way to do it: You can buy Eye-Fi memory cards, which have wireless connectivity built in. You can find out more about these cards and how to set them up to connect with your computer at the manufacturer's website: www.eye.fi. Also check the Eye-Fi details provided in the D5600 manual; look for the section related to the Eye-Fi Upload option on the Setup menu. (The menu item appears only when an Eye-Fi card is installed.) I don't cover these cards in this book.

As for the wireless communication features on the D5600, you can't use them to move files to your computer. You can only connect wirelessly to Android- and iOS-based phones, tablets, and other smart devices that can run the Nikon Snap-Bridge app. (Your device needs to run a fairly recent version of the Android or iOS operating system to run the app.) Again, check the appendix for a primer on SnapBridge and the camera's wireless features.

With those preliminaries out of the way, the next section tells you how to connect your camera and computer via USB. Following that, you can read about the steps in making the actual file transfer whether you go the USB route or use a card reader.

Connecting via USB

If you invest in the USB cable needed to download pictures directly from your camera to your computer, take these steps to connect the two devices:

1. **Check the level of the camera battery.**

WARNING

   If the battery is low, charge it before continuing. Running out of battery power during downloading can cause problems, including lost picture data. Alternatively, if you purchased the AC adapter, use it to power the camera during downloading.

2. **Turn on the computer and give it time to finish its normal start-up routine.**

3. **Turn off the camera.**

4. **Insert the smaller of the two plugs on the USB cable into the USB port on the side of the camera.**

   Look under the lower rubber door on the left side of the camera for this port, highlighted in Figure 9-10.

5. **Plug the other end of the cable into a USB port on the computer.**

6. **Turn on the camera.**

   What happens now depends on the photo software you have installed on your computer. The next section explains the possibilities and how to proceed with the transfer process.

7. **When the download is complete, turn off the camera and then disconnect it from the computer.**

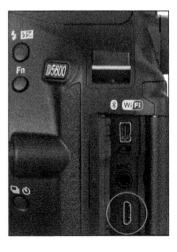

FIGURE 9-10:
The port for connecting the USB cable is hidden under the door on the left side of the camera.

Starting the file-transfer process

After you connect the camera to the computer or insert a memory card into a card reader, what happens next depends on the software installed on your computer. Here are the most common possibilities and how to move forward:

>> **On a computer running Windows, you see a message asking what software you want to use to download your pictures (or movies).** If you don't have a favorite program to use for this task, I suggest you select Nikon ViewNX-i. The program should appear as an option after you install it onto your computer. I give step-by-step instructions for downloading via this program in the next section.

>> **An installed photo program automatically displays a photo-download wizard.** For example, on a Mac computer, you may see the downloader associated with Photos (or iPhoto, on systems running some older versions of the Mac OS). Or the downloader associated with some other photo program, such as Adobe Lightroom, may leap to the forefront. Usually, the downloader that appears is associated with the software you most recently installed.

>> **Nothing happens.** Don't panic; assuming your card reader or camera is properly connected, all is probably well. Someone simply may have disabled all the automatic downloaders on your system. Just launch your photo software and then transfer your pictures using whatever command starts that process.

The next section provides details on using Nikon ViewNX-i to download files. If you use another program, the concepts are the same, but check the program manual for specifics.

Downloading using Nikon ViewNX-i

Nikon ViewNX-i has a built-in tool, Nikon Transfer, that simplifies the job of downloading files. Follow these steps to use it:

1. **Launch Nikon Transfer 2, shown in Figure 9-11, if it isn't already open.**

   Depending on how you install ViewNX-i and the computer preferences you establish, the Nikon Transfer 2 window may appear automatically when you insert a memory card into your card reader or attach the camera via USB cable. If the program doesn't launch automatically, start ViewNX-i, open the File menu, and choose Launch Transfer. You also can just click the Transfer button at the top of the ViewNX-i window. (Note that although my figures show the Windows version of the program, these steps work for the Mac version as well.)

2. **Display the Source tab to view thumbnails of your pictures, as shown in the figure.**

   Don't see any tabs? Click the Options triangle (refer to Figure 9-11) to display them. Then click the Source tab. The icon representing your camera or memory card should be selected, as shown in the figure. (My card reader shows up as Removable Disk F, but the letter of the disk varies depending on what other drives you have installed and how many slots your memory card offers.) If your camera or card isn't selected, click the icon.

Click to hide/display thumbnails

Click to hide/display Options panels

Select marked

Select all

Select protected

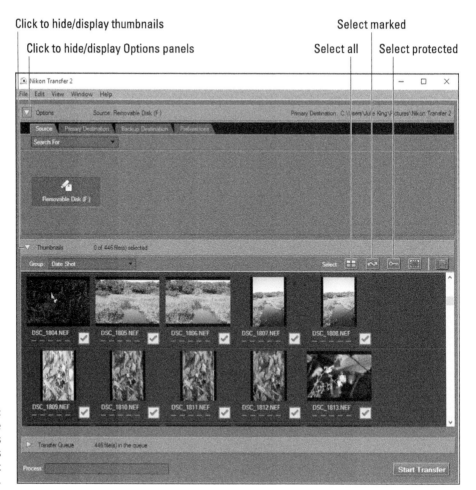

FIGURE 9-11:
Select the
check boxes
of the images
that you want
to download.

REMEMBER

Thumbnails of your files appear in the bottom half of the dialog box. If you don't see the thumbnails, click the Thumbnails triangle (refer to Figure 9-11) to open the thumbnails area.

3. **Select the files that you want to download.**

Click a thumbnail to highlight it and then click the box near its lower-right corner to select that file for downloading.

TIP

These tricks can speed up the process:

- *Select all files.* Click the Select All icon, also labeled in the figure.

- *Select files tagged for transfer to a smart device:* Through the camera's Playback menu, you can select files you want to transfer the next time you connect the camera wirelessly to your smart device. If you take that step, you can tell Nikon Transfer 2 to look for and download only the tagged files. Just click the Select Marked icon, also labeled in Figure 9-11.

- *Select protected files.* If you used the in-camera function to protect pictures, you can select just those images by clicking the Select Protected icon (refer to Figure 9-11).

4. **Click the Primary Destination tab to display options for handling the file transfer, as shown in Figure 9-12.**

Choose storage location for transferred files

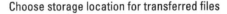

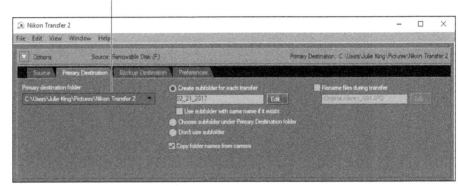

FIGURE 9-12: Specify the folder where you want to put the downloaded images.

You still see the entire Nikon Transfer window; I cropped the figure to show only the options on the tab at the top of the window.

The most important setting on this tab is Primary Destination Folder, which determines where the program puts your transferred files. (Look for the option on the left side of the tab.) Open the drop-down list and choose the folder on your computer's hard drive (or external drive) where you want to put the pictures. Other options on this tab enable you to specify how pictures should be organized inside the primary destination folder and whether to rename files during the transfer.

5. **To send copies of your pictures to a backup drive as well as to your main storage location, click the Backup Destination tab.**

TIP

This feature is a big timesaver, enabling you to download photos to your primary drive and a backup drive at the same time. After displaying the Backup Destination tab, select the Backup Files box and then use the other panel options to specify where you want the backup files to go.

6. **Click the Preferences tab to display the options shown in Figure 9-13.**

Three settings here are critical:

- *Transfer New Files Only:* This option, when selected, ensures that you don't waste time downloading images you've already transferred.

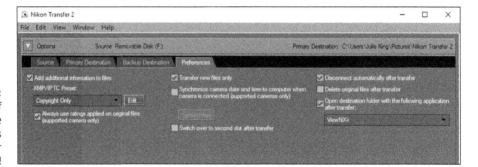

FIGURE 9-13:
Turn off
the Delete
Original Files
after Transfer
option!

WARNING

- *Delete Original Files after Transfer:* **Turn off this option.** Otherwise, your pictures are erased from your memory card when the transfer is complete. Always make sure the pictures made it to the computer before you delete them from your memory card.

TIP

DRAG-AND-DROP FILE TRANSFER

As an alternative to using a photo program to download files, you can use Windows Explorer or the Mac Finder to drag and drop files from your memory card to your computer, just as you copy files from a CD, DVD, or flash drive onto your computer. If you connect the camera's SD card through a card reader, the computer sees the card as just another drive on the system. Windows Explorer also shows the camera as a storage device when you connect the camera directly to the computer. (With some versions of the Mac OS, including the most recent ones, the Finder doesn't recognize cameras in this way.)

The downside to this method is that you may not be able to preview thumbnails of your photos. Instead, you may see only filenames in the Windows Explorer or Finder windows. So if time permits, I transfer using a photo program that lets me see my images and decide which ones I want to bother downloading. But I use the drag-and-drop method if I'm in a hurry to unload a memory card so that I can use it on my next shoot. The process is marginally faster because the photo program doesn't have to create thumbnails of each image, and I don't get distracted looking at each photo as it appears. When I return to the computer later, I can use my photo software to view and organize the files I downloaded.

Br careful to copy, and not move, the image files when you drag and drop. That way, the images remain on the memory card as a backup if something goes awry during the transfer process.

TIP

● *Open Destination Folder with the Following Application after Transfer:* You can tell the program to immediately open your photo program after the transfer is complete. Choose ViewNX-i to view and organize your photos using that program. To choose another program, open the drop-down list, choose Browse, and select the program from the dialog box that appears. Click OK after doing so.

Your choices remain in force for any subsequent download sessions, so you don't have to revisit the Preferences tab unless you want the program to behave differently.

7. **Click the Start Transfer button, found at the lower-right corner of the Nikon Transfer 2 window (refer to Figure 9-11).**

The Process bar in the lower-left corner of the program window indicates how the transfer is progressing. What happens when the transfer completes depends on the choices you made in Step 6; if you selected Nikon ViewNX-i as the photo program, it opens and displays the folder that contains your just-downloaded images.

Processing Raw (NEF) Files

Chapter 2 introduces you to the Raw file format. The advantage of capturing Raw files — NEF files on Nikon cameras — is that you make the decisions about how to translate the original picture data into an actual photograph. You take this step by using a software tool known as a *Raw converter.* To process your NEF files, Nikon offers the following free options:

» **Use the in-camera processing feature.** You can specify only limited image attributes when you go this route, and you can save the processed files only in the JPEG format. Still, having this option is a nice feature.

» **Process and convert in Capture NX-D.** For more control over how your raw data is translated into an image, use this option. Not only do you get access to tools not found on the camera, but you also can save the adjusted files in either the JPEG or TIFF format. In addition, you have the advantage of evaluating your photos on a larger screen than the one on your camera.

TECHNICAL STUFF

TIFF stands for Tagged Image File Format and has long been the standard format for images destined for professional publication. I recommend saving your converted Raw files in this format because it does a better job than JPEG of holding onto your original image data. As explained in Chapter 2, JPEG compresses the file, meaning it does away with what it considers "unnecessary" data.

Of course, you can use any third-party Raw-processing tool you prefer, such as the one provided with Adobe Photoshop and Adobe Lightroom. Just don't pay for a third-party tool until you've tried Capture NX-D — the fact that it's free doesn't mean that it isn't a good program. Also understand that third-party programs usually don't support new cameras right away, so check the program information to make sure it can open Raw files from the D5600. You may need to download a software update to make that happen.

Processing Raw images in the camera

By using the NEF (RAW) Processing option on the Retouch menu, you can create a JPEG version of a Raw file right in the camera. Follow these steps:

1. **Press the Playback button to switch to playback mode.**

2. **Display the picture in the full-frame view.**

    If necessary, you can shift from Thumbnail view to Full-Frame view by pressing OK. Press OK twice if you're in Calendar view. (Chapter 9 has details on these playback modes.)

3. **Press the i button.**

    You see the screen shown on the left in Figure 9-14.

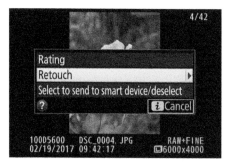
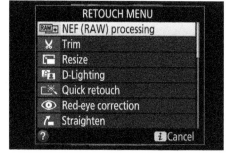

FIGURE 9-14: Select Retouch (left screen) and then select NEF (RAW) Processing option (right screen).

4. **Choose Retouch to display the Retouch menu.**

5. **Choose NEF (RAW) Processing, as shown on the right in Figure 9-14.**

    You see a screen similar to the one on the left in Figure 9-15, which is the first of two pages of options you can select for processing your file. You can use the Multi Selector to scroll to the second screen, shown on the right in the figure.

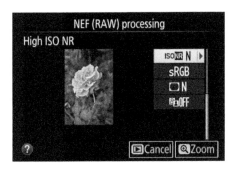

FIGURE 9-15:
You get two
pages of
options for
processing a
Raw file.

6. **Set the conversion options.**

   Along the right side of each option screen, you see a column offering the available settings. The following list identifies each setting, starting with the first option on the left screen in Figure 9-15 and continuing through the four settings shown in the right screen:

   - *EXE:* Although this option tops the list of settings, it's actually the last one to choose. You select it to create the JPEG copy of your Raw file after you work your way though all the other settings.

   - *Image Quality:* Choose Fine to retain maximum picture quality. See the Chapter 2 section related to the JPEG format for details on this option.

   - *Image Size:* Chapter 2 explains this one, too. Choose Large to retain all the original image pixels.

   - *White Balance:* Unless colors appear to be wrong, stick with the default, Auto. Otherwise, experiment with each setting to see which one renders colors most accurately. Check out Chapter 5 for details about White Balance.

   - *Exposure Compensation:* With this option, which I cover in Chapter 3, you can adjust image brightness. When using this feature for Raw conversion, you're limited to a range of —2.0 and +2.0; when shooting, you can choose from settings ranging from –5.0 to +5.0. Raise the value for a brighter image; lower it for a darker shot. The camera updates the preview to indicate how your setting will affect the picture.

   - *Picture Control:* This option, detailed in Chapter 5, enables you to adjust color saturation, contrast, and image sharpness. As with the White Balance and Exposure Compensation settings, the screen updates to show you the effect of the selected Picture Control.

   - *High ISO Noise Reduction:* If your picture looks *noisy* — that is, marred by a speckled look — enabling this feature may improve the picture. See Chapter 3 for an explanation of ISO and noise.

   - *Color Space:* This setting determines whether the camera uses the default color space, sRGB, or the larger Adobe RGB color space when converting your photo. Stick with sRGB until you digest the Chapter 5 section that details this option.

- *Vignette Control:* Does your picture appear unnaturally dark in the corners? This flaw, called *vignetting,* can sometimes be eliminated or at least diminished by applying the Vignette Control feature. Chapter 4 has more information.

- *D-Lighting:* To brighten the darkest part of your picture without also brightening the lightest areas, try adjusting this setting. It's the post-capture equivalent of the Active D-Lighting feature that's available during shooting; see Chapter 3 for help with the option. You can set the level of adjustment to High, Normal, or Low; to darken shadows, try setting the option to Off.

At any time, you can magnify the image by pressing and holding the Zoom In button or by tapping the Zoom icon at the bottom of the screen. Release the button or tap the icon again to return to the normal display.

7. **Select EXE on the first conversion screen.**

The camera records a JPEG copy of your Raw file and displays the copy in the monitor. The camera assigns the next available file number to the image, so the number of the original and the number of the processed JPEG don't match. You also see the little Retouch menu symbol (the box with a paintbrush) with the photo during playback.

TIP

You also can access the Raw processing tool by displaying the Retouch menu and then choosing NEF (RAW) Processing. The camera displays thumbnails of Raw images; use the Multi Selector to highlight an image (or just tap the image) and then press OK or tap the OK symbol to access the conversion options.

Processing Raw files in Capture NX-D

Figure 9-16 offers a look at Capture NX-D, one of the free programs you can download from the Nikon website. When you first open the program, it won't look like what you see in the figure; I customized the window layout to show before and after views of my photo and to display the panel of Raw conversion tools along the right side of the window. You can customize these and other aspects of the program window through options on the View and Window menus.

As you can see, this isn't a program for sissies; expect a little bit of a learning curve. Then again, you can't really "break" your photo no matter what you do, so don't be afraid to experiment. Your original data is never overwritten because you can't resave it in the Raw format — you can only create a copy in the TIFF or JPEG format.

Convert Files

Undo all changes

Edit panel

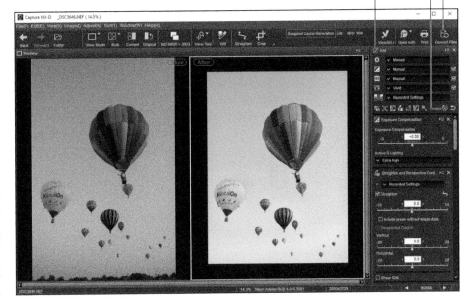

FIGURE 9-16:
Capture NX-D
offers a large
assortment
of tools for
finalizing the
look of your
Raw images.

I have room in this book only for the briefest of explanations of the Capture NX–D Raw–processing tools, but the following pointers should get you started in a good direction:

>> **Select the Raw file.** After opening Capture NX-D, click the thumbnail of the image you want to process. (If you don't see any thumbnails, open the View menu and select the Thumbnail option.)

TIP

If you're viewing images in Nikon ViewNX-i, you can ship the Raw file directly to Capture NX-D. Select the photo, open the File menu, and then choose Open in Capture NX-D. Or skip the menu operation and just click the NX-D icon found near the top-right corner of the ViewNX-i window.

>> **Display before and after views of your photo.** To arrange your original side-by-side with the edited version, open the View menu and select Compare Before and After Images.

>> **Display the Edit panel, labeled in Figure 9-16.** Controls for adjusting your Raw image appear in the Edit panel along the right side of the window, as shown in Figure 9-16. If you don't see the panel, open the Window menu and choose Edit.

>> **Use the tools in the Edit panel to adjust your photo.** You have to do a little work to uncover all the available options. See the icons along the left and bottom edges of the top pane of the Edit panel? Click those icons to display

related tools. (Pause your cursor momentarily over an icon to display a text label that tells you what the symbol represents.) Use the scroll bar on the right side of the window to scroll the display to reveal more settings if needed.

>> **To remove all adjustments you made, click the symbol labeled** *Undo all changes* **in the figure.** You also can select Recorded Settings from the drop-down list near the top of the Edit panel to restore the settings that were in force when you took the picture.

>> **When you finish adjusting the image, click the Convert Files icon, labeled in Figure 9-16.** Or open the File menu and choose Convert Files. You then see the dialog box shown in Figure 9-17. Set the File Format option, highlighted in the figure, to 8-bit TIFF. (If you choose 16-bit TIFF, you may not be able to use the image in other programs, such as Microsoft PowerPoint.) The rest of the options work as they do when you save files in most Mac or Windows programs: Specify where you want to store the file, give the file a name, and then click Save.

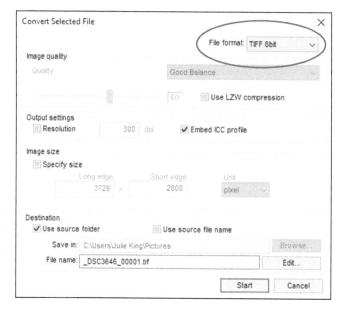

FIGURE 9-17: To retain the best picture quality, select TIFF as the file format for your processed Raw files.

TIP

One neat thing about working with Raw images is that you can easily create as many variations of the photo as you want. For example, you might choose one set of options when processing your Raw file as a color image and then a different set to create a black-and-white version of the photo. Just be sure to give each processed file a unique name so you don't overwrite the first TIFF file you create with your second version.

You can find more details on Raw processing and other NX-D features in the program's instruction manual, which is available online. To find out how to get to the manual, see the sidebar "Getting help with the Nikon software," earlier in this chapter.

Preparing Pictures for Online Sharing

Have you ever received an email containing a photo so large that you can't view the whole thing without scrolling the email window? This occurs because monitors can display only a limited number of pixels. The exact number depends on the screen resolution, but suffice it to say, today's cameras produce photos with pixel counts in excess of what monitors can handle.

Thankfully, newer email programs incorporate features that automatically shrink the photo display to a viewable size. That doesn't change the fact that a large photo file means longer downloading times, though — and if recipients choose to hold onto the picture, a big storage hit on their hard drives.

Sending a high-resolution photo *is* the thing to do if you want the recipient to be able to generate a good print. But for simple onscreen viewing, I suggest limiting your photos to fewer than 1,000 pixels on the longest side of the image so that people who use older email programs can see the entire picture (or nearly all of it) without scrolling the display.

This size recommendation means that even if you shoot at your camera's lowest Image Size setting (2992 x 2000), you wind up with more pixels than you need for onscreen viewing. Some new email programs have a photo-upload feature that creates a temporary low-res version for you, but if not, creating your own copy is easy. If you're posting to an online photo-sharing site, you may be able to upload all your original pixels, though many sites have resolution limits.

REMEMBER

In addition to resizing high-resolution images, check their file types. If the photos are in the Raw (NEF) or TIFF format, you need to create a JPEG copy for online use. Web browsers and e-mail programs can't display Raw or TIFF files.

You can tackle both bits of prep in ViewNX 2 or by using the Resize option in your camera. The next sections explain both methods.

Prepping online photos using ViewNX-i

For pictures stored on your computer, you can create small JPEG copies for online sharing using Nikon ViewNX-i. First, click the image thumbnail to select it. Next, open the File menu, select the Export option, and then choose Convert Files to display the dialog box shown in Figure 9-18.

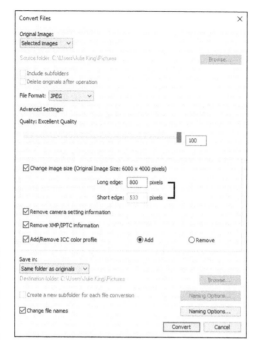

FIGURE 9-18:
Select JPEG as
the file format
and then
specify the
size for your
online copy.

Set up things as follows:

» **Select JPEG as the file type:** Make your selection from the File Format drop-down list.

» **Set the picture-quality level:** Use the Quality slider to set the picture quality, which is controlled by how much JPEG compression is applied when the file is saved. For best quality, drag the slider all the way to the right, but remember the trade-off: As you raise the quality, less compression occurs, which results in a larger file size. (See Chapter 2 for more information about JPEG compression.)

» **Set the image size (number of pixels):** To resize the photo, select the Change Image Size check box and then enter a value (in pixels) for the longest dimension of the photo. The program automatically fills in the other value.

» **Select all three Remove check boxes:** The boxes are located under the Change Image Size option. Selecting these boxes removes unnecessary camera metadata, which reduces image file size.

» **Tell the program where you want to store the reduced-size file and how you want to name the file:** Use the options in the Save In area of the Convert Files dialog box to handle this bit of business.

WARNING

If you're resizing a JPEG original, be sure to give the small version a new name to avoid overwriting the original. I like to add the words "For Web" to the filenames of my online versions; for example, if the original is DSC_0020.jpg, I name the online version DSC_0020 For Web.jpg. That way, it's easy to find the file that is ready for online use.

After working your way through the Convert Files dialog box options, click the Convert button at the bottom of the box to create the small-size JPEG version of your original.

Resizing pictures in the camera

TIP

The in-camera resizing tool, found on the Retouch menu, works on both JPEG and Raw images. With both types of files, your resized copy is saved in the JPEG format. You can get the job done in two ways:

» **Resize a single photo:** Set the camera to playback mode, display the photo in single-image view (or select it in Thumbnail or Calendar view), and press the *i* button. On the screen that appears, select Retouch to display the Retouch menu, as shown on the left in Figure 9-19.

FIGURE 9-19:
Use the
Resize option
to create a
low-resolution
version of your
picture.

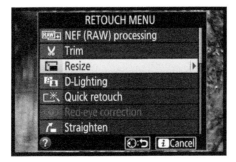
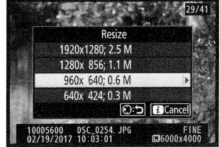

Select Resize to display possible image sizes (refer to the right side of Figure 9-19). The first value shows the pixel dimensions of the small copy; the second, the total number of pixels, measured in megapixels. After you select a size, the camera asks permission to create the resized copy; answer in the affirmative to go forward.

» **Resize a batch of photos:** Display the Retouch menu and choose Resize, as shown on the left in Figure 9-20, to display the second screen in the figure. Select Choose Size to set the pixel count of the small images. Then choose Select Image, as shown in the figure, to display thumbnails of your photos, as shown in Figure 9-21.

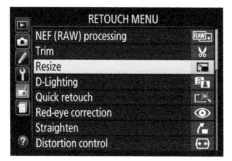

RETOUCH MENU

NEF (RAW) processing
Trim
Resize
D-Lighting
Quick retouch
Red-eye correction
Straighten
Distortion control

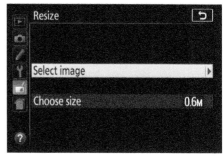

Resize

Select image

Choose size   0.6M

FIGURE 9-20:
To resize
a batch of
photos, it's
quicker to do
the job via the
Retouch menu.

Select the image you want to resize (just tap its thumbnail or use the Multi Selector to move the yellow highlight box over it). Then tap Set (bottom of screen) or press the Multi Selector up or down to tag the file with a Resize icon, labeled in the figure. Select the next photo and rinse and repeat. After tagging all the photos, tap OK or press the OK button to display the go-ahead screen. Then select Yes to create your small copies.

In both cases, the camera duplicates the selected images and *downsamples* (eliminates pixels from) the copies to achieve the size you specified. The small copies are saved in the JPEG file format, using the same Image Quality setting (Fine, Normal, or Basic) as the original. Raw originals are saved as JPEG Fine images. Either way, your original picture files remain untouched.

Small-size copies appear during playback marked by a Resize symbol next to the file size (lower-right corner), as shown in Figure 9-22. Next to the symbol, you see the resolution (pixel count) of the resized image. You also see the standard Retouch symbol, which appears anytime you alter a photo via a Retouch menu option.

Resize symbol

Resize
Select image
100D5600
100-16   100-17   100-18
100-19   100-20   100-21
Set   Zoom   OK

FIGURE 9-21:
After selecting a photo, press the Multi Selector up or down or tap the set icon to tag the file for resizing.

Retouch symbol

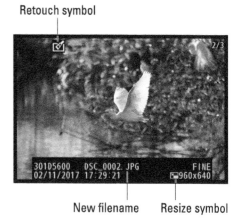

301D5600   DSC_0002.JPG   FINE
02/11/2017 17:29:21   960x640

New filename   Resize symbol

FIGURE 9-22:
The Resize icon indicates a small-size copy.

4

The Part of Tens

IN THIS PART . . .

Add text comments and copyright notices to camera metadata (hidden file data).

Customize the Information display, Function button, and other camera features.

Find out how to use the Retouch menu editing tools.

Repair red-eye, fix lens distortion, straighten tilting horizon lines, and crop to a better composition.

Correct minor exposure and color problems.

Create special effects by using the Effects exposure mode or by applying Retouch menu effects tools.

IN THIS CHAPTER

» **Tagging files with image comments and copyright notices**

» **Creating custom folders and filenames**

» **Customizing the Information display**

» **Designing your own menu**

» **Altering the camera's automatic shutdown timing**

» **Changing the function of some controls**

Chapter **10**

Ten More Ways to Customize Your Camera

As you've no doubt deduced, Nikon is more than eager to let you customize almost every aspect of the camera's operation. This chapter discusses customization options not considered in earlier chapters, including ways to embed a copyright notice in your picture files, create custom folder and file names, and even tweak the function of external controls.

Adding Comments and Copyright Notices

Through two Setup menu options, Image Comment and Copyright Information, you can add hidden text to your picture files. Suppose, for example, that you're on vacation and visiting a different destination every day. With Image Comment, you can annotate all the pictures you take on a particular outing with the name of the location. Similarly, Copyright Information enables you to tag files with your name and other copyright data.

REMEMBER

By *hidden text*, I mean that the text doesn't appear on the photo itself; instead, it's stored in the image file with other *metadata* (extra data, such as shutter speed, date and time, and so on). You can view metadata during playback in the Shooting Data display mode (see Chapter 8) or along with other metadata in Nikon ViewNX-i and Nikon Capture NX-D (see Chapter 9).

The next two sections explain both features.

Adding an image comment

Select Image Comment from the Setup menu, as shown on the left in Figure 10-1. Then select Input Comment, as shown on the right in the figure, to display the keyboard screen shown on the left in Figure 10-2.

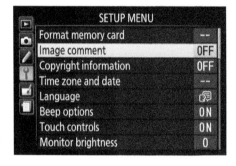
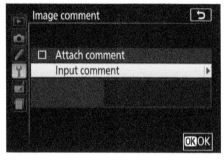

FIGURE 10-1:
You can tag pictures with hidden text comments through this feature.

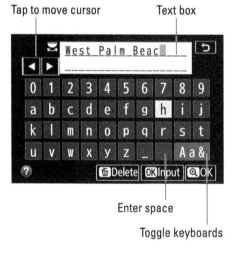
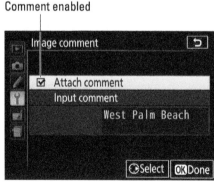

FIGURE 10-2:
After entering comment text (left), select the Attach Comment box (right) and then press OK or tap Done.

Enter text using these methods:

>> **Enter a character:** If the touch screen is enabled (check the Touch Controls setting on the Setup menu), just tap a character in the keyboard. You also can use the Multi Selector to highlight a character and then tap the OK Input symbol at the bottom of the screen or press the OK button. Either way, the characters appear in the text box, labeled on the left side of Figure 10-2. Your comment can be up to 36 characters long.

To cycle from the keyboard shown in the figure, to screens that contain uppercase characters and symbols, select the Aa& key, which is the last one on the keyboard. Select the empty box just to the left of that key to enter a space. I labeled both keys in Figure 10-2.

>> **Move the cursor in the text box:** Tap the cursor arrows (see figure) or rotate the Command dial. (The symbol just above the arrows represents the Command dial.) For big cursor moves, rotating the Command dial is the fastest option.

>> **Delete a letter:** Move the cursor under the letter in the text box and then tap the Delete symbol at the bottom of the screen or press the Delete button.

After entering your comment, tap the rightmost OK symbol (the one marked with a magnifying glass) or press the Zoom In button to display the screen shown on the right in Figure 10-2. Your text comment appears underneath the Input Comment line. You're not done, however: You still need to place a check mark in the Attach Comment box, as shown in the figure. To toggle the check mark on and off, tap the Attach Comment box or press the Multi Selector right. Finally, press the OK button or tap the OK Done symbol to exit to the Setup menu. The Image Comment menu item should now read On, and any new pictures you take will include the comment data.

To disable the feature, remove the check mark from the Attach Comment box. Press or tap OK to make your decision official.

Adding a copyright notice

To add a copyright notice, choose Copyright Information from the Setup menu, as shown on the left in Figure 10-3. You then see the screen shown on the right in the figure. (If you have not yet entered copyright data, the Artist and Copyright lines will appear empty.)

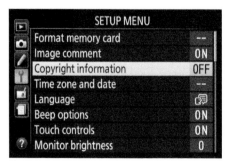
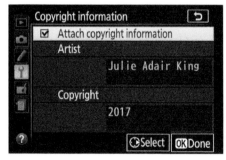

Select Artist to display the keyboard screen and then use the techniques outlined in the preceding section to enter your name. Select Copyright Data to add that information. The Artist field can hold 36 characters; the Copyright field, 54 characters.

After entering your data, select Attach Copyright Information and turn on the check mark in the accompanying box, as shown on the right in Figure 10-3. To toggle the check mark on and off, press the Multi Selector right or tap the box or the Select icon at the bottom of the screen. Then press the OK button or tap OK Done. Your copyright notice will now be included in the metadata of all future files until you uncheck the Attach Copyright Information box.

Creating a Custom Storage Folder

By default, your camera stores all images in one folder, which it names 100D5600. Folders have a storage limit of 999 images; when you exceed that number or the last photo you stored in that folder has the file number 9999, the camera creates a new folder, assigning a name that indicates the folder number — 101D5600, 102D5600, and so on.

If you choose, you can create your own folder-numbering scheme. For example, perhaps you sometimes use your camera for business and sometimes for personal use. To keep your images separate, you can set up one folder numbered 200D5600 for work images and use the regular 100D5600 folder for personal photos.

To create a new storage folder, follow these steps:

1. **Display the Shooting menu and select Storage Folder.**

   If you haven't yet created a new folder (or reached the limit that causes the camera to do it for you), the number displayed next to the option is 100, representing the first three numbers of the folder name. During picture playback, you see the entire folder name (100D5600, for example) in display modes that show the folder name.

2. **Choose Select Folder by Number.**

You see the screen shown in Figure 10-4, with the current folder number shown in the middle of the screen.

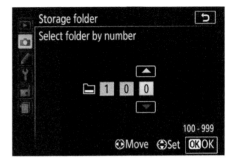

FIGURE 10-4:
Use this screen to create a new folder.

REMEMBER

A folder icon next to the folder number indicates that the folder already exists. A half-full icon like the one in Figure 10-4 shows that the folder contains images. A full icon means the folder is stuffed to its capacity (999 images) or contains a picture with the file number 9999. Either way, that full icon means that you can't put any more pictures in the folder.

3. **Assign the new folder a new number.**

To select the box for the digit you want to change, tap the box or press the Multi Selector right or left. Change the value by tapping the triangles above and below the box or by pressing the Multi Selector up/down.

When you create a new folder, the little folder icon disappears because the folder doesn't yet contain any photos.

4. **Tap the OK symbol or press the OK button.**

The camera creates your new folder and automatically selects it as the current storage folder.

WARNING

Each time you shoot, verify that the folder you want to use is shown for the Storage Folder option. If not, select that option and then choose Select Folder by Number to enter the folder number (if you know it) or choose Select Folder from List to pick from a list of all available folders.

Customizing Filenames

Normally, image filenames begin either with the characters DSC_, for photos captured in the sRGB color space, or _DSC, for images that use the Adobe RGB color space. (Chapter 5 explains color spaces.) But you can change to any three-letter prefix you prefer. So, for example, you could replace DSC with TIM before you take pictures of your brother Tim's family.

Follow these steps:

1. **Open the Shooting menu and select File Naming, as shown on the left in Figure 10-5.**

   You see the screen shown on the right in the figure. The current file naming structure for sRGB and Adobe RGB files appears on the screen.

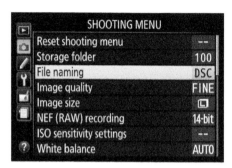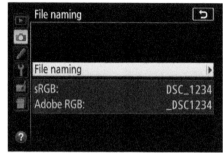

FIGURE 10-5: This option enables you to change the first three characters of filenames.

2. **Select File Naming to display a text-entry keyboard.**

3. **Enter three characters.**

   Use the same techniques as you do when adding image comments, explained at the start of this chapter. The only difference is that this keyboard limits you to a single screen of numbers and letters. You can't use a space, underscore, or other special characters in the filename.

4. **Press the Zoom In button or tap the rightmost OK symbol at the bottom of the screen.**

   You return to the Shooting menu; the File Naming option should reflect the changes you just made.

Changing the Information Display Style

By default, the Information display that appears when you shoot in the P, S, A, and M exposure modes appears as shown on the left in Figure 10-6. The three large circular graphics represent, from left to right, the shutter speed, f-stop, and ISO settings. As you adjust the f-stop setting, the center of its circle grows or shrinks to represent the opening and closing of the aperture. In other exposure modes, the default design is the same as for the P, S, A, and M modes, but the background is light gray.

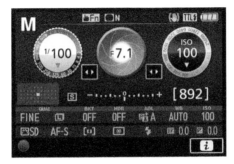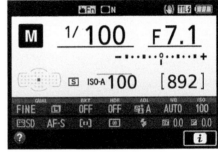

FIGURE 10-6:
You can alter
the display
style of the
Information
screen.

For those of us with less-than-perfect eyesight, the default Information Display design makes some data a tad difficult to see. You can't alter the design of the top and bottom of the screen, but you can switch the middle of the display to the layout shown on the right in the figure, which presents the critical settings at a larger size. You also can change the background color from black to blue or light gray.

To select the design you want to use, open the Setup menu and choose Info Display Format. On the next screen, you can specify a design for the P, S, A, and M exposure modes separately from the one used for the other modes.

Keeping the Information Display Hidden

Also found on the Setup menu, the Auto Info Display option offers another way to customize the Information display. When this option is On, as it is by default, the Information display appears whenever you press the shutter button halfway and release it. If you disable the Image Review feature (via the Playback menu), the display also appears after you take a picture.

Turn off the Auto Info Display option, and the Information screen appears briefly when you first turn on the camera, but after that, you must press the Info button to display it. Instructions in this book assume that you stick with the default setting (On). But because the monitor is one of the biggest drains of battery power, you may want to set the option to Off if the battery is running low.

REMEMBER

Directly below this Setup menu option is the similarly named Info Display Auto Off setting. This setting, when enabled, tells the camera to shut off the monitor display as soon as the eye sensor atop the viewfinder detects that you put your eye to the viewfinder. I see no reason to turn this option off. You can only look at one display at a time, and having the monitor turned on while you're looking through the viewfinder is just wasting battery power. In addition, turning off Auto Info Display disables the Touch Function feature, which I explain in the upcoming section "Assigning a Touch Function Role."

Creating Your Own Menu

Keeping track of how to access all the D5600's options can be a challenge, especially when it comes to those that you adjust through menus. To make things a little easier, you can build a custom menu that holds up to 20 of the options you use most frequently. Here's how:

1. **Display the My Menu menu, shown on the left in Figure 10-7.**

REMEMBER

This menu shares a slot in the menu list with the Recent Settings menu. The menu icon for the My Menu menu is labeled in the figure. If the Recent Settings menu appears instead, scroll to the end of that menu, select Choose Tab, and select My Menu. The My Menu screen then appears.

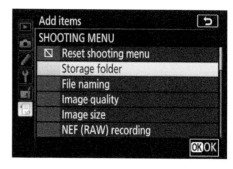

FIGURE 10-7:
You can create
a custom
menu to hold
up to 20 of the
settings you
access most
often.

My Menu icon   Select to switch back to
                Recent Settings menu

2. **Choose Add Items, as shown on the left in Figure 10-7.**

A screen listing all the other camera menus appears.

3. **Select the menu that contains an option you want to add to your menu.**

You see a list of all available options on the selected menu. A few items can't be added to a custom menu; a box with a slash through it appears next to those items.

4. **Select the item you want to add.**

Either tap the item or use the Multi Selector to highlight it and then press the OK button or tap the OK symbol. You then see the Choose Position screen, shown on the left in Figure 10-8; more about that screen momentarily. For now, just press OK or tap the return arrow at the top of the screen to return to the My Menu screen. The item you just added appears at the top of that screen.

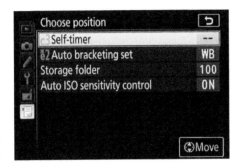

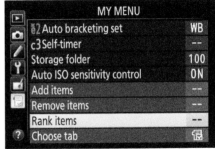

5. **Repeat Steps 2–4 to add more items to your menu.**

When you get to Step 3, a check mark appears next to any item that's already on your menu.

6. **Arrange the menu items on the Choose Position screen (first screen in Figure 10-8).**

After you add your second item to the menu, the Move symbol at the bottom of the Choose Position screen becomes available. You can then rearrange the position of the menu item you just added if you want. While that item is highlighted, press the Multi Selector up or down or tap the Move icon at the bottom of the screen to display a yellow line. Position the line just above where you want to put the just-added item. (You'll have the opportunity to rearrange items later, so don't get too hung up on this step.)

7. **Press OK.**

Your menu is saved, and the initial My Menu screen appears.

After creating your menu, you can reorder and remove menu items as follows:

>> **Change the order of menu options.** Display the My Menu screen and highlight Rank Items, as shown on the right in Figure 10-8. If your menu contains more than a handful of items, you need to scroll to the second screen of the menu to get to the Rank Items option.

After choosing Rank Items, you see a screen that lists all your menu items in their current order. You can then use the touchscreen or Multi Selector and OK button to shuffle the list:

* *Touchscreen:* Tap an item to select it and then tap the line where you want the item to go. After reordering all items, tap OK to lock the moved item into its new home.

- *Multi Selector:* Highlight the item you want to move, press OK, press the Multi Selector up/down to choose the new list position, and then press OK again.

When you're happy with the order of the menu items, tap the exit arrow (top right of the screen) or press the Multi Selector left to return to the My Menu screen.

>> **Remove menu items.** On the My Menu screen, shown on the right in Figure 10-8, select Remove Items and press OK. (Again, you may need to scroll to the second page of the menu to get to the Remove Items option.) You then see a list of current menu items, with an empty box next to each item. To remove an item, check its box. (You can tap the box or use the Multi Selector to highlight the item and then press the Multi Selector right.) After tagging all the items you want to remove, press or tap OK. You see a confirmation screen asking permission to remove the item; select OK to go forward.

Adjusting Automatic Shutdown Timing

When the camera is in shooting mode, its *standby timer* feature saves battery power by shutting off the Information display and viewfinder after a period of inactivity. Similarly, the camera limits the Image Review period (the length of time your picture appears immediately after you press the shutter button), the length of time the Live View display remains active, how long a picture appears in playback mode, and how long menus remain onscreen.

You can control the auto-shutdown timing through the Custom Setting menu. Choose the Timers/AE Lock item from the main Custom Setting menu and then select Auto Off Timers, as shown on the left in Figure 10-9. You then see the screen shown on the right.

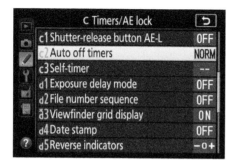
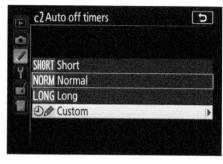

FIGURE 10-9: Customize auto shutdown timing here.

You get four choices, which produce the following shutdown times:

>> **Short:** Standby Timer (affects Information display and viewfinder), 4 seconds; Live View, 5 minutes; Image Review, 4 seconds; playback/menus, 20 seconds.

>> **Normal (default setting):** Standby Timer, 8 seconds; Live View, 10 minutes; Image Review, 4 seconds; playback/menus, 5 minutes.

>> **Long:** Standby Timer, 1 minute; Live View, 20 minutes; Image Review, 20 seconds; playback/menus, 10 minutes.

>> **Custom:** Choose this setting to specify delay times for the Standby Timer, Live View display, Image Review period, and Playback/menu display individually.

TIP
To disable Image Review altogether, head for the Playback menu and set the Image Review item to Off.

Customizing a Few Buttons

You can modify a few camera buttons to perform functions different from their default purposes. Again, instructions in this book assume you haven't modified the buttons, but after you master your camera, you may want to take advantage of these options. You can customize the following buttons through options on the Custom Setting menu:

>> **Function (Fn) button:** Establish this button's behavior via the Assign Fn Button option, found on the Controls submenu of the Custom Setting menu and shown in Figure 10-10.

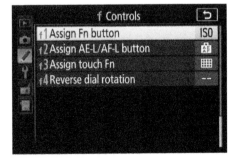
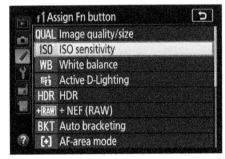

FIGURE 10-10:
You can assign any number of jobs to the Function (Fn) button.

By default, pressing the button accesses the ISO setting; press the button while rotating the Command dial to change the ISO value. You also can choose from a list of other options, as shown on the right in Figure 10-10. (Scroll to the second page of the list to access all the options.)

To see an information screen that tells you what each Fn button setting does, tap the question mark icon at the bottom of the screen or press the Zoom Out button. To exit the information screen, tap the return arrow or press the Zoom Out button again.

» **AE-L/AF-L button:** This button is related to the autoexposure and autofocusing systems. You can set the button to perform the following functions via the Assign AE-L/AF-L Button option, also found in the Controls section of the Custom Setting menu:

- *AE/AF Lock:* This is the default setting. Focus and exposure remain locked as long as you press the button.

- *AE Lock Only:* Autoexposure is locked as long as you press the button; autofocus isn't affected. (You can still lock focus by pressing the shutter button halfway.)

- *AE Lock (Hold):* This one locks exposure only with a single press of the button. The exposure lock remains in force until you press the button again or the exposure meters turn off.

- *AF Lock Only:* Focus remains locked as long as you press the button. Exposure isn't affected.

- *AF-On:* Pressing the button activates the camera's autofocus mechanism. If you choose this option, you can't focus by pressing the shutter button halfway.

» **Shutter button:** The Timers/AE Lock section of the Custom Setting menu offers an option called Shutter-Release Button AE-Lock. This option determines whether pressing the shutter button halfway locks focus only or locks focus and exposure.

At the default setting, Off, only focus is locked; exposure is adjusted up to the time you take the shot. If you change the setting to On, your half-press of the shutter button locks both focus and exposure. (Remember that you also have the option of using the AE-L/AF-L button to lock exposure and focus together, as outlined in Chapters 3 and 4.)

Assigning a Touch Function Role

You may be wondering about the purpose of the little Fn symbol that appears by default at the top of the Information display, labeled in Figure 10-11. Tapping the symbol does nothing, so what gives?

Touch Function assigned

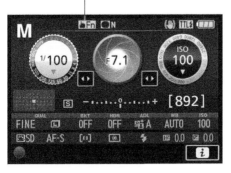
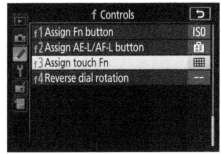

FIGURE 10-11:
The Touch
Function
symbol (left)
indicates that
you assigned
a role to the
Touch Function
feature (right).

The symbol indicates that a feature Nikon refers to as Touch Function is enabled. That means that when you are looking through the viewfinder, you can use your thumb or another finger to tap a specific region of the Information display to quickly adjust a setting. By default, your tap toggles the viewfinder grid display on and off. (In order for the feature to work, the Auto Info Off option on the Setup menu must be set to On.)

REMEMBER

Where you can tap to activate the assigned function depends on the position of the monitor. When the monitor is flat on the camera back, you can tap any empty area within the right half of the screen. If you swing the monitor out and away from the camera, you can tap any empty area throughout the whole screen.

To determine what functions you can assign, open the Controls submenu of the Custom Settings menu, as shown on the right in Figure 10-11. Then choose Assign Touch Fn to display the list of settings, as shown in Figure 10-12. Don't forget: If you need help, tap the question mark symbol or press the Zoom Out button to display a text screen that contains information about each option.

Scroll to the second page of the options list to reveal the None setting. If you

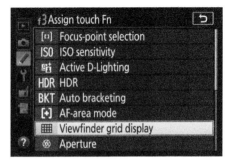

FIGURE 10-12:
By default, the Touchscreen Function is set to toggle the viewfinder grid display on and off.

select this setting, the Touch Function symbol disappears from the top of the Information display, indicating that tapping the Touch Function area of the screen has no result. This setting is perfect for those of us whose noses sometimes touch the screen, resulting in an unintended Touch Function action.

REMEMBER

The Touch Function setting *does not* enable or disable the rest of the touchscreen functions. To control those functions, use the Touch Controls option on the Setup Menu. Choose Enable to enable all touch operations; Playback Only to turn on touch control only during playback; and Disable to turn off the touchscreen altogether.

Reversing the Command Dial Orientation

When you shoot in certain exposure modes, you rotate the Command dial to adjust some exposure-related settings. For example, in the S exposure mode, you rotate the dial to change the shutter speed.

By default, rotating the dial to the right raises the value that's being adjusted. But you can tell the camera that you prefer to rotate the dial to the left to increase the value. Open the Custom Setting menu, select Controls, and choose Reverse Dial Rotation. You then see a screen where you can modify the dial orientation separately for Exposure Compensation and for shutter speed/aperture adjustment. (The Exposure Compensation setting you choose also affects Flash Compensation.) Place a check mark in the box next to the option to reverse the dial orientation. To toggle the check mark on and off, tap it or highlight it and press the Multi Selector right. Tap OK or press the OK button to finalize things.

IN THIS CHAPTER

» **Using in-camera editing tools to retouch photos**

» **Having fun with special effects**

» **Taking advantage of a dust-busting tool**

» **Printing directly from the camera**

» **Creating slide shows**

Chapter **11**

Ten Fun (And Practical) Features to Explore on a Rainy Day

Consider this chapter the literary equivalent of the end of one of those late-night infomercial offers — the part where the host exclaims, "But wait! There's more!"

The features covered here fit the category of "interesting bonus." They aren't the sort of features that drive people to choose one camera over another, and they may come in handy only for certain users, on certain occasions. Still, they're included at no extra charge, so check 'em out when you have a few spare moments. Who knows; you may discover a hidden gem that provides just the solution you need for one of your photography problems.

Applying the Retouch Menu Filters

Every photographer produces a clunker now and then. When it happens to you, don't be too quick to press the Delete button, because many common problems are surprisingly easy to fix. In fact, you often can repair your photos right in the camera, thanks to tools found on the Retouch menu. You also can create special effects with some of the menu items.

I have enough room in this book to detail only a few of the most helpful Retouch tools. Should you need more help, you can find it in the electronic camera manual available for download from the Nikon website. To be honest, though, alterations you can make via the in-camera tools are better done in a photo-editing program. It's nigh on impossible to make precise changes to a picture with some Retouch menu tools and it's also hard to get a good view of your results, given the size of the camera monitor.

That said, I want to provide a quick overview to give you the basics you need to start exploring the Retouch menu. The first thing to know is that you can access the retouching tools in two ways:

>> **Press Menu, display the Retouch menu, select the tool you want to try, and then select the photo you want to alter.** The left screen in Figure 11-1 shows the D-Lighting tool selected, for example. After you choose a tool, you see thumbnails of your photos, as shown on the right in the figure. The currently selected photo is indicated by a yellow frame. To select a different photo, tap it or use the Multi Selector to move the frame over the thumbnail. Then press the OK button or tap the OK symbol. You then see a full-screen view of your photo along with the options available for the selected retouching tool.

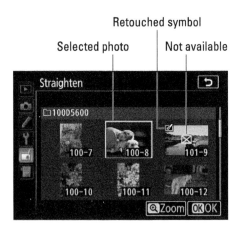

FIGURE 11-1:
After selecting a Retouch menu option (left), select the photo you want to edit (right).

TIP

If a photo can't be altered, an X appears over the thumbnail, as shown on the right side of Figure 11-1. Normally, you get the no-go signal because you already applied a certain Retouch menu option to a picture. For example, you can't edit a photo after you crop it using the Trim tool. (A Retouch symbol like the one labeled in the figure indicates a previous edit to the photo.) Nor can you edit photos taken by a camera other than the D5600, even if you can display them in Playback mode.

>> **Use the Playback mode *i*-button menu.** Switch the camera to playback mode, display your photo in single-frame view, and press the *i* button. The screen shown on the left in Figure 11-2 appears. Select Retouch to display the Retouch menu superimposed over your photo, as shown on the right in the figure. Select a tool to display your photo along with the options related to the tool. Any tools that can't be used on the photo appear dimmed in the menu.

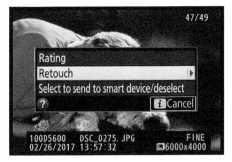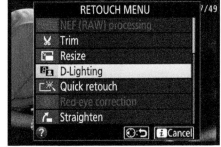

FIGURE 11-2:
In single-frame playback view, press the *i* button to access the Retouch menu.

A few other facts to remember about the Retouch menu:

>> **All menu items except Edit Movies apply to still photographs only.** The end of Chapter 7 explains how to use the Edit Movies tool.

>> **Two tools work only with Raw (NEF) files only.** The Raw (NEF) Processing tool converts a Raw file to the JPEG format; I detail this feature in Chapter 9. The Image Overlay tool blends two Raw photos to create a composite image. Check out the section "Adding Special Effects to Existing Photos," later in this chapter, for more about that possibility.

>> **Changes are made to a copy of the photo; your originals remain intact.** The camera assigns the next available file number to the retouched image. Make note of the filename of the retouched version so you can track it down later.

>> **Certain tools enable you to temporarily display a magnified preview of the results produced by the current tool settings.** If so, you see the word *Zoom* at the bottom of the screen. Tap that symbol or hold down the Zoom In button to get the magnified view. To return to the normal view, release the button or tap the exit arrow in the top-right corner of the magnified display.

>> **In Playback mode, you can display the retouched version and the original side by side.** First, display either the original or the retouched photo. Then press the *i* button to display the i-button menu, choose Retouch, and scroll the menu to get to Side-by-Side Comparison, as shown on the left in Figure 11-3. After selecting that option, you see the original on one side of the screen and the retouched version on the other, as shown on the right in the figure. The label above the previews indicates the Retouch tool that you applied to create the "after" photo.

FIGURE 11-3:
Side-by-Side
Comparison,
available only
via the Playback
i-button
menu, lets you
compare the
before and
after versions
of your photo.

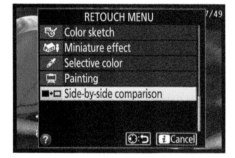 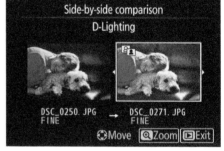

TIP

Try these tricks in Side-by-Side Comparison display:

• If you applied more than one tool to the picture, press the Multi Selector right and left to display thumbnails that show how each tool affected the picture.

• If you create multiple retouched versions of the same original — for example, you create a monochrome version, save it, and then crop the original image and save that — use a different technique to compare the versions. First, press the Multi Selector right or left to surround the After image with the yellow highlight box. Now press the Multi Selector up and down to scroll through the retouched versions.

To exit Side-by-Side Comparison view and return to normal playback, move the highlight box over the image you want to display (the original or the altered version). Then press the Playback button or tap the Exit symbol in the lower-right corner of the screen.

Side-by-Side Comparison is available *only* via the i-button path; you can't access it through the normal menu route.

REMEMBER

Removing Red-Eye

For portraits marred by red-eye, give the Red-Eye Correction filter a whirl. If the camera detects red-eye, it applies the filter and displays the retouched images. Be sure to press the Zoom In button or tap the Zoom icon to magnify the display so you can verify that the corrected eye colors look good. If you're cool with the results, tap or press OK to exit the magnified view and then again to create the retouched version of the image. To instead cancel the repair, press the Playback button.

Fixing Tilting and Distorted Images

Try these Retouch filters to level a tilting horizon line or remove distortion that can occur with some lenses and subjects:

>> **Straighten:** Even with the viewfinder grid displayed as a guide, I have trouble keeping the horizon level in the frame. Luckily, the Straighten tool can rotate images into proper alignment.

When you select the tool, a grid appears to guide you in making the repair, as shown on the left in Figure 11-4. The yellow marker on the scale at the bottom of the screen shows the current degree of rotation, with 0 degrees (no change) at the center point.

To rotate the picture clockwise, press the Multi Selector right or tap the box at the right end of the scale. To rotate the image counterclockwise, press left or tap the box at the left end of the scale. Each press or tap spins the picture by 0.25 degrees; the maximum rotation is 5 degrees. Press OK or tap the OK symbol to create the straightened copy.

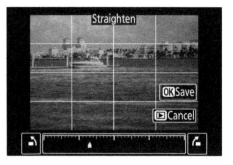

FIGURE 11-4:
Use the
Straighten tool
to level a tilting
horizon line.

>> **Distortion Control:** Try this filter to conquer *barrel distortion,* which causes straight lines to bow outward, as shown in Figure 11-5. You can also correct the opposite problem, *pincushion distortion* (lines curving inward). The filter offers two options: Auto and Manual. For the most control, choose Manual, which displays the same sort of adjustment scale as the Straighten filter. Move the yellow marker to the right to reduce barrel distortion; move it left to reduce pincushioning.

Slight barrel distortion   After Distortion Control filter

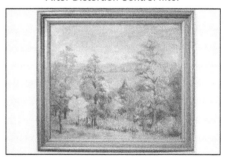

FIGURE 11-5:
You may
be able to
fix barrel
distortion by
applying the
Distortion
Control tool
from the
Retouch menu.

TIP

If a particular lens consistently produces either kind of distortion, also try enabling the Distortion Control option found on the Shooting menu. When you do, the camera tries to fix the problem as it's saving the shot you just took to the memory card. See Chapter 4 for details.

>> **Perspective Control:** When you photograph a tall building and tilt the camera upward to fit it all into the frame, an effect that's referred to as *convergence* or *keystoning* occurs. This effect causes vertical structures to tilt toward the center of the frame. Buildings sometimes even appear to be falling away from you, as shown in the left image in Figure 11-6. (If the lens is tilting down, vertical structures instead lean outward, and the building appears to be falling toward you.) Using the Perspective Control feature, you can right those tilting vertical elements, as I did to create the corrected image shown on the right in the figure.

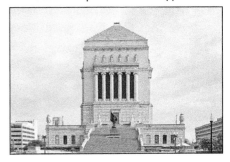

FIGURE 11-6:
I used the Perspective Control to remove the illusion that the monument was leaning backwards.

This filter offers two scales. Move the yellow marker on the bottom scale to rotate the scene horizontally; shift the marker on the vertical scale to rotate the object toward or away from you. When you're happy with the results, tap OK or press the OK button.

WARNING

To do their magic, all three tools must crop your image and enlarge the remaining area to fill the frame. (The same thing occurs if you use similar tools in a photo-editing program.) The camera updates the display as you rotate the photo so that you can get an idea of how much of the original scene may be lost.

When shooting subjects that you anticipate might need some help from these tools, frame the subject a little loosely. That way, you don't lose important parts of the scene due to the correction.

Manipulating Exposure and Color

The following Retouch tools tweak exposure and color:

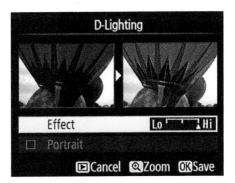

>> **D-Lighting:** Chapter 3 explains Active D-Lighting, which brightens too-dark shadows in a way that leaves highlight details intact. You can apply a similar adjustment to an existing photo by choosing D-Lighting from the Retouch menu. You then see before-and-after views of the image, as shown in Figure 11-7. Press the Multi Selector left or right to adjust the Effect option, which sets the strength of the adjustment.

FIGURE 11-7:
With the D-Lighting tool, you may be able to brighten areas that are too dark without blowing out highlights.

Also note the Portrait option, which is underneath the Effect option and dimmed in the figure. If the camera recognizes faces in the photo, you can select this option to limit the exposure adjustment to areas around the face (or faces). However, only three faces (maximum) are considered for this special exposure change. Also, you must have captured the photo with the Auto Image Rotation option on the Playback menu enabled.

WARNING

You can't apply D-Lighting to a picture taken using the Monochrome Picture Control, introduced in Chapter 5. Nor does D-Lighting work on images that you created by applying the Quick Retouch filter, covered next, or the Monochrome filter, detailed later in this list.

>> **Quick Retouch:** This tool increases contrast and color saturation and, if your subject is backlit, also applies a D-Lighting adjustment to restore some shadow detail that otherwise might be lost. As with D-Lighting, you can choose from three levels of Quick Retouch correction. And the same restrictions apply: You can't apply the filter to monochrome images or to pictures that you created by applying the D-Lighting tool.

>> **Filter Effects:** Choose this option to access two *warming filters*, which enhance warm (red and yellow) tones and reduce the intensity of blues. Select Skylight for a subtle warming effect; select Warm for a more noticeable change.

>> **Monochrome:** When you choose this tool, you can opt to create a black-and-white copy of a color original or to create a sepia or *cyanotype* (blue and white) image.

You can't apply certain Retouch menu options to an image that you create using the Monochrome tool: D-Lighting, Quick Retouch, and Soft filters are among those that don't work. Obviously, filters related to color adjustment also are no longer available. So use those filters before heading to the Monochrome option.

Cropping Your Photo

Cropping means to trim away some of the perimeter of a photo. You might crop a photo for compositional reasons, removing excess background so the subject fills more of the frame. Or you may need to crop a photo to create an image that has proportions other than the 3:2 aspect ratio of original images captured by the D5600.

The Retouch menu's Trim tool enables you to create a cropped copy of a photo right in the camera. However, always make this your *last* editing step because you can't apply any other Retouch menu tools to cropped images.

After you select Trim from the menu, you see the screen shown in Figure 11-8. The yellow box represents the boundaries of the crop frame. Adjust the aspect ratio, size, and position of the frame as follows:

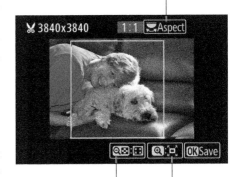

Set aspect ratio of crop frame

Reduce crop frame   Enlarge crop frame

FIGURE 11-8:
The yellow box indicates the cropping frame.

>> **Set the aspect ratio:** You can choose 3:2, 4:3, 5:4, 1:1, and 16:9. (Hint: Use 1:1, as in the figure, to fit the frame size used for Facebook profile pictures.) To cycle through the settings, tap that Aspect symbol, labeled in the figure, or rotate the Command dial.

>> **Adjust the size of the crop frame:** The current size, stated in pixels, appears in the upper-left corner of the screen. To reduce the frame size, press the Zoom Out button or tap the Zoom Out icon; to enlarge the frame, press the Zoom In button or tap the Zoom In icon. Each press or tap further shrinks or enlarges the frame. The range of sizes available depends on the original pixel count (resolution) of the photo. (See Chapter 2 for help understanding resolution.)

>> **Reposition the frame.** Drag your finger inside the crop frame or press the Multi Selector up, down, right, or left.

To create the cropped copy of your photo, press the OK button or tap OK Save on the touchscreen.

TIP

When viewing your photos in the default playback display mode (as well as certain other display modes), you see a scissors symbol near the Image Size readout. This symbol is different from the one that appears if you use the Resize option, which creates a lower-resolution version of the entire image, maintaining the original 3:2 proportions. For details on resizing photos, see Chapter 9. Chapter 8 covers playback display modes.

Adding Special Effects to Existing Photos

In addition to its image–correction tools, the Retouch menu also offers the following special effects tools:

» **Fisheye:** Apply this tool to distort the image so that it appears to have been taken with a fisheye lens. The look is similar to what you see when you look through a security peephole in a door.

» **Cross Screen:** This tool adds a starburst effect to the brightest part of the image. To access it, choose the Filter Effects option on the Retouch menu.

» **Soft:** Also accessed via the Filter Effects option, the Soft filter blurs your photo to give it a dreamy, watercolor-like look.

» **Image Overlay:** This option enables you to select two Raw images and then overlay one over the other to create a composite image that shows each original at half opacity. Figure 11-9 shows an example. The composite image is saved in the Raw format, so if you have the urge, you can select the composite Raw image, select another Raw image, and combine *those* images into a new composite. You can merge as many photos as you want; just remember that this tool works only with Raw (NEF) originals.

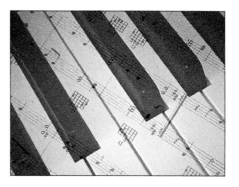

REMEMBER

Image Overlay isn't available from the i-button menu that's available during picture playback. You must use the standard menu process: Press Menu, open the Retouch menu, and choose Image Overlay.

Also understand that you can't adjust the positioning or the opacity of the images in the composite. So if you enjoy creating this type of imagery, you're better off using a photo-editing program that provides more sophisticated compositing tools. The free Nikon programs that I discuss in Chapter 9 don't fill the bill, unfortunately.

» **Color Outline:** Select this option from the Retouch menu to turn your photo into a black-and-white line drawing. (And please don't ask me why this filter isn't called Black-and-White Outline.)

» **Photo Illustration:** This effect produces a cross between a photo and a bold, color drawing .

>> **Color Sketch:** This filter creates an image similar to a drawing done in colored pencils.

>> **Miniature Effect:** Have you ever seen an architect's small-scale models of planned developments? The Miniature Effect filter attempts to create a photographic equivalent by applying a strong blur to all but one portion of an image. (When you apply the filter, you indicate the area you want to keep in focus by moving a yellow frame over that part of the photo.) Figure 11-10 offers an example. The left photo is the original; the right shows the result of keeping focus sharp in the part of the street occupied by the cars.

Original | Miniature Effect filter

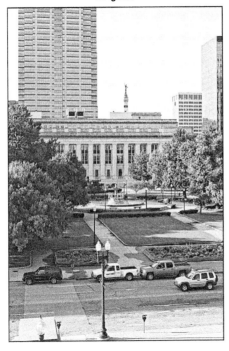 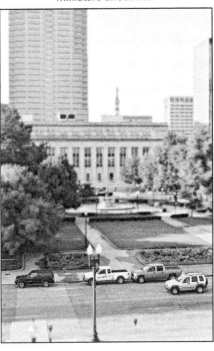

FIGURE 11-10:
The Miniature Effect filter throws all but a small portion of a scene into very soft focus.

TIP

The Miniature Effect filter works best if you shoot your subject from a high angle — otherwise, you don't get the miniaturization result.

>> **Selective Color:** This effect *desaturates* (removes color from) parts of a photo while leaving specific colors intact. For example, in an image of a red rose against a green background, you might desaturate the background and leave only the rose petals in color.

TIP

Not only is this tool less than intuitive to use, but it's also difficult to precisely adjust only specific parts of the image. First, it affects all objects that have the same colors as the ones you choose to desaturate. So, for example, if there's a red ball in the background that you'd like to turn black and white along with the green grass, you're out of luck. Also, if there is any green (or greenish tones) in the rose, those, too, become gray. For this kind of effect, you really need to do the job in a photo-editing program so that you can accurately select the parts of the photo you want to change.

>> **Painting:** The last special effect on the Retouch menu, this one produces a vividly colored, loosely rendered version of your photo.

Shooting in Effects Mode

When you set the Mode dial to Effects, as shown in Figure 11-11, you can apply special effects on the fly. That is, the effect is added as the camera writes the picture to the memory card.

For still photos, I prefer to capture my originals sans effect and then work from the Retouch menu to alter them. That way, I wind up with one normal image and one with the effect applied, just in case I decide that I prefer the unaltered photo to the effects version. Shooting in Effects mode also brings up another problem: To create the effects, the camera puts most picture-taking controls, such as White Balance and Metering mode, off-limits.

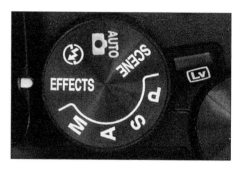

FIGURE 11-11:
Effects mode lets you apply special effects to movies and still photos.

However, Effects mode does offer some artistic filters not available on the Retouch menu. In addition, it enables you to add effects to movies, which isn't possible from the Retouch menu. So even though I suspect that you won't find a use for Effects mode very often, I'd be remiss if I didn't spend a little time discussing it.

TIP

The best way to take advantage of Effects mode is to turn on Live View (rotate the LV switch on the right edge of the Mode dial). You have to use Live View to shoot movies anyway, but it's beneficial for still photography, too. Several effects offer settings you can tweak to alter the result, and you can get to those settings only in Live View mode. Live View also enables you to preview the selected effect.

As soon as you set the Mode dial to Effects, an icon representing the currently selected effect appears in the upper-left corner of the display, as shown in Figure 11-12. (The VI represents the Super Vivid effect.) Tap that icon or rotate the Command dial to display the left screen shown in Figure 11-13. A ribbon containing icons representing each effect appears near the top of the screen. To scroll through the available effects, tap the left/right touchscreen arrows on either side of the ribbon or rotate the Command dial. The preview updates each time you scroll to a new setting.

Current Effects mode

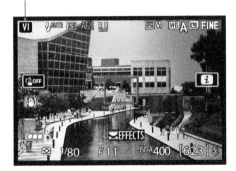

FIGURE 11-12:
Set the camera to Live View mode to access Effects mode adjustments or to apply effects when recording movies.

FIGURE 11-13:
Rotate the Command dial to scroll through available effects (left); the OK Set symbol tells you that you can adjust the impact of the effect (right).

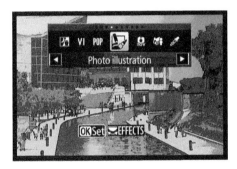 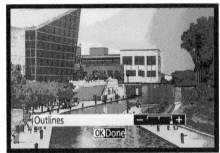

If an effect offers tools for altering the final look of the image, you see an OK Set icon in the lower part of the screen, as shown in the figure. (The Effects label and the accompanying graphic are there to remind you that you can rotate the Command dial to cycle through the effects.)

When you find an effect you like, press the shutter button halfway and release it to return to shooting mode. If an effect offers adjustments, tap the OK Set symbol or press the OK button to display a screen containing the adjustment controls. For example, the Photo Illustration effect offers the single control shown on the right in Figure 11-13. As you change the control setting, the preview updates to show how the new setting affects the image. Usually, you adjust options by moving a marker along a bar like the one shown in the figure. Press the Multi Selector right or left to make that happen. You can also tap the bar to place the marker at the spot you tap.

After making your adjustments, tap OK Done or press OK to return to the live preview. (If you see the OK Set sign on the preview, you can tap it at any time to readjust the effect settings.)

REMEMBER

Now for a review of the various effects:

>> **Night Vision:** Use this setting in low-light situations to produce a grainy, black-and-white image like the one shown in Figure 11-14.

A few critical points about Night Vision mode:

- *Autofocusing is available only in Live View mode.* For viewfinder photography, you must focus manually.

- *Flash is disabled, as is the AF-assist lamp.* The whole idea is to create a picture taken in little light, after all.

- *Use a tripod to avoid blur.* A slow shutter speed is needed to capture the image in dark conditions, and you must be careful to avoid camera movement during the exposure. If your subject is moving, it can appear blurry even if the camera is on a tripod.

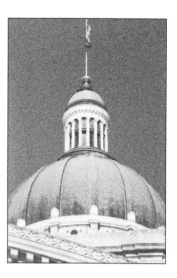

FIGURE 11-14:
The Night Vision effect creates an exceptionally noisy black-and-white image.

- *You can capture the photo only in the JPEG format.* You select this setting via the Image Quality option on the Shooting menu. Raw (NEF) files aren't compatible with the Night Vision effect.

>> **Super Vivid:** Choose this setting for hypersaturated, super-contrasty images.

>> **Pop:** One step less intense than Super Vivid, this mode amps up saturation only.

>> **Photo Illustration:** This setting produces a bright, poster-like effect; refer to Figure 11-13 for an example.

WARNING

Autofocusing is not available during movie recording in this mode. Additionally, the resulting movie looks more like a slide show made up of still images than a standard movie.

>> **Toy Camera Effect:** This mode, also compatible only with the JPEG Image Quality setting, is designed to create a photo or movie that looks like it was shot by a toy camera — specifically, the type of toy camera that produces images that have a vignette effect (corners of the scene appear darker than the rest of the image).

In Live View mode, you can adjust two options: Vividness, which affects color intensity; and Vignetting, which controls the amount of vignetting.

>> **Miniature Effect:** This one is also a duplicate of the one on the Retouch menu; refer to Figure 11-10 for an example of the result. Again, the filter works by blurring all but a small portion of the scene, which you specify by positioning the red focus frame that appears in Live View mode.

To set up this effect, press OK or tap the OK icon to display horizontal markings that indicate the width of the sharp-focus region. Use the Multi Selector or touchscreen controls to adjust the width and position of the in-focus region. When you achieve the look you want, press or tap OK again.

A few limitations apply: Flash is disabled, as is the AF-assist lamp. If you use the Continuous Release mode, the frames per second rate is reduced. You must set the Image Quality option (Shooting menu) to JPEG for still photography, and when autofocusing, you can't use any AF-area mode except Single-point. (Chapter 4 discusses this autofocus option.)

For movies, sound recording is disabled, autofocus is disabled during recording, and movies play back at high speed. (The high-speed playback means a movie that contains about 45 minutes of footage is compressed into a 3-minute clip, for example.)

>> **Selective Color:** Like the Selective Color filter on the Retouch menu, this effect enables you to desaturate (turn black and white) all but a few colors. And as with the Retouch menu filter, the Effects mode version is complex to use — even more so, in fact — and doesn't give you enough control to precisely desaturate just the colors you want to alter. If I were you, I wouldn't waste my time; instead, shoot the photo in a regular exposure mode and then create the effect in a photo-editing program that offers tools that make it easier to control which part of your photo is affected by the desaturation.

>> **Silhouette:** Choosing this setting ensures that backlit subjects will be captured as dark silhouettes against a bright background, as illustrated in Figure 11-15. To help ensure that the subject is dark, flash is disabled.

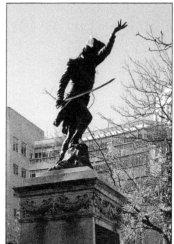

FIGURE 11-15:
The Silhouette effect can produce an interesting result when you photograph dark subjects set against a bright background.

- » **High Key:** A *high key* photo is dominated by white or very light areas, such as a white china cup resting on a white doily in front of a sunny window. This setting is designed to produce a good exposure for this type of scene, which the camera otherwise tends to underexpose in response to all the high brightness values. Flash is disabled.

How does the name relate to the characteristics of the picture? Well, photographers refer to the dominant tones — or brightness values — as the *key tones*. In most photos, the *midtones,* or areas of medium brightness, are the key tones. In a high key image, the majority of tones are at the high end of the brightness scale.

- » **Low Key:** The opposite of a high key photo, a low key photo is dominated by shadows. Use this mode to prevent the camera from brightening the scene too much and thereby losing the dark and dramatic nature of the image. Flash is disabled.

After selecting an effect, you can exit Live View to take the picture using the viewfinder if you prefer. Or, to record a movie, remain in Live View mode and press the red movie-record button on top of the camera to stop and start recording.

Creating a Dust Reference File

If you notice spots appearing in the same place on every photo, they're likely caused by dust that made its way onto the camera's image sensor. The best remedy is to take your camera to a qualified technician for sensor cleaning, but until you have time to do that, the Image Dust Off Ref Photo option on the Setup menu may be worth trying.

Here's how it works: You shoot a picture of a blank piece of paper, the idea being that only the dust spots will show up in the resulting image. You then load that image into Nikon Capture NX-D, one of the free Nikon programs I introduce in Chapter 9. From the reference image, the program creates a file noting the position of the dust spots. When you open a photo in Capture NX-D, you enable the program's Image Dust Off tool, which then applies some corrective magic just to the dust spots, consulting the reference file to know where those spots are located.

Unfortunately, the tool works only on photos that you shoot in the Raw format. In fact, you apply the Image Dust Off tool as you process the Raw file in Capture NX-D. Also bear in mind that the tool isn't always successful, sometimes resulting in a blurred area that's more problematic than the original dust spot. There's also a chance that the dust on the sensor may move slightly between photo shoots, making the reference photo inaccurate.

For specifics on capturing the reference photo, check the camera manual, available for download from the Nikon website. Chapter 9 provides an overview of Raw processing in Capture NX-D and points you to sources for additional information.

Printing Directly from the Camera

Your camera is compatible with printers that offer *PictBridge,* a technology that enables you to connect the camera to the printer and then print any images on the installed memory card. The connection is made via USB, so you need to purchase the Nikon USB cable that works with the D5600 (the UC-E20 cable, which is about $12). After you connect the camera to the printer, screens appear on the camera monitor to guide you through the steps of selecting images to print and setting other print options. For details on how to make things work with your printer, consult the printer's user manual.

Presenting a Slide Show

Through the Slide Show feature, found on the Playback menu and shown in Figure 11-16, you can set the camera to automatically display photos and movies one by one. You can view the show on the camera monitor or, by connecting your camera to a tv, enjoy it on an HDTV screen.

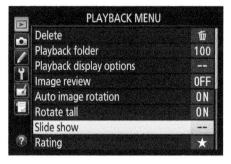
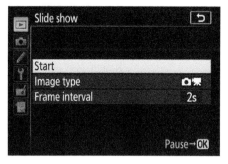

FIGURE 11-16: Choose Slide Show to set up automatic playback of pictures and movies.

REMEMBER

Which files are available for inclusion in the slide show depends on the Playback Folder setting, also found on the Playback menu. By default, that option is set to All, so any photos on the card are available, regardless of their folder location, as long as they're stored in a format that the D5600 can display. I explain other Playback Folder options in Chapter 8.

After you select Slide Show from the Playback menu, you see the screen shown on the right in Figure 11-16. Use the following options to set your preferences for the show:

>> **Image Type:** Specify which types of files you want to include: photographs and movies, photos only, movies only, or files to which you assigned a particular rating. (Chapter 9 explains how to rate files.)

>> **Frame Interval:** Select the amount of time you want each photograph to appear. Movies always play in their entirety.

To begin playing the show, select Start (highlighted on the right screen in Figure 11-16). Control playback as follows:

>> **Pause/restart:** Press OK to pause; select Restart to resume playback. While the show is paused, you can adjust the frame interval if needed.

>> **Skip to the next/previous image:** Press the Multi Selector right or left.

>> **Change the information displayed with the image:** Press the Multi Selector up or down to cycle through the display modes. See Chapter 8 for help understanding the various modes.

>> **Adjust movie sound volume:** Press the Zoom In button to increase the volume; press Zoom Out to decrease it.

>> **Exit the show before the last slide:** You have three options:

- *To return to regular playback,* press the Playback button.

- *To return to the Playback menu,* press the Menu button.

- *To return to picture-taking mode,* press the shutter button halfway.

If you play the show through to the end, you're given the option to restart the show, adjust the frame interval, or exit to the Playback menu.

Appendix

Intro to Nikon SnapBridge

Your D5600 enables you to connect your camera wirelessly to a smartphone or tablet. After establishing the connection, you can upload photos to the device and use the device as a wireless remote control.

To enjoy these features, you must install the Nikon SnapBridge app on your smart device. The app is free, but is available only for devices that run recent versions of the Android OS (operating system) or Apple iOS. Visit Google Play for Android apps; go the App Store for iOS apps. The current OS requirements appear on the download page for that app.

Your smart device also must offer Bluetooth low-energy (BLE), a special Bluetooth feature that minimizes the battery power required to handle wireless data transmission. (Look for Bluetooth version 4.0 or later.)

I can't provide detailed instructions for using SnapBridge because things vary depending on your device and its operating system. In addition, when Nikon issues updates to the app — which it is likely to do as it introduces new cameras that offer SnapBridge support — some aspects of the app itself may change. As I write this, the most current versions of the SnapBridge app are 1.2.0.3001 for Android and Version 1.2.0 for iOS.

That said, this appendix provides you with some general guidance. For additional help, including video tutorials that explain various setup steps and features, point your web browser to www.snapbridge.nikon.com.

What Can I Do with SnapBridge?

Here are just some of the functions that you can enjoy after making the wireless connection between your camera and the SnapBridge app:

>> **Use your device as a wireless remote control.** When the camera and device are connected, the device's screen becomes an extension of the camera's Live View display. You can set focus, view a few camera settings, and then tap a button on the device to trigger the camera's shutter release. See the last bit of the appendix for more information on this cool tool.

>> **Transfer photos and movies from the camera to your smart device.** You can then view photos on the device or use the device's Wi-Fi or cellular Internet connection to upload them to social media sites or share them via email. Note that you can't upload Raw photos; the app can handle only JPEG and movie files. You can transfer full-resolution images or smaller versions that are 2MB in size (which is plenty large for online sharing). In either case, the camera sends copies of your images; your originals remain on your memory card.

WARNING

Before transferring photos, check the camera's battery level; transmission is suspended when the battery level is low.

>> **Ship photos to Nikon Image Space.** Your D5600 purchase entitles you to a free account at Nikon Image Space, an online photo storage and sharing site. After registering for an account at the site (www.nikonimagespace.com), you can use SnapBridge to upload transferred files to your Image Space gallery. You also can connect to the website via your computer and upload photos from your hard drive or other storage device.

If you use Image Space, you may want to download its standalone app, also free and available for iOS and Android devices. The app enables you to view, organize, and share your Image Space files.

>> **Add credits and other text information to photos that you transfer to the device.** You can add a copyright notice, the location and date and time, a logo, or certain bits of shooting data (shutter speed, ISO, and so on). This data is attached only to the transferred images.

TIP

You also can use options on the camera's Setup menu to tag files with comments and copyright notices. Going that route adds the data to all new photos you shoot. See Chapter 10 to find out more.

Setting Up the Camera for SnapBridge

You'll find all camera settings related to using SnapBridge on the Setup menu. I highlighted the options in Figure A-1.

Here's what each option does:

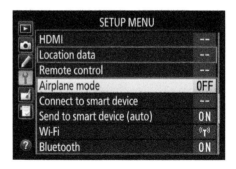

FIGURE A-1:
These Setup menu options provide ways to customize the camera's interaction with your device.

>> **Location Data:** Choose this option and then set the Download from Smart Device option to On if you want SnapBridge to tag photos with your current location — that is, the current location of your phone or tablet. (The app uses the location-data service of your smart device.) After you connect the camera to the smart device, location data is then added to any pictures you take in the next 2 hours.

>> **Airplane Mode:** Set this option to On to disable wireless transmission from the camera, as you might when, say, on an airplane. The feature is disabled by default.

   If you use Eye-Fi memory cards, turning on Airplane mode also shuts down wireless transmission from the cards.

>> **Connect to Smart Device:** Choose this setting to start the process of connecting your camera to your phone or tablet. I offer assistance with that task later in the next section.

>> **Send to Smart Device (Auto):** Select On if you want the camera to automatically send all new photos you shoot to your smart device. Turn the feature off if you prefer to select specific pictures to send to the device.

   If you choose the second option, you can tag pictures in two ways:

   • *Open the Playback menu and choose Select to Send to Smart Device.* On the next screen, choose Select Images to view photo thumbnails, as shown on the left in Figure A-2. Use the Multi Selector to move the selection box over a photo you want to transfer and then press the Zoom Out button to apply the Send to Smart Device tag, labeled in the figure. To remove the tag, press the button again. For a quick way to remove the tag from a batch of selected photos, exit the screen (tap the exit arrow in the upper-right corner of the screen) to return to the initial Select to Send to Smart Device screen. On that screen, choose Deselect All.

FIGURE A-2:
Choose Select to Send to Smart Device from the Playback menu to tag multiple images for transfer (left); in Playback mode, press the i button and choose the same option to tag only the currently displayed photo (right).

Selected for transfer

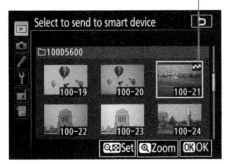
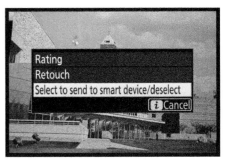

Alternatively, put the camera in Playback mode, display a photo you want to tag for transfer, press the *i* button, and choose Select to Send to Smart Device/Deselect, as shown on the right in Figure A-2. The transfer symbol appears on the photo. To remove it, repeat the process.

Either way, the next time you initiate a transfer of photos to your smart device, only selected photos are sent.

» **Bluetooth:** Choose this option to turn Bluetooth functionality on or off, to see a list of devices currently paired with the camera, and to choose whether you want the connection to remain on even after you turn off the camera. (By default, transmission of photos does take place when the camera is off or has gone into sleep mode.)

Connecting to Your Smart Device

Before you start the process of connecting your camera to your smartphone or tablet, here are some tips for making sure things go as smoothly as possible:

» **Enable Wi-Fi and Bluetooth on your smart device.** The camera connects via Bluetooth, but using the SnapBridge remote control feature requires Wi-Fi.

» **Download and install the latest version of Nikon SnapBridge on your smart device.** Again, Google Play has the Android version; the Apple store has the iOS version. Remember to check the app specs before you download to ensure your device will be able to run it.

» **Make sure that your camera is running the latest firmware.** Open the Setup menu and choose Firmware Version to check the version number. Nikon released an update shortly after the camera came to market, and that update resolves some issues that prevented the camera from connecting to devices running certain versions of the Apple operating system (iOS). Specifically, the C firmware item should be 1.01 or later. If your camera is still running version 1.0, head for the D5600 support pages on the Nikon website and follow the instructions to download and install the updated firmware.

» **Turn on the camera's Wi-Fi and Bluetooth functions; turn off Airplane mode.** All three options live on the Setup menu, as shown in Figure A-1. The default settings enable both Wi-Fi and Bluetooth and disable Airplane mode, but double-check to be sure.

With those preliminaries out of the way, here are the basic steps to connect your camera to your smartphone or tablet:

1. **Open the camera's Setup menu and choose Connect to Smart Device.**

   You see a welcome screen; press OK. You then see a message explaining that if your device offers NFC wireless connection, you can just touch the device to the NFC symbol on the right side of the camera. It's the gray N printed near the HDMI port cover. (Check the device's instruction manual for information about enabling and using its NFC functions.)

   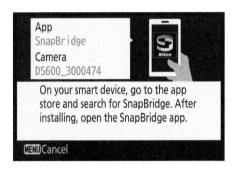

   FIGURE A-3:
   When you see this screen, open the Snap-Bridge app on your smart device.

   No NFC? Press OK again to display the screen shown in Figure A-3.

2. **Open SnapBridge on your device.**

   The first time you take these steps, the screen looks similar to what you see in Figures A-4 (iOS version) and A-5 (Android version). The Connect tab should be selected; if not, tap the Connect icon, labeled in both figures.

3. **Tap the plus sign (iOS) or the exclamation point (Android), labeled in Figures A-4 and A-5.**

   The device searches for your camera; if it detects the camera's signal, the camera name appears on the screen. When prompted, tap the camera name. Then give the device a few minutes to display the Select an Accessory menu. Tap the camera name when it appears. (It may take a little while for the name to appear, too.)

4. **When the Bluetooth Pairing Request appears on your device, tap Pair and then press OK on the camera.**

The devices should now be connected. If this is the first time you've connected them, the camera will present two more screens, one asking whether you want to download location data from the smart device and one asking whether you want to sync the camera clock with the one on the smart device. After you make your choices (which you can adjust later if needed), you're returned to the initial Connect screen.

Tap to connect to camera

Tap to connect to camera

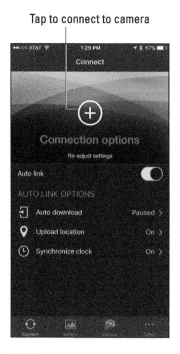
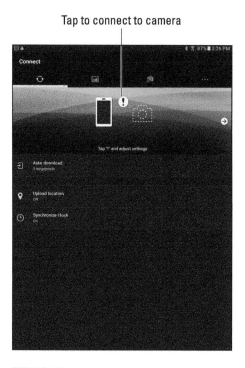

FIGURE A-4:
On an Apple iOS device, tap the Connect icon at the bottom of the screen to access options for connecting your camera.

FIGURE A-5:
Here you see the Android version of the Connect screen. The Connect icon (and other tab icons) appear at the top of the screen.

Taking a Look at SnapBridge Functions

SnapBridge features are organized into four tabs, which I describe briefly in the following sections. To switch between the tabs on an iOS device, tap the icons at the bottom of the screen (Connect, Gallery, Camera, and Other). On an Android device, the icons are near the top of the screen.

Connect tab

In addition to using this screen to establish the connection to the camera, you can set a few important options related to image transfers. When the Auto Link option is enabled, as it is by default, choose Auto Download to access the following settings:

>> **Auto download:** Turn the option on if you want photos to be transferred automatically whenever you connect the camera to your device.

>> **Choose download size:** You can specify whether you want to transfer photos from the camera at their original size or a more online-friendly, 2MP copy.

>> **Nikon Image Space:** You also can enable or disable automatic upload to your Nikon Image Space account on this screen.

If auto download is enabled, the device starts transferring photos immediately, either copying all photos on your memory card or those you selected by tagging them in the camera. However, this is not your only avenue to downloading images to the device; you also can select photos to transfer via the Camera tab, explained a block or two from here.

Gallery tab

Tap the Gallery icon to view thumbnails of images you've transferred to your device. You can view photos stored on your device as well as those you transferred from the camera. Use the standard tablet and smartphone picture-viewing gestures — swipe to scroll through your photos, pinch out to magnify the display, and pinch in to reduce the display size.

Camera tab

Through this tab, you can access two features:

>> **Use the device as a camera remote control.** This feature applies to still photography only and works via a Wi-Fi connection. Before making that connection, set the camera to P, S, A, or M exposure mode and select the picture settings you want to use. Then return to the SnapBridge screen and choose Remove Photography, as shown on the left in Figure A-6. When the app finds your camera, it prompts you to open your device's Wi-Fi settings and select the camera as your Wi-Fi source. You need to enter the camera's network password: NIKOND5600. (Be patient; the connection process can take a while.)

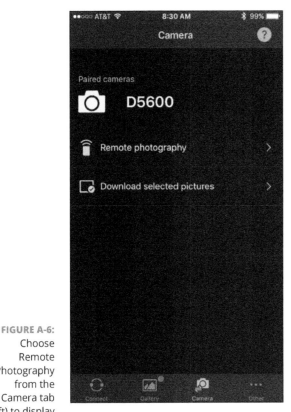

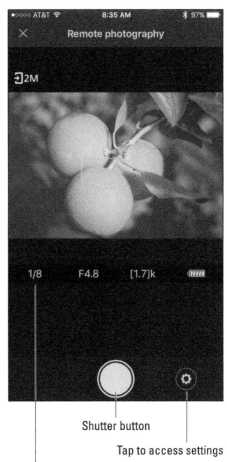

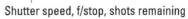

Shutter button

Tap to access settings

Shutter speed, f/stop, shots remaining

FIGURE A-6: Choose Remote Photography from the Camera tab (left) to display a live preview (right). Tap the shutter button icon to take a picture.

REMEMBER

When the connection is made, you see the screen shown on the right in the figure with a live view of the scene in front of the camera lens. You also see some shooting data, such as the shutter speed and f-stop. A focus box appears on the preview; tap your subject to place the focus box over it and set focus. The focus box turns green when focus is achieved.

To take a picture, press the shutter-button icon, labeled in the figure. The picture is saved to the SnapBridge gallery. A thumbnail of the photo appears under the live preview. Tap the thumbnail to see the images at a larger size and access icons that enable you to share or delete the image.

WARNING

Don't turn the camera off or choose another tab in the SnapBridge app between shots; either action breaks the Wi-Fi link and you have to go through the connection process all over again.

» **Download selected pictures from the camera memory card.** If you didn't set up automatic download and you didn't tag pictures in the camera for transfer, choose the Download Selected Pictures option (left screen in Figure A-6). You see thumbnails of your pictures. Tap Select and then tap each image or movie file you want to transfer. Next, choose the download size (either original resolution or 2MB) and then OK.

You can transfer movie files *only* via a Wi-Fi connection. If the camera isn't connected to the device via Wi-Fi, movie files won't appear in the list of files you can transfer.

Other tab

Tap this icon, found just to the right of the camera icon on the SnapBridge home page, to display the screen shown in Figure A-7. The two most useful features you can access via this screen are the following:

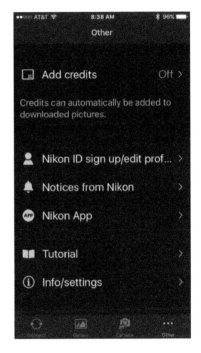

» **Add Credits:** Choose this option to access the features that enable you to embed copyright data and other information into your picture files.

» **Info/Settings:** Tap this option and then tap Instructions to launch the web browser on your device and access the SnapBridge Help site.

FIGURE A-7:
Tap the Other icon to access a variety of features, including a tutorial for using the app.

Because the Help site information is very thorough, I won't waste any more space in this book explaining the myriad SnapBridge features. I offer just one more word of advice: In my experience, the camera-connection process isn't always reliable, and it's difficult to sort out where the issue lies. My best advice is to uninstall the app, reinstall it, and start fresh. If you previously connected but can't seem to reconnect, another fix that sometimes works is to visit your device's Bluetooth and Wi-Fi connection settings, locate the camera name, and then choose Forget This Device.

REMEMBER

While you're online, also visit www.dummies.com and enter the title of this book in the Search box. The search results should include a link to download a copy of the Cheat Sheet created for this book. The Cheat Sheet offers a guide to your camera's external features as well as to some important picture-taking settings.

Index

Symbols and Numerics

* (asterisk), 104

3D-tracking, 136

9-point Dynamic-area, 135

21-point Dynamic-area, 135

24 fps, 203, 206

25 fps, 203, 206

30 fps, 204, 206

39-point Dynamic-area, 136

50 fps, 204, 206

60 fps, 204, 206

A

A (aperture-priority autoexposure) mode
  about, 49
  adjusting aperture and shutter speed in,
    105–106
  automatic bracketing in, 124
  checking exposure meter in, 98
  flash in, 73
  for shooting dynamic close-ups, 191–193
  for shooting scenic vistas, 189–191
  for shooting still portraits, 178–185
  using, 96–98
accessing
  Live View control strip, 44
  Retouch menu, 292–293
  Scene modes, 47
accessory terminal, 17, 18
action shots, shooting, 185–188
activating
  automatic picture rotation, 227–229
  control strip, 132
  Exposure Smoothing, 58
  flash, 72–73
  Shooting Data display mode, 242

touchscreen, 18–21
  Wind Noise Reduction option, 209–210
Active D-Lighting
  about, 297–298
  applying, 115–118
  settings for, 178
adding
  comments, 277–280
  copyright notices, 277–280
  flash, 72–83
  special effects to photos, 300–302
adjusting
  auto-shutdown timing, 286–287
  color, 297–298
  crop frame size, 299
  depth of field, 152–156
  exposure, 297–298
  Flash mode, 78–79
  flash output, 79–82
  Focus mode setting, 132–134
  Information display style, 282–283
  ISO, 212
  movie exposure, 212–214
  playback timing, 226–227
  playback volume, 216
  settings via control strip, 27–28
  video settings, 202–206
  viewfinder, 10
  White Balance setting, 157–169
Adobe (website), 258
Adobe RGB color space, 169
advanced exposure modes, 96–98
advancing movie playback frame by frame, 216
AE Lock (autoexposure lock)
  for recording movies, 214
  using, 123–124
AE-L/AF-L button, 15, 143, 288

AF-A (auto-servo autofocus), 133
AF-area mode
    about, 132
    for recording movies, 211
    selecting, 134–139, 148–150
    settings for, 178
AF-assist lamp, 12, 13
AF-C (continuous-servo autofocus), 133–134,
        140–141
AF-F (full-time servo AF)
    for movies, 200
    using in Live View mode, 147
AF-P lens, 30, 130–131
AF-S (single-servo autofocus)
    about, 133, 139–140
    for movies, 199
    using in Live View mode, 146–147
AF-S lens, 30–31, 130, 131
Airplane Mode option (Setup menu), 35–36
alignment grid, 20
aperture
    about, 49, 88–89
    effect on depth of field of, 90–91, 153–154
    for recording movies, 213
    setting, 103–107
    viewing, 103
aperture-priority autoexposure (A) mode
    about, 49
    adjusting aperture and shutter speed in,
        105–106
    automatic bracketing in, 124
    checking exposure meter in, 98
    flash in, 73
    for shooting dynamic close-ups, 191–193
    for shooting scenic vistas, 189–191
    for shooting still portraits, 178–185
    using, 96–98
applying
    Active D-Lighting, 115–118
    Exposure Compensation, 111–114
    Retouch menu filters, 292–295

aspect ratio, 299
assigning
    ratings in Playback mode, 248–249
    Touch Function roles, 289–290
asterisk (*), 104
attaching lenses, 8
audio, controlling for movies, 206–210
Auto Distortion Control feature, 156
Auto flash mode, 74
Auto Flash Off mode, 46, 72
Auto Image Rotation option (Playback menu), 228
Auto Info Display option, 283
Auto ISO Sensitivity Control, 109
Auto mode
    about, 46
    flash in, 73
    Live View in, 40–44
    shooting in, 38–44
    using viewfinder in, 38–40
Auto Sensitivity setting, 207
autoexposure lock (AE Lock)
    for recording movies, 214
    using, 123–124
autofocus lock, 143
autofocusing, 31, 49
automatic bracketing, 124
automatic picture rotation, enabling, 227–229
auto-servo autofocus (AF-A), 133
auto-shutdown timing, adjusting, 286–287
Autumn Colors mode, 72

B

backlighting, shooting in strong, 194–195
back-of-the-body controls, 13–16
balancing exposure, 94–95
barrel distortion, 156, 296
Basic Photo Indicators display, 43
Battery status indicator, 26
Beach/Snow mode, 72
Beep Options (Setup menu), 34–35

beeps, disabling, 51

bit depth, with Raw (NEF), 68

blinkies (Highlights) mode, 237–238

Blossom mode, 72

blown highlights, 237–238

Bluetooth, 18, 309–317

bracketing

  Active D-Lighting exposures, 124–127

  white balance, 166–169

Brightness histograms, reading, 239–240

buffer, 53

Bulb setting, 106

burst mode (Continuous) shooting, 52–53

buttons, customizing, 287–288

buying SD cards, 32–33

C

Calendar playback mode, 215, 230–234

cameras, printing directly from, 307

camera-to-subject distance, depth of field and, 154–155

Candlelight mode, 72

Capture NX-D, processing Raw files in, 268–271

car windows, shooting from, 194

center-weighted metering mode, 101

changing

  auto-shutdown timing, 286–287

  color, 297–298

  crop frame size, 299

  depth of field, 152–156

  exposure, 297–298

  Flash mode, 78–79

  flash output, 79–82

  Focus mode setting, 132–134

  Information display style, 282–283

  ISO, 212

  movie exposure, 212–214

  playback timing, 226–227

  playback volume, 216

  settings via control strip, 27–28

  video settings, 202–206

  viewfinder, 10

  White Balance setting, 157–169

Cheat Sheet (website), 3

checking

  exposure meter, 98–100

  image quality, 61–72

  image size, 61–72

choosing

  AF-area mode, 134–139, 148–150

  autofocus combinations, 139

  automatic focusing, 130–131

  color spaces, 169

  from Custom Setting menu, 23

  exposure metering modes, 101–103

  exposure modes, 46–49

  Flash mode, 73–79

  Focus mode in Live View mode, 146–148

  Frame Size/Frame Rate, 203–204

  images to view, 225–226

  Live View autofocusing pairs, 151

  manual focusing, 130–131

  thumbnails, 230

Clean Image Sensor option (Setup menu), 35

clipped highlights, 237–238

Close Up mode, 42

closing

  movie playback, 215

  Shooting Time screen, 60

Cloudy symbol, 160

color

  about, 49, 157

  adjusting, 297–298

  adjusting White Balance setting, 157–169

  choosing color spaces, 169

  flash and, 80

  in Live View mode, 159

  Picture Controls, 170–175

  troubleshooting, 159

Color Outline tool, 300

Color Sketch filter, 301

color spaces, choosing, 169

color temperature, 158

Command dial

  about, 12, 14

  adjusting exposure compensation using, 113

  adjusting Flash Compensation from, 82

  adjusting Flash mode with, 78–79

  adjusting shutter speed with, 106

  reversing orientation, 290

comments, adding, 277–280

computers, downloading pictures to, 258–265

Conformity Marking option (Setup menu), 36

connections

  hidden, 17–18

  via USB, 260

Continuous (burst mode) shooting, 52–53

continuous-servo autofocus (AF-C), 133–134, 140–141

control strip

  accessing in Live View, 44

  activating, 132

  adjusting exposure compensation using, 114

  adjusting Flash Compensation from, 82

  adjusting Flash mode with, 79

  adjusting microphone settings from, 209

  adjusting settings from, 27–28, 70–71

  adjusting White Balance setting from, 160

  applying Active D-Lighting from, 117

  enabling HDR from, 120–121

controlling

  audio for movies, 206–210

  flash output manually, 82–83

convergence, 296

copyright notices, adding, 277–280

cover, for viewfinders, 44

creating

  custom menus, 23–24

  custom storage folders, 280–281

  dust reference files, 306–307

  menus, 284–286

  white balance presets, 163–166

creative control, with Raw (NEF), 68

crop factor, 32

crop frame size, adjusting, 299

cropping photos, 233–234, 298–299

Cross Screen tool, 300

cross-type sensors, 138

custom menus, creating, 23–24

Custom Setting menu

  about, 22

  options on, 36–37

  selecting from, 23

custom storage folders, creating, 280–281

customizing

  buttons, 287–288

  filenames, 281–282

  tips for, 277–290

cyanotype, 298

D

date

  deleting files by, 254–255

  setting, 9–10

Date (File Information mode), 236

Date Stamp option (Custom Setting menu), 37

decibels (dB), 208

default settings

  for movies, 198–202

  restoring, 37–38

Delete button, 14, 15

deleting files, 252–255

depth of field

  about, 49, 129–130

  adjusting, 152–156

  camera-to-subject distance and, 154–155

  defined, 90, 152

  effect of aperture on, 90–91, 153–154

  lens focal length and, 154

  for shooting dynamic close-ups, 191–193

desaturates, 301

Detailed Photo Indicators display, 42

difficult-to-focus subjects, choosing Live View autofocusing pairs for, 151

diopters, 193

direct measurement, setting white balance with, 164–165

Direct Sunlight symbol, 160

disabling
  beeps, 51
  Exposure Smoothing, 58
  flash, 72–73
  Image Review, 227

displaying
  gridlines, 25
  photos in Calendar view, 230–234
  thumbnails, 229

distorted images, fixing, 295–297

Distortion Control filter, 156, 296

DK-5 Eyepiece Cap, 44

D-Lighting, 297–298

downloading pictures to computers, 258–265

drag gesture, 19

drag-and-drop file transfer, 264

Dusk/Dawn mode, 72

dust reference files, creating, 306–307

dynamic close-ups, shooting, 191–193

dynamic range, 115

Dynamic-area autofocusing mode, 135–136, 140–141

E

[-E-] symbol, 33

Effects mode
  about, 46
  flash in, 72
  Live View and, 302
  shooting in, 302–306

eliminating vignetting, 121–123

enabling
  automatic picture rotation, 227–229
  control strip, 132
  Exposure Smoothing, 58

flash, 72–73

Shooting Data display mode, 242

touchscreen, 18–21

Wind Noise Reduction option, 209–210

EV (exposure value) numbers, 79

exiting
  movie playback, 215
  Shooting Time screen, 60

expanding tonal range, 115

expose for the highlights, 115

exposure
  about, 87–88
  adjusting, 297–298
  advanced modes for, 96–98
  aperture, 88–89, 90–91, 103–107
  aperture-priority autoexposure (A) mode, 49, 73, 96–98, 105–106, 124, 178–185, 189–193
  balancing, 94–95
  bracketing, 124–127
  checking exposure meter, 98–100
  choosing exposure metering modes, 101–103
  defined, 88
  depth of field, 49, 90–91, 129–130, 152–156, 191–193
  ISO, 88, 89–90, 93–94, 107–109, 185–188, 212
  manual (M) exposure mode, 49, 73, 96–98, 106–107, 124, 193–194
  motion blur, 91–92
  noise, 110
  programmed autoexposure (P) mode, 49, 73, 96–98, 104, 124
  for recording movies, 211, 212–214
  for shooting action, 185–188
  for shooting scenic vistas, 189–191
  for shooting still portraits, 180–185
  shutter speed, 49, 77, 80, 88, 89, 91–92, 103–107, 185–193, 212
  shutter-priority autoexposure (S) mode, 49, 73, 96–98, 104–105, 124, 185–188
  stops, 96
  troubleshooting, 110–124

Exposure Compensation
  accessing, 213
  applying, 111–114
  for recording movies, 213–214
Exposure Compensation button
  about, 12, 13
  adjusting aperture with, 106–107
  changing exposure compensation using, 113
Exposure Delay mode, 56
exposure meter, checking, 98–100
Exposure mode. *See also specific exposure modes*
  advanced, 96–98
  choosing, 46–49
  for recording movies, 211, 212
  settings for, 178
Exposure Smoothing, 58
exposure value (EV) numbers, 79
extending lenses, 10, 28
external controls
  about, 11
  back-of-the-body, 13–16
  front-left, 16–17
  hidden connections, 17–18
  topside, 11–13
eye sensor, 14
Eye-Fi memory cards, 34, 259

F

Face Priority AF-area mode, 41
Face-priority mode, 149
fast-forwarding movie playback, 216
50 fps, 204, 206
file format, 65–69, 201. *See also specific types*
File Information mode, 235–237
File Number Sequence option (Custom Setting menu), 36–37
file transfer process, starting, 260–261
Filename (File Information mode), 236
filenames, customizing, 281–282

files
  deleting, 252–255
  protecting, 251–252
  size of, 64
Fill Flash mode, 74
Filter Effects, 298
filters, on Retouch menu, 292–295
fine-tuning White Balance settings, 162–163
fireworks, shooting, 193–194
Firmware Version option (Setup menu), 36
Fisheye tool, 300
fixing
  distorted images, 295–297
  tilted images, 295–297
FL (Flat) mode, 171
flash
  about, 49
  adding, 72–83
  adjusting output, 79–82
  color and, 80
  Continuous (burst mode) shooting and, 53
  controlling output of manually, 82–83
  disabling, 72–73
  enabling, 72–73
  for shooting action, 185–188
  for shooting dynamic close-ups, 191–193
  for shooting still portraits, 180–185
  shutter speed and, 77, 80
  using outdoors, 80
Flash button, 16, 78–79
Flash Compensation, 79–82
flash hot shoe, 12, 13
Flash mode
  changing, 78–79
  choosing, 73–79
  setting, 78
Flash Off mode, 74
Flash symbol, 160
Flat (FL) mode, 171
flick gesture, 19

Fluorescent symbol, 160
Fn (Function) button
    about, 16, 17
    adjusting ISO with, 108
    customizing, 287–288
focal length, 32
focal plane indicator, 12, 13
focal-length indicator, 28, 29
focus
    about, 129–130
    auto-, 31, 49
    choosing automatic or manual, 130–131
    lenses, 31
    in Live View mode, 145–152
    manual, 31
    for recording movies, 211
    setting method of, 28–31
    standard options for, 131–145
Focus mode
    about, 29, 132
    changing setting for, 132–134
    choosing in Live View mode, 146–148
    for recording movies, 211
    settings for, 178
    viewing setting, 199
Folder name (File Information mode), 236
formatting memory cards, 33
frame, repositioning, 299
frame by frame advancing, for movies, 216
Frame number/Number frames (File Information mode), 235–236
Frame Size/Frame Rate, choosing, 203–204
Framing Grid display, 43
front-left controls, 16–17
f-stops, 89, 105–106, 213
full-time servo AF (AF-F)
    for movies, 200
    using in Live View mode, 147
Function (Fn) button
    about, 16, 17
    adjusting ISO with, 108
    customizing, 287–288

G

gestures, 19
glass, shooting through, 194
graduated neutral-density filter, 190
gridlines, displaying, 25

H

handling
    memory cards, 33
    special situations, 193–195
HDMI port, 17, 18
HDR (high dynamic range) photography, 118–121
Help button, 14, 15–16
hidden connections, 17–18
hidden text, 278
Hide Indicators display mode, 42, 43, 201–202
hiding information, 283
high dynamic range (HDR) photography, 118–121
High ISO Noise Reduction filter, 110
High Key mode, 306
highlights, 115, 237–238
Highlights (blinkies) mode, 237–238
histograms
    about, 239
    Brightness, 239–240
    RGB, 240–241
hot shoe, 12, 13

I

i button, 14, 15
icons, explained, 3
Image Overlay tool, 300
Image Quality setting (File Information mode)
    about, 65–69, 178, 236
    using, 69–72
Image Review settings, 227
Image Size setting (File Information mode)
    about, 61–65, 178, 236
    using, 69–72

images
  about, 247–248
  adding special effects to, 300–302
  choosing which to view, 225–226
  cropping, 233–234, 298–299
  displaying in Calendar view, 230–234
  downloading to computers, 258–265
  playback of, 15–16
  preparing for online sharing, 271–274
  rating, 248–250
  resizing in-camera, 273–274
  rotating, 295
  viewing on television, 244–245
  viewing playback of. See playback mode
  viewing settings for, 24–26
  zooming, 232–234
incandescent bulbs, 158
Incandescent symbol, 160
Info button, 14–15, 42, 201–202
Information display
  adjusting ISO from, 108
  adjusting style of, 282–283
  creating direct-measurement presets via, 165
  viewing exposure setting from, 113
  viewing settings in, 24–25
Information screen, adjusting shutter speed
      from, 105
inserting memory cards, 9
interlaced format, 204
Interval Timer Shooting, 56–59
ISO
  about, 88, 89–90
  adjusting, 212
  effect on noise of, 93–94
  for recording movies, 212
  setting, 107–109
  for shooting action, 185–188
ISO Sensitivity, settings for, 178

J

JPEG artifacting, 66
JPEG Basic, 67

JPEG file format, 62, 65–69, 218–219
JPEG Fine, 66, 69
JPEG Normal, 67

K

Kelvin scale, 158
keystoning, 296

L

Landscape (LS) mode
  about, 42, 47, 171, 228
  flash in, 72
language, setting, 9–10
lens distortion, 156
lens focal length, depth of field and, 154
lens lock button, 29
lenses
  about, 8, 28–31
  AF-P, 30, 130–131
  AF-S, 30–31, 130, 131
  attaching, 8
  crop factor, 32
  extending, 10, 28
  focal length, 32
  focusing, 31
  removing, 31
  retracting, 28
  for shooting dynamic close-ups, 192–193
  unlocking, 10
  zooming, 28
lens-release button, 16, 17, 29
light fall-off, 121–123
lighting
  Live View display and, 44
  for shooting action, 185–188
  for shooting dynamic close-ups, 191–193
  for shooting scenic vistas, 189–191
  for shooting still portraits, 180–185
Live View mode
  about, 16
  accessing control strip, 44

adjusting shutter speed in, 105
in Auto mode, 40–44
autofocus, 146–151
color in, 159
Effects mode and, 302
exposure metering in, 100
focusing in, 145–152
lighting and, 44
manual focusing in, 151
viewing exposure setting from, 113
viewing settings in, 25
Live View switch, 12, 13
Lock Mirror Up for Cleaning option (Setup menu), 35
locking memory cards, 34
Long Exposure Noise Reduction filter, 110
lossy compression, 66
Low Key mode, 306
LS (Landscape) mode
about, 42, 47, 171, 228
flash in, 72

M

M. *See* manual (M) exposure mode
managing
memory cards, 33
special situations, 193–195
manual (M) exposure mode
about, 49
adjusting aperture and shutter speed in, 106–107
automatic bracketing in, 124
checking exposure meter in, 98
flash in, 73
for shooting fireworks, 193–194
using, 96–98
manual focus (MF), 31, 134, 143–145, 147, 151
manual focusing ring, 29
Manual Sensitivity setting, 207
matching white balance to existing photos, 165–166

matrix metering mode, 101
Maximum Sensitivity option, 109
MB (megabytes), 71
MC (Monochrome) setting, 170–171
megabytes (MB), 71
memory buffer, Continuous (burst mode) shooting and, 53
memory card reader, 258–259
memory card warning, 26
memory cards
inserting, 9
working with, 32–34
Menu button, 13
menus
creating, 284–286
custom, 23–24
navigating, 21–24
metadata, 37, 278
metering modes
about, 100
choosing, 101–103
settings for, 178
MF (manual focus), 31, 134, 143–145, 147, 151
Micro-Nikkor Lenses, 193
microphone, 12, 13, 207–209
microphone jack, 17, 18
Microphone Off setting, 207
Miniature Effect filter, 301, 305
Miniature mode, 136
Minimum Shutter Speed option, 109
mirror-lockup shooting, 56
Mode dial, 12
modes. *See also* aperture-priority autoexposure (A) mode; Live View mode; manual (M) exposure mode; playback mode; programmed autoexposure (P) mode; shutter-priority autoexposure (S) mode
advanced exposure, 96–98
AF-area mode, 132, 134–139, 148–150, 178, 211
Auto, 38–44, 46, 73
Auto flash, 74
Auto Flash Off, 46, 72

modes *(continued)*
  Autumn Colors, 72
  Beach/Snow, 72
  blinkies (Highlights), 237–238
  Blossom, 72
  burst, 52–53
  Calendar playback, 215
  Candlelight, 72
  center-weighted metering, 101
  Close Up, 42
  Continuous, 52–53
  Dusk/Dawn, 72
  Dynamic-area autofocusing, 135–136, 140–141
  Effects, 46, 72, 302–306
  Exposure, 46–49, 96–98, 178, 211, 212
  Exposure Delay, 56
  Face Priority AF-area, 41
  Face-priority, 149
  File Information, 235–237
  Fill Flash, 74
  Flash, 73–79
  Flash Off, 74
  Flat (FL), 171
  Focus, 29, 132–134, 146–148, 178, 199, 211
  Hide Indicators display, 42, 43, 201–202
  High Key, 306
  Highlights (blinkies), 237–238
  Landscape (LS), 42, 47, 72, 171, 228
  Low Key, 306
  matrix metering, 101
  metering, 100, 101–103, 178
  Miniature, 136
  Night Landscape, 72
  Night Portrait, 42
  Night Vision, 136, 304
  Normal-area, 149
  Overview, 242–244
  Pet Portrait Scene, 53
  Photo Illustration, 72, 73, 300, 304
  Pop, 72, 304
  Portrait (PT), 42, 47, 171
  Quiet Shutter, 49, 51
  Rear-Sync, 75–76
  Rear-Curtain Sync, 76–77
  Red-Eye Reduction, 75
  Release, 49–60, 127, 178
  RGB Histogram, 238–241
  Scene, 42, 47–48
  Self-Timer, 49, 54–55
  Shooting Data display, 241–242
  Silhouette, 305
  Single Frame, 51
  single-point autofocusing, 134–135, 139–140
  Slow-Rear, 77
  Slow-Sync, 75–76
  Slow-Sync with Red-Eye Reduction, 77
  Sports, 72
  spot metering, 101
  Subject-tracking, 149–150
  Sunset, 72
  Super Vivid, 72, 304
  Thumbnail playback, 215
  Toy Camera Effect, 72, 304–305
  Wide-area, 148
monitor, rotating, 9
Monitor Brightness option (Setup menu), 35
monitor shutdown, 44
Monochrome (MC) setting, 170–171
Monochrome tool, 298
motion blur, effect of shutter speed on, 91–92
mounting index, 8
MOV format, 201
Movie Indicators display, 42, 43
movie-record button, 12, 13
movies
  about, 197, 247–248
  adjusting exposure, 212–214
  adjusting settings, 202–206
  controlling audio, 206–210
  maximum recording times, 206

playback of, 16

quality of, 204–206

rating, 248–250

recording options, 210–211

saving frames as still images, 218–219

screening, 214–216

shooting using default settings, 198–202

trimming, 216–218

moving subjects, choosing Live View autofocusing pairs for, 151

Multi-Selector/OK button, 14, 15, 22

My Menu/Recent Settings menu, 22

N

N symbol, 18

navigating menus, 21–24

Near Field Communication (NFC), 18

NEF (Raw) format, 62, 65–69, 265–271

neutral density filter, 189

Neutral (NL) setting, 170

NFC (Near Field Communication), 18

NFC antenna mark, 17

Night Landscape mode, 72

Night Portrait mode, 42

Night Vision mode, 136, 304

Nikon (website), 36, 55, 193, 258

Nikon Capture NX-D, 257–258

Nikon ViewNX-i

about, 255–258

downloading using, 261–265

9-point Dynamic-area, 135

NL (Neutral) setting, 170

noise

about, 44

defined, 90

effect of ISO on, 93–94

reducing, 110

Normal-area mode, 149

number of frames per second, Continuous (burst mode) shooting and, 53

O

OK button, 14, 15

online sharing, preparing pictures for, 271–274

On/Off switch, 11, 12

Optical Vibration Reduction, 202

Overview mode, 242–244

P

P (programmed autoexposure) mode

about, 49

adjusting aperture and shutter speed in, 104

automatic bracketing in, 124

checking exposure meter in, 98

flash in, 73

using, 96–98

Painting filter, 302

pausing movie playback, 215–216

Perspective Control, 296–297

Pet Portrait Scene mode, 53

Photo Illustration mode, 72, 73, 300, 304

photos

about, 247–248

adding special effects to, 300–302

choosing which to view, 225–226

cropping, 233–234, 298–299

displaying in Calendar view, 230–234

downloading to computers, 258–265

playback of, 15–16

preparing for online sharing, 271–274

rating, 248–250

resizing in-camera, 273–274

rotating, 295

viewing on television, 244–245

viewing playback of. *See* playback mode

viewing settings for, 24–26

zooming, 232–234

PictBridge, 307

Picture Controls

about, 170–175

for recording movies, 211

picture data, viewing, 234–244
picture quality, with Raw (NEF), 68
pictures
  about, 247–248
  adding special effects to, 300–302
  choosing which to view, 225–226
  cropping, 233–234, 298–299
  displaying in Calendar view, 230–234
  downloading to computers, 258–265
  playback of, 15–16
  preparing for online sharing, 271–274
  rating, 248–250
  resizing in-camera, 273–274
  rotating, 295
  viewing on television, 244–245
  viewing playback of. See playback mode
  viewing settings for, 24–26
  zooming, 232–234
pinch in/out gesture, 19
pincushion distortion, 156, 296
pixel, 61
pixel dimension, 61
playback
  of movies, 16
  of pictures, 15–16
Playback button, 14, 15
Playback menu, 22, 249–250
Playback mode
  about, 223–225
  adjusting timing, 226–227
  assigning ratings in, 248–249
  choosing what pictures to view, 225–226
  displaying pictures in Calendar view, 230–234
  enabling automatic picture rotation, 227–229
  switching to Thumbnails display, 229–230
  viewing picture data, 234–244
  viewing pictures on television, 244–245
playing movies, 214–216
Pop mode, 72, 304
Portrait (PT) mode, 42, 47, 171
portrait orientation, 228
portraits, focusing frame for, 41

ports, 17, 18
power switch/Shutter button, 12
preparing
  for initial use, 7–11
  pictures for online sharing, 271–274
presenting slide shows, 307–308
Preset symbol, 160
presets, white balance, 163–166
print size, 62–63
printing directly from camera, 307
processing Raw (NEF) files, 265–271
programmed autoexposure (P) mode
  about, 49
  adjusting aperture and shutter speed in, 104
  automatic bracketing in, 124
  checking exposure meter in, 98
  flash in, 73
  using, 96–98
progressive video format, 204
Protect feature, 248, 251–252
Protected symbol (File Information mode), 237
protecting files, 251–252
PT (Portrait) mode, 42, 47, 171

Q
quality
  image, 61–72, 69–72
  movie, 204–206
Quick Retouch tool, 298
Quiet Shutter mode, 49, 51

R
rangefinder, 144–145
rating photos and movies, 248–250
Rating symbol (File Information mode), 237
Raw converter, 265
Raw (NEF) files, 62, 65–69, 265–271
reading
  Brightness histograms, 239–240
  exposure meters, 99–100

Rear-Sync mode, 75–76

Rear-Curtain Sync mode, 76–77

Record button, 12, 13

recording times, 206

red-eye, removing, 75, 295

Red-Eye Reduction mode, 75

reducing
  exposure stops, 96
  noise, 110
  wind noise, 209–210

Release mode
  bracketing in, 127
  settings for, 49–60, 178

Release Mode button, 16, 17, 50

Remember icon, 3

remote control shooting, 55–56

removing
  lenses, 31
  memory cards, 33
  red-eye, 295

repositioning frame, 299

resizing pictures in-camera, 273–274

resolution, 61–65

restoring default settings, 37–38

resuming movie playback, 215–216

Retouch menu
  about, 22
  accessing, 292–293
  filters on, 292–295

Retouch symbol (File Information mode), 237

retracting lenses, 28

reversing Command dial orientation, 290

rewinding movie playback, 216

RGB Histogram mode, 238–241

RGB histograms, 240–241

RGB images, 240

Rotate Tall option (Playback menu), 228

rotating
  monitor, 9
  pictures, 295

S

S (shutter-priority autoexposure) mode
  about, 49
  adjusting aperture and shutter speed in,
    104–105
  automatic bracketing in, 124
  checking exposure meter in, 98
  flash in, 73
  for shooting action, 185–188
  using, 96–98

saving movie frames as still images, 218–219

Scene modes, 42, 47–48

scenic vistas, shooting, 188–191

screen display size, 64

screening movies, 214–216

scrolling, 229

SD (Secure Digital) memory card
  about, 8
  buying, 32–33

SD (Standard) setting, 170

SD Speed Class, 33

Secure Digital memory card. *See* SD (Secure
    Digital) memory card

selecting
  AF-area mode, 134–139, 148–150
  autofocus combinations, 139
  automatic focusing, 130–131
  color spaces, 169
  from Custom Setting menu, 23
  exposure metering modes, 101–103
  exposure modes, 46–49
  Flash mode, 73–79
  Focus mode in Live View mode, 146–148
  Frame Size/Frame Rate, 203–204
  images to view, 225–226
  Live View autofocusing pairs, 151
  manual focusing, 130–131
  thumbnails, 230

Selective Color filter, 301–302, 305

Self-Timer mode, 49, 54–55

Send to Smart Device symbol (File Information mode), 237
sensitivity, setting for microphone, 207–209
setting(s)
    about, 178–179
    adjusting via control strip, 27–28
    aperture, 103–107
    date, 9–10
    default, 37–38, 198–202
    Flash mode, 78
    focus method, 28–31
    focus with touchscreen, 146
    image quality, 69–72
    image size, 69–72
    language, 9–10
    microphone sensitivity, 207–209
    Release mode, 49–60
    shutter speed, 103–107
    time zone, 9–10
    video, 202–206
    viewing for pictures, 24–26
    white balance with direct measurement, 164–165
Setup menu, 22, 34–36
Shade symbol, 160
sharpening, 170
shooting
    action shots, 185–188
    in Auto mode, 38–44
    from car windows, 194
    dynamic close-ups, 191–193
    in Effects mode, 302–306
    fireworks, 193–194
    movies using default settings, 198–202
    remote control, 55–56
    scenic vistas, 188–191
    still portraits, 179–185
    in strong backlighting, 194–195
    through glass, 194
Shooting Data display mode, 241–242
Shooting menu
    about, 22

    adjusting ISO from, 108–109
    adjusting microphone settings from, 208
    adjusting Release mode from, 51
    adjusting settings from, 71
    adjusting White Balance setting from, 160
    applying Active D-Lighting from, 117
    enabling HDR from, 120–121
Shooting Time screen, 60
Shots remaining, 26
Shutter button/power switch, 11–12, 288
shutter speed
    about, 49, 88, 89
    effect on motion blur of, 91–92
    flash and, 77, 80
    for recording movies, 212
    setting, 103–107
    for shooting action, 185–188
    for shooting dynamic close-ups, 191–193
    for shooting scenic vistas, 189–191
    for shooting still portraits, 181–185
    viewing, 103
shutter-priority autoexposure (S) mode
    about, 49
    adjusting aperture and shutter speed in, 104–105
    automatic bracketing in, 124
    checking exposure meter in, 98
    flash in, 73
    for shooting action, 185–188
    using, 96–98
Silhouette mode, 305
Single Frame mode, 51
single-point autofocusing mode, 134–135, 139–140
single-servo autofocus (AF-S)
    about, 133, 139–140
    for movies, 199
    using in Live View mode, 146–147
60 fps, 204, 206
size, image, 61–72, 69–72
Slide Show feature, 307–308
Slot Empty Release Lock option (Setup menu), 35

Slow-Rear mode, 77

slow-shutter blur, 142

Slow-Sync mode, 75–76

Slow-Sync with Red-Eye Reduction mode, 77

Soft filter, 300

SnapBridge, 35, 55, 242–243, 259, 309–317

speaker, 12, 13

special effects, adding to photos, 300–302

special situations, handling, 193–195

Sports mode, 72

spot metering mode, 101

sRGB color space, 169

Standard (SD) setting, 170

standby timer feature, 286–287

starting file transfer process, 260–261

stationary subjects, choosing Live View autofocusing pairs for, 151

still images, saving movie frames as, 218–219

still portraits, shooting, 179–185

stop down the aperture, 90–91

stops, 96

Straighten tool, 295–296

Subject-tracking mode, 149–150

Sunset mode, 72

Super Vivid mode, 72, 304

swipe gesture, 19

switching to Thumbnails display, 229–230

T

Tagged Image File Format (TIFF), 265

tap gesture, 19

Technical Stuff icon, 3

television, viewing photos on, 244–245

30 fps, 204, 206

39-point Dynamic-area, 136

3D-tracking, 136

through the lens (TTL), 78

Thumbnail playback mode, 215

Thumbnails display, switching to, 229–230

TIFF (Tagged Image File Format), 265

tilted images, fixing, 295–297

Time (File Information mode), 236

Time setting, 106

time zone, setting, 9–10

Time-Lapse Movie option, 59–60

time-lapse photography, 56–59

timing
   auto-shutdown, 286–287
   playback, 226–227

Tip icon, 3

toggling between thumbnails, 230

tonal range, expanding, 115

topside controls, 11–13

Touch Function, assigning roles, 289–290

Touch Shutter feature
   about, 41, 43
   Continuous (burst mode) shooting and, 53
   using, 52

touchscreen
   accessing menus from, 22
   enabling, 18–21
   setting focus with, 146

Toy Camera Effect mode, 72, 304–305

Trim tool, 298–299

trimming movies, 216–218

tripod
   advantages of using, 76
   for shooting fireworks, 193
   for slow-shutter blur, 142

troubleshooting
   color, 159
   exposure problems, 110–124

TTL (through the lens), 78

tungsten photo lights, 158

21-point Dynamic-area, 135

24 fps, 203, 206

25 fps, 203, 206

U

unlocking lenses, 10

upsampling, 62

USB cable, 259, 260

USB port, 17, 18

V

V (Vivid) setting, 170
Vibration Reduction (VR) feature, 92, 142
Vibration Reduction symbol, 26
videos
  about, 197, 247–248
  adjusting exposure, 212–214
  adjusting settings, 202–206
  controlling audio, 206–210
  maximum recording times, 206
  playback of, 16
  quality of, 204–206
  rating, 248–250
  recording options, 210–211
  saving frames as still images, 218–219
  screening, 214–216
  shooting using default settings, 198–202
  trimming, 216–218
viewfinder
  adjusting, 10
  cover for, 44
  shutter speeds in, 104
  using in Auto mode, 38–40
  viewing exposure setting from, 113
  viewing settings in, 25
Viewfinder adjustment dial, 13, 14
viewfinder photography, standard focusing
  options in, 131–145
viewing
  aperture, 103
  Focus mode setting, 147, 199
  ISO setting, 108
  photos on television, 244–245
  picture data, 234–244
  picture settings, 24–26
  pictures. See playback mode
  shutter speed, 103
  White Balance setting, 159

ViewNX-i, preparing online photos using,
  271–273
vignetting, eliminating, 121–123
Vivid (V) setting, 170
volume, playback, 216
VR (Vibration Reduction) feature, 92, 142

W

waking exposure meters, 99
Warning icon, 3
websites
  Adobe, 258
  Cheat sheet, 3
  Eye-Fi memory cards, 259
  Nikon, 36, 55, 193, 258
white balance
  settings for, 178
  for shooting still portraits, 183–185
White Balance setting
  adjusting, 157–169
  for recording movies, 211
  viewing, 159
Wide-area mode, 148
Wi-Fi, 18, 309–317
Wind Noise Reduction option, 209–210
wired remote control, 55
wireless remote control, 55

Z

zoom barrel, 28, 29
Zoom In button, 14, 15–16
Zoom Out/Help button, 14, 15–16
zooming
  focus and, 152
  lenses, 28
  photos, 232–234

About the Author

Julie Adair King is the author of many books about digital photography and imaging, including the best-selling *Digital Photography For Dummies.* Her most recent titles include a series of *For Dummies* guides to popular digital SLR cameras, including the *Nikon D3400, D5500, D7200,* and *D600.* Other works include *Digital Photography Before & After Makeovers, Digital Photo Projects For Dummies,* and *Shoot Like a Pro!: Digital Photography Techniques.* A native of Ohio and graduate of Purdue University, she resides in West Palm Beach, Florida.

Author's Acknowledgments

I am deeply grateful for the chance to work with a wonderful publishing team, which includes Kim Darosett, Steve Hayes, and Mary Corder, to name just a few. I am also indebted to technical editor Theano Nikitas, without whose insights and expertise this book would not have been the same.

Publisher's Acknowledgments

Executive Editor: Steven Hayes

Project Editor: Kim Darosett

Technical Editor: Theano Nikitas

Editorial Assistant: Serena Novosel

Sr. Editorial Assistant: Cherie Case

Production Editor: Magesh Elangovan

Cover Image: Julie Adair King

Apple & Mac

iPad For Dummies,
6th Edition
978-1-118-72306-7

iPhone For Dummies,
7th Edition
978-1-118-69083-3

Macs All-in-One
For Dummies, 4th Edition
978-1-118-82210-4

OS X Mavericks
For Dummies
978-1-118-69188-5

Blogging & Social Media

Facebook For Dummies,
5th Edition
978-1-118-63312-0

Social Media Engagement
For Dummies
978-1-118-53019-1

WordPress For Dummies,
6th Edition
978-1-118-79161-5

Business

Stock Investing
For Dummies, 4th Edition
978-1-118-37678-2

Investing For Dummies,
6th Edition
978-0-470-90545-6

Personal Finance

Personal Finance
For Dummies, 7th Edition
978-1-118-11785-9

QuickBooks 2014
For Dummies
978-1-118-72005-9

Small Business Marketing
Kit For Dummies,
3rd Edition
978-1-118-31183-7

Careers

Job Interviews
For Dummies, 4th Edition
978-1-118-11290-8

Job Searching with Social
Media For Dummies,
2nd Edition
978-1-118-67856-5

Personal Branding
For Dummies
978-1-118-11792-7

Resumes For Dummies,
6th Edition
978-0-470-87361-8

Starting an Etsy Business
For Dummies, 2nd Edition
978-1-118-59024-9

Diet & Nutrition

Belly Fat Diet For Dummies
978-1-118-34585-6

Mediterranean Diet

Mediterranean Diet
For Dummies
978-1-118-71525-3

Nutrition For Dummies,
5th Edition
978-0-470-93231-5

Digital Photography

Digital SLR Photography
All-in-One For Dummies,
2nd Edition
978-1-118-59082-9

Digital SLR Video &
Filmmaking For Dummies
978-1-118-36598-4

Photoshop Elements 12
For Dummies
978-1-118-72714-0

Gardening

Herb Gardening
For Dummies, 2nd Edition
978-0-470-61778-6

Gardening with Free-Range
Chickens For Dummies
978-1-118-54754-0

Health

Boosting Your Immunity
For Dummies
978-1-118-40200-9

Diabetes

Diabetes For Dummies,
4th Edition
978-1-118-29447-5

Living Paleo For Dummies
978-1-118-29405-5

Big Data

Big Data For Dummies
978-1-118-50422-2

Data Visualization
For Dummies
978-1-118-50289-1

Hadoop For Dummies
978-1-118-60755-8

Language & Foreign Language

500 Spanish Verbs
For Dummies
978-1-118-02382-2

English Grammar
For Dummies, 2nd Edition
978-0-470-54664-2

French All-in-One
For Dummies
978-1-118-22815-9

German Essentials
For Dummies
978-1-118-18422-6

Italian For Dummies,
2nd Edition
978-1-118-00465-4

Available in print and e-book formats.

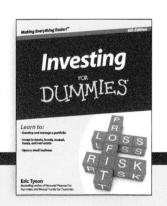
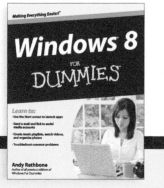
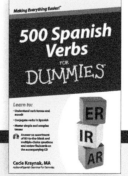
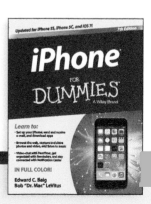

Available wherever books are sold. **For more information or to order direct visit www.dummies.com**

Math & Science

Algebra I For Dummies, 2nd Edition
978-0-470-55964-2

Anatomy and Physiology For Dummies, 2nd Edition
978-0-470-92326-9

Astronomy For Dummies, 3rd Edition
978-1-118-37697-3

Biology For Dummies, 2nd Edition
978-0-470-59875-7

Chemistry For Dummies, 2nd Edition
978-1-118-00730-3

1001 Algebra II Practice Problems For Dummies
978-1-118-44662-1

Microsoft Office

Excel 2013 For Dummies
978-1-118-51012-4

Office 2013 All-in-One For Dummies
978-1-118-51636-2

PowerPoint 2013 For Dummies
978-1-118-50253-2

Word 2013 For Dummies
978-1-118-49123-2

Music

Blues Harmonica For Dummies
978-1-118-25269-7

Guitar For Dummies, 3rd Edition
978-1-118-11554-1

iPod & iTunes For Dummies, 10th Edition
978-1-118-50864-0

Programming

Beginning Programming with C For Dummies
978-1-118-73763-7

Excel VBA Programming For Dummies, 3rd Edition
978-1-118-49037-2

Java For Dummies, 6th Edition
978-1-118-40780-6

Religion & Inspiration

The Bible For Dummies
978-0-7645-5296-0

Buddhism For Dummies, 2nd Edition
978-1-118-02379-2

Catholicism For Dummies, 2nd Edition
978-1-118-07778-8

Self-Help & Relationships

Beating Sugar Addiction For Dummies
978-1-118-54645-1

Meditation For Dummies, 3rd Edition
978-1-118-29144-3

Seniors

Laptops For Seniors For Dummies, 3rd Edition
978-1-118-71105-7

Computers For Seniors For Dummies, 3rd Edition
978-1-118-11553-4

iPad For Seniors For Dummies, 6th Edition
978-1-118-72826-0

Social Security For Dummies
978-1-118-20573-0

Smartphones & Tablets

Android Phones For Dummies, 2nd Edition
978-1-118-72030-1

Nexus Tablets For Dummies
978-1-118-77243-0

Samsung Galaxy S 4 For Dummies
978-1-118-64222-1

Samsung Galaxy Tabs For Dummies
978-1-118-77294-2

Test Prep

ACT For Dummies, 5th Edition
978-1-118-01259-8

ASVAB For Dummies, 3rd Edition
978-0-470-63760-9

GRE For Dummies, 7th Edition
978-0-470-88921-3

Officer Candidate Tests For Dummies
978-0-470-59876-4

Physician's Assistant Exam For Dummies
978-1-118-11556-5

Series 7 Exam For Dummies
978-0-470-09932-2

Windows 8

Windows 8.1 All-in-One For Dummies
978-1-118-82087-2

Windows 8.1 For Dummies
978-1-118-82121-3

Windows 8.1 For Dummies, Book + DVD Bundle
978-1-118-82107-7

Available in print and e-book formats.

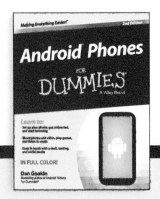
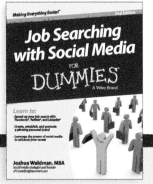
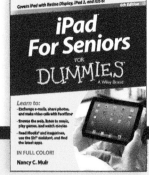
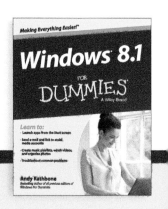

Available wherever books are sold. **For more information or to order direct visit www.dummies.com**

Take Dummies with you everywhere you go!

Whether you are excited about e-books, want more from the web, must have your mobile apps, or are swept up in social media, Dummies makes everything easier.

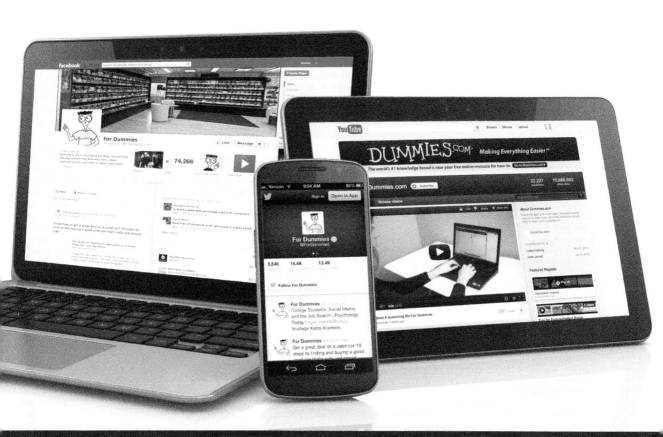

Leverage the Power

For Dummies is the global leader in the reference category and one of the most trusted and highly regarded brands in the world. No longer just focused on books, customers now have access to the For Dummies content they need in the format they want. Let us help you develop a solution that will fit your brand and help you connect with your customers.

Advertising & Sponsorships

Connect with an engaged audience on a powerful multimedia site, and position your message alongside expert how-to content.

Targeted ads • Video • Email marketing • Microsites • Sweepstakes sponsorship

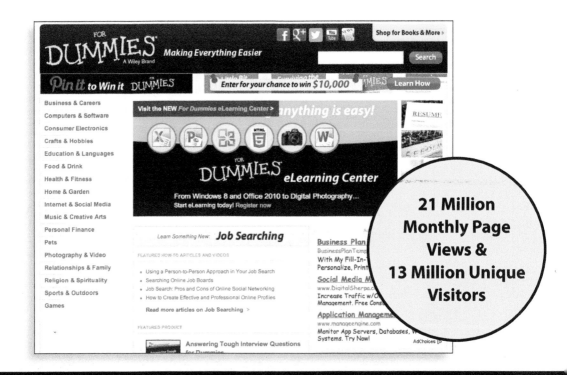